Education
Philosophy and Practice

Education

Philosophy and Practice

Edited by
Indrani Sanyal
Anirban Ganguly

Centre for Sri Aurobindo Studies
Jadavpur University
Kolkata

in collaboration with

Decent Books
New Delhi

Cataloging in Publication Data — DK
[Courtesy: D.K. Agencies (P) Ltd. <docinfo@dkagencies.com>]

Education : philosophy and practice / edited by
Indrani Sanyal, Anirban Ganguly.
p. cm.
Contributed articles.
Includes bibliographical references and index.
ISBN 13: 9788186921562

1. Education — India — Philosophy. 2. Educators — India. 3. Ghose, Aurobindo, 1872-1950. I. Sanyal, Indrani. II. Ganguly, Anirban. III. Jadavpur University. Centre for Sri Aurobindo Studies.

DDC 370.954 22

ISBN 13: 978-81-86921-56-2 **ISBN 10: 81-86921-56-7**

First published in India in 2011

Published and printed by:
Decent Books
D-36/A-1, Mohan Garden
Najafgarh Road, New Delhi - 110 059
Ph. (011) 2535 3435

in association with
Centre for Sri Aurobindo Studies
Jadavpur University
Kolkata (West Bengal)

Distributed by:
D.K. Printworld (P) Ltd.
Regd. Office: 'Vedaśrī', F-395, Sudarshan Park
Ramesh Nagar Metro Station
New Delhi – 110 015-11
Phones: (011) 2545 3975; 2546 6019; *Fax*: (011) 2546-5926
E-mail: indology@dkprintworld.com
Website: www.dkprintworld.com

Preface

EDUCATION: *Philosophy and Practice* participates in the process of expounding philosophy of education of Sri Aurobindo in its generalities with reference to the classical Indian model and in its relation to the views of his contemporary educationists of India. This is a great venture no doubt and in the present volume consisting of twelve essays, we make no pretensions to have covered all the dimensions of Sri Aurobindo's thought on the subject.

The articles entitled "Sri Aurobindo and his Philosophy of Education" by Aparna Banerjee; "Sri Aurobindo's Views on Education and its Relevance" by Sushmita Bhowmik; "Physical Education: An Essential Item of Integral Education" by Indrani Sanyal; "Roots of Violence: Negating the Individual's Self-determination in Education — Alternative Insights from Sri Aurobindo" by Anirban Ganguly; "Sri Aurobindo's Integral Education in Contemporary Higher Education" by Debashish Banerjee; "Education for a Faith in the Future" by Manoj Das, are all explications and analyses to give substance to Sri Aurobindo's perspective on education. Anirban Ganguly in his second article in this volume draws our attention to the vast panorama of Indian nationalism and its incessant search for the national education. The viewpoints of some distinguished nationalist thinkers and luminaries like Rabindranath Tagore, Mohandas Karamchand Gandhi, and Jiddu Krishnamurti have also been included. Without reference to Rabindranath Tagore's contribution towards ideology of education and his experiment with his philosophy at the soil of Santiniketan the present effort would remain incomplete; Shefali Moitra's "The Indian Education System and Tagore's Unmitigated Pain" develops Rabindranath's ideas on education. Two more essays, Mohit Chakrabarti's "Gandhian Education: Aesthetic Perspectives" and Atashee Chatterjee Sinha's "A New Philosophy of Education : by J. Krishnamurti" as included in this volume, contribute towards laying the Indian theoretical perspective of education. Of the collection of essays, entitled "Sri Aurobindo and Dilip Kumar Roy" by Sachidananda Mohanty and "Harindranath Chattopadhyay's 'Spiritual Education' and Sri Aurobindo" are different in their contents being more of the nature of biographical details narrating some instances of relationship between a great *ācārya* and his *śiṣya*s. This is also an important aspect of the whole enterprise of education.

Working on a group project on education, the Centre for Sri Aurobindo Studies, Jadavpur University, held seminars on the subject and had invited distinguished scholars as visiting faculties to deliver lectures in this Centre. The present volume is the outcome of our various academic activities mentioned above. As a Centre for Sri Aurobindo Studies our focus has been mainly in understanding Sri Aurobindo's views on education and their practical relevance. This explains why in this collection of essays, mostly articles are on one aspect or the other of Sri Aurobindo's philosophy of education. We have also included some other articles which do not have any direct bearing upon Sri Aurobindo's views but in many ways indirectly offer important clues to Sri Aurobindo's philosophy of education.

We have special debt to all the authors of the present volume who have readily agreed to share his or her views with us and took the trouble to put on record their deliberations. Our sincere thanks are due to the University Grants Commission, New Delhi, for providing us financial support for carrying on our various research activities under the Epoch-making Social Thinkers of India — Programme. Thanks are due to Decent Books, New Delhi, for bringing out this publication jointly with Jadavpur University, Kolkata.

Kolkata **Indrani Sanyal**

Contents

Introduction

EDUCATION is associated with umpteen philosophical ideologies and their implications in practice. The right to education has been accepted as one of the basic human rights throughout the world, though many millions have been deprived of this right even in recent times in some countries like ours. The concept of education, as we shall find, is a very much philosophically loaded expression and to a certain extent its connotation is culture-specific. In the classical Indian tradition, expressions like *śikṣā, vidyā, jñāna* are inter-related and often co-referential expressions. The appropriate expression for "education" is *śikṣā*. The verbal root *śikṣa* as shown by Monier Monier-Williams may be taken to have various senses such as "to wish to be able to effect for others," "to inform," "to instruct," "to cause to learn," "to impart knowledge," "to teach." According to lexicography, *śikṣā* also implies *vidyāsampradānam* and *grahaṇam,* i.e. giving or bestowing of knowledge and accepting or taking knowledge. Education is a conglomerate of several items which include thinking subjects in separate roles as the givers of knowledge, and as the takers of knowledge, who have the capability for accepting or partaking knowledge, the interrelationship between the givers of knowledge and the takers, the content provided through education, methodology to be adopted for furnishing the content and the end envisioned. The study concerning education may concentrate on all these aspects of education or many of these aspects or any of these aspects specifically. The very title of the volume *Education: Philosophy and Practice* indicates the main focus here is upon accommodating both the theoretical framework for education and also bringing to light some of its practical implications. Now discussing about theories of education is not an easy task nor is it easy to cite and discuss different aspects of its practice. In this volume we have dealt with the philosophy of education of Sri Aurobindo who was undoubtedly one of the greatest educationists that the world knows, and also have attempted to explore his ways of practising ideologies through his relationship with his disciples. In this context, a brief reference to Sri Aurobindo's biographical details may unravel some clues as to the perspective that he had acquired on education. Aurobindo Ghose in the year 1879 at the age of seven years was sent to England along with his two brothers for education and stayed there for fourteen years. After returning to India, he was appointed by the Gaekwar of Baroda in the Baroda Service. From the year 1893 to 1906, Aurobindo spent these thirteen years in the Baroda Service in different positions among which worth-mentioning are as Professor of English in Baroda College and also as Vice-Principal of the same College. During his tender years in his school and college period, he was nurtured in the European classical tradition, and subsequent to his return to Baroda, he bloomed in the tradition of classical India through his initiation into the realm of the Vedas, the Upaniṣads, the *Mahābhārata*, and the *Rāmāyaṇa*. He learnt Sanskrit and other Indian languages like Marathi, Gujarati and his mother tongue Bengali during this period. His contact with two spheres of different culture, access to two different sorts of educational experiences had lasting influence in the development of his philosophy of education. In course of analysing Sri Aurobindo's philosophy of education, the role of history, the very political characteristic feature of the period when it was a colonial India, can hardly be ignored. The aspiration for national education was intertwined with the nationalist struggle for independence. The programme for national education was originally conceived as a measure for national liberation. Under the direction of Satish Chandra Mukherji, the editor of *The Dawn*, the movement for national education received inspiration and a special institution, known as Dawn Society, for providing training to the youths, was founded. The resolution that was adopted at the Education Conference of 1905, held in Bengal is as follows: "That in the opinion of this conference it is desirable and necessary that a National Council of Education should be established to organise a system of education — literary, scientific and technical — on national lines and under national control." Aurobindo Ghose had returned from Baroda to Bengal in 1906 and was appointed as the first principal of Bengal National College along with Satish Chandra Mukherji as the first superintendent. The nationalist leaders of Bengal were all dissatisfied with the then-prevailing system of education and were earnestly in search of a right model for adoption. The historians generally earmark the period between 1900 and 1921 as witnessing the rise of the spirit of nationalism and giving shape to the nationalist agenda for education in India. The leaders of the nationalist movement were united against the educational policy of the British government and demanded control over the educational policy of the country. The leaders strongly urged for the development of a national character of education in India. Even today, after nearly sixty-four years of Independence, we find Government of India to bear greater responsibility for reinforcing the national and integrated nature of education. However, in all these cases whenever the discussion about national education does arise, it should not be supposed that one uniform clear-cut model of such education is available. From the writings of Sri Aurobindo,

Rabindranath Tagore, Mahatma Gandhi, Vivekananda, Lajpat Rai and many other distinguished educationists the nationalist educational discourse gained impetus, though these thinkers differed among themselves in detail. It remains an unresolved issue as to whether British education made any enriching contribution to Indian culture or had cast a doom over Indian culture.

Sri Aurobindo's perspective on education reached its profound philosophical dimension since his post-Pondicherry period. His view on education is often nicknamed as "integral education." According to Sri Aurobindo, a true education is one that integrates man, nation and Spirit. Sri Aurobindo sees in man, the individual, a soul, a portion of the divinity enwrapped in mind and body. Though man is the highest of the created beings, he is not the last word in the evolutionary process. A great possibility awaits man. The aim of education is to be understood in the light of the remark, "There is a supreme Divine Consciousness and we want to manifest this Consciousness in physical life." But it may be asked how it is possible to manifest this consciousness in physical life. Some may feel his notion of education is impractical, for it is associated with some abstruse metaphysical jargons. Critics express their disillusionment regarding this notion of education. But there are others who are curious to know how genuine education would prepare "the future of humanity to receive the supramental light that will transform the elite of today into a new race."

The true education as conceived by Sri Aurobindo is one of the processes by which man can increase his capacity as substratum of the infinite energy, or *prakṛti*, or *māyā* or *śakti*, or by whatever name it is called. According to Sri Aurobindo any education to be regarded as true education must aim at developing five main types of human activities, like the physical, the vital, the mental, the psychical and the spiritual. These may be regarded as the five aspects of education and these physical, vital, mental, psychic and spiritual aspects may succeed each other in the growth of the individual. But it should not be supposed that once one aspect has been developed it will continue in that phase, but rather the process of developing each of these aspects must continue throughout the life.

Among the different domains of human consciousness the physical domain is "most completely governed by method, order, discipline and procedure." The total perfection of the body and nothing short of it would meet the requirement of Sri Aurobindo for whom education is the other name for evocation of potentialities, and when talking about physical body, it is to be understood that specifically the entire and full development of the potentialities of the physical body is implied here. The education of the vital is considered to be indispensable and for that matter very important. Two aspects of vital education have received much consideration, one relating to the development and utilisation of sense organs and the other relating to acquiring mastery over one's character and vital transformation. The adoption of any coercive measures for suppression of senses is never encouraged; nor the path of asceticism has been ever advocated. The powers of the mind have to be developed. Sri Aurobindo states that mind or *antaḥkaraṇa* consists of four layers: *Citta,* the reservoir of past mental impressions or the storehouse of memory. *Manas,* the sixth sense of some schools of Indian psychology. The function of the mind is to receive the images of things translated into sight, sound, taste, and touch and translate these again into thought sensations. *Buddhi* or intellect is the real instrument of thought and that which orders and disposes of knowledge acquired by the outer parts of mind.

Bodhi, the fourth layer of the mind is not yet fully developed in man and is gradually attaining to a wider development and more perfect evolution. Sri Aurobindo admits that education concerning physical, vital and mental is necessary, for that helps in developing human personality as a "well-defined self-conscious entity." Sri Aurobindo maintains that "psychic education is required for making an individual conscious of his psychic presence in the depths of his being that which carries in it the sense of universality, limitless expansion, timeless continuity." "It is through the psychic process that truth of an individual being comes into contact with him and the circumstances of his life." Psychic education will facilitate the discovery of the psychic being, which requires as much fortitude and endurance as the discovery of "the new continents." The step that an individual has to take to reach the summit is through spiritual education, which is another part of the integral education that Sri Aurobindo had envisaged. Sri Aurobindo insists on drawing a sharp line of demarcation between the psychic education and the spiritual education, though both of these aspects of education are brought under the "yogic discipline." The objective of psychic education is not the same as the objective of spiritual education, for the psychic education aims at higher realisation on the earth, but the aim of the spiritual education is to escape from all earthly manifestations. "They dream that others should profit by the wonders they have discovered in their inner explorations." The supramental education will progress from above to downwards. It will not merely progressively develop human nature, it will transform nature itself, heightening the consciousness and bringing down the higher consciousness into the lower. According to Sri Aurobindo, the transformation when it is supramental as a result of the descent of the supermind, the body, life and mind of man are also greatly transformed. The supramental education, he believes, will bring about ascent of the species, leading in the end to the appearance of a divine race upon the earth. According to Sri Aurobindo, true education as a process of self-development through physical education, vital education, and mental education may be the goal of ordinary men. This process of self-development, if carried further, leads to a total transformation. The true education will establish life divine upon earth. True education will be an instrument for real working of the spirit in the mind and body of the individual and the nations. Thus understood, education would be an instrument for social change.

Sri Aurobindo is critical of the type of education that was being provided to the students. He in his "Education," draws distinctions among the intellectual aspect of education, the physical training and the edification of character. In his opinion these three aspects together constitute education. Intellectual aspect of education is larger and more difficult but it is a mistake to consider this to be the whole aspect of education.

The ultimate destiny of man is very beautifully brought out by Sri Aurobindo in his epic *Savitri*:

> Thus shall the earth open to divinity
> And common natures feel the wide uplift,
> Illumine common acts with Spirits ray
> And meet the deity in common things,
> Nature shall live to manifest secret God,
> The Spirit shall take up the human play,
> The earthly life becomes the life divine.

Another interesting thing is that Sri Aurobindo is regarded as the great master, *guru*; it may be looked into what makes him a great teacher? This enquiry would clearly bring out how education has been viewed in the Vedic-Upaniṣadic tradition and also by the later Indian thinkers on education like Sri Aurobindo and many of his contemporaries. In the recent past we find that some Western educationists have understood teaching in a new light and have defined it as facilitation of learning and consequently the teacher's role has been defined as the facilitator of learning. A strong awareness is gaining ground among the educationists to abandon the earlier model of education wherein teaching is considered as narration and the role of teacher as narrator, and the role of a pupil is to memorise mechanically the content of the narration. The teacher in this model is just to fill the students with the contents of his narration. Thus the relation between the student and the teacher is that of a container and filler of the container. In recent times in the Western circle we come across the name of Paulo Friere as the critique of this model of the "banking concept of education." This is no doubt an interesting area of research but all these discussions do not come within the purview of this introduction. The Upaniṣadic model of education, which had been pursued by Sri Aurobindo, may be viewed as a way for the development of the human. In this connection it has to be kept in mind that the Western libertarian educationists would also view education as a way for the growth and development of individual-human. But in the Indian context, in the writings of Sri Aurobindo, and some others, we find the notion of human growth and development has some greater significance to convey.

The *ācārya* of the Upaniṣad delivers knowledge as inspired by the spiritual energy. The *ācārya* is regarded as the Śākta, i.e. one who is capable of bringing about the strength in those who are being educated by him. In order to strengthen with *śakti,* i.e. power or energy, the teacher or preceptor must be capable of placing himself at the level of *prajñānam,* i.e. transcendental energy. The pupil is *śikṣamana,* i.e. one who is being educated. The preceptor energises the pupil, the pupil accepts it. There are passages at the very beginning in the *Taittirīya Upaniṣad*, and also in some other places, where we find that prayers are offered jointly by the teachers and students. *Brahmānandavallī* begins with a *Śāntimantra* as follows:

> Hari Oṁ. Together may He protect us,
> Together may He possess us,
> Together may we make unto us strength and virility.
> May our study be full to us of light and power.
> May we never hate.

The student-teacher relationship reaches its height through the close bond between the teacher and the student. The following prayers of the *ācārya* are important in this connection:

> O Glorious Lord, into That which is Thou may I enter, *Svāhā*!
> (*tam tvā bhaga praviśāni, svāhā*)[1]
>
> Do Thou also enter into me, O Shining One, *Svāhā*!)
> (*sa ma bhaga pravisa, svāhā*!)[2]

The *ācārya* and the pupils are not poles apart where the *ācārya* teaches and students are taught. This, however, is not to be confused with the libertarian educationists' model of the West which, vehemently speaks against the teacher-student contradiction, generated in the narrative model of teaching, and seek to view education as a drive towards the reconciliation among the poles of contradiction, viz. the teacher and the student. The sentence quoted above from the Upaniṣad carries deeper philosophical import. The intimacy of the student-teacher relationship may culminate into revealing oneself to the other and another's appropriating the

1. "Taittirīya Upaniṣad" in *The Upaniṣads*, vol. II, Sri Aurobindo, Pondicherry: Sri Aurobindo Ashram, 2004, pp. 208-9.
2. Ibid.

other self into its own self. Sri Aurobindo's contribution as a great master is beyond doubt. Many more explorations are yet to be done covering this pronounced aspect of Sri Aurobindo as an educationist. *Education: Philosophy and Practice* is a humble attempt to cover multifarious aspects of one of the greatest educationists that the world has ever known and also of some of his contemporaries situating in a historical background.

Indrani Sanyal

1

Sri Aurobindo and his Philosophy of Education

Aparna Banerjee

In this paper I have discussed Sri Aurobindo's philosophy of education within the context of some debates about the aim of education. I have tried to show that Sri Aurobindo's broader philosophy of integral evolution, of which his philosophy of education is a part, solves such issues satisfactorily. One problem that is very contemporary is about the aim of moral education. It seems to involve a choice between sectarianism and universalism. Sri Aurobindo has consistently mentioned a view of education that does not allow the problem to arise at all.

II

A very common idea about the aim of education is that it should be designed to develop certain attitudes and skills that are recognised to be useful in society. It is, thereby, also presupposed that such attitudes and skills need to be cultivated, ideally, by all members of the society. In different societies the understanding of what is useful will, no doubt, differ. It will vary, for example, between a primitive agricultural society on the one hand and a modern technological society on the other, at least to some extent. However, there is also an altogether different view about the aim of education. There are some philosophers of education who have emphasised upon the development of inner maturation of the student to be the true aim of education rather than moulding his personality to suit the purpose of society. This debate implicitly involves the debate between individualism and socialism. It may then seem natural to suppose that ultimately framing an idea about the aim of education involves a choice between the above-mentioned norms. Similarly, it may be asked as to what are the dimensions in which a person's nature needs to be developed? What is the common minimum that should be learnt by one in order to be known as educated? One may hold that human excellence is the prerogative of the educated person. In what case one could be an educated person even if he did not display any human excellence? In fact, the concept of human excellence, like the concept of education, is basically evaluative. In both cases some ideal conception of a human being is presupposed. However, there is one model which seems to be compatible with all the conflicting norms. This is known as model of integrated education. The word "integration" means a unity of parts into a whole in such a way that the parts themselves are blended and transformed into a new character. Now, one problem in this agenda is that even if we accept both maturation of the individual and being useful to society as our aims in formulating the ideal of education, a successful integration between the two may not seem to be possible. It may be argued that development in some areas may conflict with development in other areas. Hence, a total and integrated development of both the individual and the society without compromises and adjustments, in all respects that are recognised to be good, may be taken to be an impossible ideal in education.

Generally, education may be viewed as an investment into the future. When a society deliberately devotes much of its resources in order to improve the abilities of its young members it can expect a great increase in the quality of performance in all fields. It is generally accepted that education helps to develop skills and knowledge so that the reservoir of human wisdom may increase. But today we realise that apart from skilled technicians and first-rate scientists and business leaders we need moral leaders who with their intellectual, moral and spiritual wisdom will help eradicate or at least lessen conflicts both among people and also among nations. When we take human development to be our primary objective, such development should be given primary importance.

One striking feature of Sri Aurobindo's philosophy of education is that the underlying evolutionary thesis accommodates solution to the complexity of the problem of integrated education. Similarly, in the ultimate analysis, the conflict between the individual-centred education as against an educational curriculum aimed at the upliftment of the society does not arise; for evolution itself, according to Sri Aurobindo, is a process of transition from ignorance to a greater evolution in knowledge for both the individual and the society as a whole. In this process the evolution of man himself is only a stage in his growth and achievement of excellence. The supreme absolute consciousness is at the same time the one and the many. The world is manifested through a double process of descent of the one into the many and the rise of the latter once again to its original state through successive stages. Hence, even matter, the first stage in the ascending process of evolution is the same in essence as the Absolute Consciousness. The world is the field of experiment in which one of the infinite possibilities of the Absolute is actualising itself through a particular mode of evolution. ". . . Life is already involved in Matter and Mind in Life because in essence Matter is a form of veiled Life, Life a form of veiled Consciousness."[1] In man self-consciousness first appears in so far as apart from being of the nature of an organism, that is, being material, he is also mental. This feature is the basic characteristic of man just as life characterises primarily plants and animals. Just as these features of matter, life and mind are integrated in human nature, his further evolutionary route lies in a wider integration in a spiritual direction. However, even in man, his consciousness does not appear abruptly.

> This consciousness is at first rudimentary, mostly a half subconscious or just conscious instinct; it develops slowly till in more organised forms of living matter it reaches its climax or intelligence and exceeds itself in Man, the thinking animal who develops into the reasoning mental being but carries along with him even at his highest elevation the mould of original animality. . . . This control by the original Inconscience over the consciousness emerging from it takes the general shape of a mentality struggling towards knowledge. . . .[2]

The conflict that we see between man and man and within man himself is due to this struggle of the evolutionary principle working through him. Man's urge towards transcendence of his limitations finds its expression in many ways. The proper model of education should be based on this human urge for achieving harmony and integration both within himself and also in his interaction with others. In fact, the whole cosmos is a field of experiment of the Absolute or the Divine.

However, the ideal of human perfection in this field does not mean artificiality fitting man into a mould; for that is not the way to achieve proper development.

---

1. Pavitra (P.B. Saint-Hilaire), *Education and the Aim of Human Life*, Pondicherry: Sri Aurobindo Ashram, 1961, 2002, p. 33.
2. Sri Aurobindo, *The Life Divine*, Pondicherry: Sri Aurobindo Ashram, 1939-40, 2006, p. 857.

Conformity to imposed rules is always mechanical and artificial. On the other hand, evolutionary growth is natural. The ideal of education finds its meaning in integrated and natural self-transcendence.

III

Even before arriving at his philosophy of integral evolution, we find that Aurobindo as a nationalist educationist had already the vision of a very integrated education. Similarly, he already worked out a balance between the growth of the individual and the growth of the community. As a successful teacher in the early stage of his life at the Baroda College in Gujarat, Sri Aurobindo was involved in his education system during 1893-1906. Later he was involved in the education system of the National College in Calcutta which was established to provide education to the Indian youth along the *svadeśī* line of thinking. Although he was not directly involved in formal teaching after he went to Pondicherry, his views on education can be found in various writings also in this later stage. In fact, even during the nationalist period, when his main aim was to instil nationalist feelings in the minds of the young people, he was completely against indoctrination in the narrow sense. He says,

> it is a fundamental and deplorable error by which we . . . have confused education with the acquisition of knowledge and interpreted knowledge itself in a singularly narrow and illiberal sense. To give the student knowledge is necessary, but it is still more necessary to build up in him the power or knowledge.[3]

In his unfinished essay, "Education: Intellectual,"[4] he lays great emphasis upon bringing out the natural abilities in the students.

3. Sri Aurobindo, *Sri Aurobindo Birth Centenary Library* (*SABCL*), vol. 3, "Education: Intellectual" (Incomplete), Pondicherry: Sri Aurobindo Ashram, 1972, p. 127.

4. Ibid.

He advises that instead of training the storing faculty and encouraging storage of facts the three great powers which are present to a certain extent in all men should be trained. These are the power of reasoning, the power of comparison and differentiation and the power of expression. In any stereotyped education system knowledge is forced into the student's resisting brain without any consideration for the child's individuality and interest; on the other hand, Sri Aurobindo says that nine-tenth of the energy of the teacher should be spent on the education of the active mental faculties while the passive retaining faculty should occupy a place subordinate to this. This is remarkable, though apparently paradoxical, that an educationist who was soon to have a nationalist programme of education should hold such views about indoctrination. But, we find that Sri Aurobindo's vision of a national education even during this phase was not based on narrow propaganda or one-sided emphasis on the glory of the Indian past. In *Bande Mataram* in February 1908, while writing on the necessity of a National University he says,

> National education cannot be defined briefly in one or two sentences, but we may describe it tentatively as the education which starting with the past and making full use of the present builds up a great nation. Whoever wishes to cut off the nation from its past is no friend of our national growth. Whoever fails to take advantage of the present is losing us the battle of life. We must therefore save for India all that she has stored up of knowledge, character and noble thought in her immemorial past. We must acquire for her the best knowledge that Europe can give her and assimilate it to her own peculiar type of national temperament.[5]

In spite of his nationalist zeal he wanted to introduce the best methods of teaching that as a whole humanity had. He wanted

5. *SABCL*, vol. 1, pp. 717-18.

to harmonise it all into a system which would be characterised by a spirit of self-reliance. Such a system, he was convinced, would develop.

> . . . national men, able men, men fit to curve out a career for themselves by their own brain power and resource fit to meet the shocks of life and breast the waves of adventure. So shall the Indian people cease to sleep and become once more a people of heroes, patriots, originators, so shall it become a nation. . . .[6]

Clearly, his programme for developing an educational system along nationalist lines does not involve the exclusion of other cultures. This may seem to be a wrong line of plan for instilling nationalism. But Sri Aurobindo's philosophy of integral evolution development later on does not depend upon a narrow conception of education. Nor was his nationalism in conflict with universalism.

One reason for this is that Sri Aurobindo does not equate nation with the state. National identity is an identity with a nature of one's own but continuous with the human race as a whole. We have noted in section I that the aim of education has both an individualistic aspect and a universalistic aspect. The individual or the particular is no doubt central in Sri Aurobindo's scheme of education and development; but this does not mean that the universal — the greater humanity — is to be neglected. Such conclusions follow if we fail to distinguish between collectivism which is incompatible with individualism and universalism which is not. We often tend to forget that an individualist may be a committed altruist too.[7] Considered from this perspective true education helps the individual to turn into a person who can have harmonious

6. *SABCL*, vol. 1, pp. 717-18.
7. Karl Popper, *The Open Society and its Enemies*, vol. 1, London: Routledge and Kegan Paul, 1945, 1984, pp. 100ff.

and peaceful relations with other members of both his specific community and ultimately the whole of mankind. It helps the child to build up his character supplying him good opportunities to develop his natural abilities which become beneficial for the society as a whole. ". . . (T)he chief aim of education should be to help the growing soul to draw out that in itself which is best and make it perfect for a noble use."[8] However, as long as we are imperfect in our outlook we tend to emphasise one aspect neglecting the other. In fact, we find in the view of Sri Aurobindo two main reasons why it is essential to start education with the development of an individual. First, if education is to be real development into the Divine, as Sri Aurobindo believed, then each man has to grow through his own individual being.

Otherwise, whatever is taught remains an imposition. Secondly, this is a process that culminates in a unity with the others because that too is a necessity of his being. Never does Sri Aurobindo consider the individual and the society as opposing entities. In and through his proper education an individual can achieve harmonious relations with other members of both his specific community and ultimately with the whole of humanity. Hence, a national education is no less important. But in "A Preface to National Education" he points out a possible objection against this. This argument is to the effect that, ". . . mankind and its needs are the same everywhere and truth and knowledge are one and have no country"[9]; hence it may be argued that education too should be without nationality. But Sri Aurobindo points out that the main question is not what science we learn but what we do with our learning. The aim of true national education is not to ignore truth which means that it should be founded on our own being, our own mind and our own spirit. In the first

8. *SABCL, The Human Mind*, vol. 17, p. 204.

9. Ibid., p. 198.

essay, in *A System of National Education: Some Preliminary Ideas,* he answers the above argument in the following way. Enumerating the principles of true teaching, he says that one important principle "is to work from the near to the far, from that which is to that which shall be. The basis of man's nature is almost always, in addition to his soul's past, his heredity, his surroundings, his nationality, his country, the soil, from which he draws sustenance. . . ."[10] In Sri Aurobindo's view from such roots a true education should begin. However great and profound our ideals may be, if they are alien to the mind in which they are implanted, they are either rejected or accepted only superficially. In his view, our future is created on the foundation of our past, the material being supplied by the present. Since, as compared to one's society, one's culture, the state is an artificial construct, Sri Aurobindo was opposed to any educational system that was controlled by the state. As a nationalist he was opposed to Annie Besant's expressed intention to form a national university because she wanted a charter from the British government for it. He says against this that, ". . . she has not realised what national control implies. No government will give a charter which excludes them from all control."[11] Although, this is an expression primarily against foreign control, he retained the same opinion, in principle, against any state control even later in *The Ideal of Human Unity.*

He says,

> The state tends always to uniformity, because uniformity is easy to it and natural variation is impossible to its essentially mechanical nature; but uniformity is death, not life. A national culture, a national religion, a national education, may still be useful things provided they do not interfere with the growth of human solidarity on the one side and

10. *SABCL, The Human Mind,* vol. 17, pp. 204-5.
11. *SABCL,* vol. 1, p. 719.

> individual freedom of thought and conscience and development on the other; for they give form to the communal soul and help it to add its quota to the sum of human advancement; but a state education, a state religion, a state culture are unnatural violences.[12]

This distinction between state and nation is very crucial for Sri Aurobindo's vision of a national education. Narrowly construed, a national education too may appear to be sectarian and partial like state education. But Sri Aurobindo's conception of national education is broad enough to be compatible with the ideal of development that has through the ages been pursued in India involving some key notions like *puruṣārtha, paramārtha, svabhāva* and *svadharma,* which are based on the vision of the spirit of humanity as advancing through diversity towards oneness.

> The only true education will be that which will be an instrument for this real working of the spirit in the mind and body of the individual and the nation. That is the principle on which we must build, that is the central motive and guiding ideal. It must be an education that for the individual will make its own central object the growth of the soul and its powers and possibilities, for the nation will keep first in view the preservation, strengthening and enrichment of the nation-soul and its *dharma* and raise both into powers of the life and ascending mind and soul of humanity.[13]

IV

We have seen that even early in his life, when his thoughts were primarily directed towards national development, the ideal of an inclusive education that encompasses all that is

12. Makarand Paranjape (ed.), *The Penguin, Sri Aurobindo Reader,* Penguin Books, India, 1999, p. 116.
13. *SABCL,* vol. 17, p. 204.

commendable in the past and the present, east and west is upheld. However, this view achieves a stronger and explicit support later in his evolutionary philosophy of man and the whole cosmic order. In his major writings, like *The Life Divine, The Human Cycle,* and *The Ideal of Human Unity*, Sri Aurobindo has described the different aspects and stages of transformation that he could foresee for mankind. There are two main pillars of his philosophy of man; one is that human existence is full of possibilities; the other is that man has an unavoidable tendency to go beyond his present accomplishments. In Sri Aurobindo's philosophy that is a reflection of the underlying evolutionary principle of the diversified oneness of the Divine. The path of gradual realisation of his possibilities is for each man his growth into the Divine. But this is felt as incomplete as long as unity with others is not achieved. In his free and spontaneous growth from within he feels the need for unity with others although it is often beset with conflict and misunderstanding. But true unity is possible only when he comes to see the Divine in himself equally in others. In Sri Aurobindo's philosophy diversification of the Divine is only the process of involution which gains completeness in the return journey of evolution from the many to the one. Growing into an inner unity with others is therefore not merely an external necessity for man but the inner necessity of his being. Evolution proceeds through a successive chain of emergent-matter, life, animal consciousness and human consciousness. As man is the final evolute in the evolutionary chain, the entire complexity of the previous stages lies within him. In this context, the observation of Pavitra, one of his early disciples, is worth noting.

> Sri Aurobindo asserts that we have arrived at a great crucial moment in human evolution, where the descent of new powers of consciousness and their establishment on the earth have begun to occur. The present world crisis is nothing

> but the break-up of the past indispensable to the forward movement. On the crest of an evolutionary wave man has to yield place to a new type of being.[14]

But this does not involve the evolution of a completely new type of being beyond human existence. Instead the change will bring in a transformation in the nature of man. At present the immense complexity of man's nature stems from the fact that all the lower principles of evolution are included in his being. Man's present stage of self-knowledge is too imperfect for integrating all these diverse elements. The growth in this process of self-knowledge will usher in greater processes of integration. Hence, along with the growth of the mental, the psychic, and the spiritual domains in one's being, which manifest the higher levels of consciousness, an integral education should also include the proper development and harmonising of all these aspects.

One may wonder about the role of reason in the whole process. It is natural for the modern educationist to expect that education involves the development of the rational faculty in man. Most of our academic programmes centre around this emphasis on the rational as the key feature. But reason has a strong tendency for simplicity and orderliness that can hardly do justice to the complexity of life. This, however, does not mean that reason has no contribution to make to help us draw up the projects of life. In fact, up to a certain point it is highly useful. Science satisfies this norm of rationality very well. It is also highly useful in our practical life. But both reason and science are committed to tailor-made orderliness and uniformity. In spite of his acceptance of the pragmatic role of both reason and science in systematising our experience and organising our lives, Sri Aurobindo does not think that the rational or intellectual man is the last and highest ideal of

14. Pavitra (P.B. Saint-Hilaire), op. cit. p. 34.

manhood. In Sri Aurobindo's view human nature, in spite of its intellectual orientation, is open to larger possibilities of knowledge and self-realisation. Any programme of education that falls short of bringing out the possibilities in man is incomplete. The customary opposition between the humanities and the sciences on the one hand and the acceptance of the superiority of scientific knowledge on the other may be primarily traced to the centrality of the norm of rationality in education. The modern man has a craze for systematic and technical knowledge; but he cannot go beyond them in order to co-ordinate them at a more fundamental level. In his observations on rational education, Sri Aurobindo notes that

> . . . a rational education means necessarily three things, first, to teach men how to observe and know rightly the facts on which they have to form a judgement; secondly, to train them to think fruitfully and soundly; thirdly, to fit them to use their knowledge and their thought effectively for their own and the common good. Capacity of observation and knowledge, capacity of intelligence and judgement, capacity of action and high character are required for the citizenship of a rational order of society; a general deficiency in any of these difficult requisites is sure source of failure. Unfortunately, even if we suppose that any training made available to the millions can ever be of this rare character — the actual education given in the most advanced countries has not had the least relation to these necessities.[15]

The main reason for this, according to Sri Aurobindo, is that reason is not the master of itself in human life. On the one hand man is infrarational and not fully rational. On the other hand, the rational lies midway between two possibilities, the infrarational and the suprarational. In so far as man is dominated by his physical and vital needs reason works to

15. Sri Aurobindo, *The Human Cycle, The Ideal of Human Unity, War and Self-Determination*, Pondicherry: Sri Aurobindo Ashram, p. 198.

satisfy them. In order to make reason serve the suprarational in us, the soul has to discover itself in its highest reality. Reason functions by adopting fixed viewpoints, each of which is only temporarily true. The spiritual truth is the ultimate integral truth.

> If reason were the secret highest law of man and the mental being were limited by mentality, it might be possible for him by the power of the reason to evolve out of the dominance of infrarational nature which he inherits from the animal. He could then live securely in his best human self as a perfected rational and sympathetic being, balanced the well-ordered in all parts, the sāttvic man of Indian philosophy; that would be his summit possibility, his consummation. But his nature is rather transitional; the rational being is only a middle term of nature's evolution. A rational satisfaction cannot give him safety from the pull from below nor deliver him from the attraction from above. If it were not so, the ideal of intellectual anarchism might be more feasible as well as acceptable as a theory of what human life might be in its reasonable perfection but, man being what he is, we are compelled in the end to aim higher and go farther.[16]

In the beginning of the paper we have raised the question about the final aim of education. In the view of Sri Aurobindo, it should be based on the concept of real development. A real development for him is integrated growth in every sphere of human life. A major criterion for such an ideal education would be harmony. Our present systems of education have been intellectually developed, no doubt. But that in the opinion of Sri Aurobindo is not enough. He observes that,

> At present mankind is undergoing an evolutionary crisis in which is concealed a choice of its destiny; for a stage has been reached in which the human mind has achieved in

16. Sri Aurobindo, *The Human Cycle, The Ideal of Human Unity, War and Self-Determination*, Pondicherry: Sri Aurobindo Ashram, p. 219.

> certain directions an enormous development, while in others it stands arrested and bewildered and can no longer find its way.[17]

The solution to such crisis, according to Sri Aurobindo, lies in man's transition from the infrarational and rational stages into the spiritual.

Another important question is whose development is the final aim of education? Should the individual's free development be given maximum importance or is the proper growth of society more important? In the view of Sri Aurobindo, in human development, there are three equally important elements — the individual himself, the community to which he belongs and the larger humanity as a whole. Each of these terms has the laws of its own development and mode of self-consciousness. But each must take into consideration the interest of the other, because they are the expressions of the same transcended reality at different levels. Thus, while there is a line of development which each nation has to follow in accordance with its own nature or as Sri Aurobindo calls the nation-soul, similarly the individual too has to follow his own nature. Each has to take the other into account in its path of progress. Similarly, humanity itself is marching in the process towards an ideal social order which is marked by free development. The individual, the community and humanity are all modes of one transcendent reality. Thus, their natural interdependence does not annul the autonomy of any of them. In the view of Sri Aurobindo, just as the free development of individuals from within is the best condition for the growth and perfection of the community, so the free development of the community or the nation from within is the best condition for the growth and perfection of mankind.

---

17. Sri Aurobindo, *The Life Divine*, p. 933.

V

From the time of his proposal of the model of national education, one feature that has remained central in Sri Aurobindo's philosophy has been his view that the mind must be consulted in its own growth. Hence no system of education can be successful if it interferes in one's natural growth. The aim of education in a given society should be determined both by the nature of the student and the society he lives in. On the other hand, the necessity of moral education has also been recognised by Sri Aurobindo. He says,

> The discovery that education must be a bringing out of the child's own intellectual and moral capacities to their highest possible value and must be based on the psychology of the child-nature was a step forward towards a more healthy because a more subjective system; but it still fell short because it still regarded him as an object to be handled and moulded by the teacher, to be educated. But at least there was a glimmering of the realisation that each human being is self-developing and that the business of both parent and teacher is to enable and to help the child to educate himself, to develop his own intellectual, moral, aesthetic and practical capacities and to grow freely as an organic being, not to be kneaded and pressured into form like an inert plastic material.[18]

Sri Aurobindo points out that teaching should be imparted by setting personal example, through regular conversations and books. In this context, he has emphasised upon the necessity of *satsaṅga* — the company of good people and good books. For the younger students the past history in its glorious accounts should be presented. The stories about the lives, ideas and activities of great men from the past should be presented to the older students so that their inner interests may be aroused. In this way the good qualities of a brāhmaṇa, kṣatriya,

18. *SABCL*, vol. 15, *The Coming of the Subjective Age*, pp. 27-28.

vaiśya or śūdra may be suggested to the young Indians. He points out that, "the danger of moral textbooks is that they make the thinking of high things mechanical and artificial, and whatever is mechanical and artificial is inoperative for good."[19] Now since one's own family or community is near to him that is where education should begin if it is not to turn artificial.

Although Sri Aurobindo is explicitly against moral education as the imposition of moral ideal, one problem that suggests itself is that at least in the context of moral education, the examples that should be set up from histories and biographies should be ones that are accepted by one's community as substantively moral. In that case the possibility of encouraging different moral ideals in different societies seems to be encouraged by Sri Aurobindo. Is such an ideal of moral education compatible with his larger goal of united humanity? In this context one is reminded of a related debate in both political and moral philosophy; this is the debate between the communitarians and the liberals regarding minority rights. Minority rights are often opposed not simply because they may violate liberal principles, but also because they will be a source of disunity and inhibit the development of a sense of shared political identity. What holds true at the national level should apply equally at the international level as well. They could lead to the dissolution of a nation or at least to a reduced willingness to make the mutual sacrifices and accommodation necessary for a human society to function. When Sri Aurobindo was writing on national education, he was writing specifically for a nation like India that was still under British rule. In fact, more generally he was formulating the ideal manner of imparting education for all human societies. The problem is if groups are encouraged to turn inwards and

19. *SABCL*, vol. 17, *The Moral Nature*, p. 209.

focus on their differences whether religious, linguistic, racial or ethnic what happens to the broader goal of human integration which Sri Aurobindo had taken to be the final goal for humanity? No doubt this goal became dominant in his later writings; but they were not absent even in his earlier essays. In his project of national education he did not ask for a rejection of Western knowledge. He says, "The aim and principle of a true national education is not certainly to ignore modern truth and knowledge but to take our foundation in our own belief, our own mind, our own spirit."[20] Similarly, he did not suggest that one should remain confined within his own culture for gaining knowledge. His main suggestion was to move gradually from the familiar to the unfamiliar, from the near to the far. Sectarianism is not consistent with his philosophy primarily because he believed in an inner unity of the whole humankind. This we have noted in our discussion of the outlines of his philosophy of integral evolution which while accepting the importance of diversity is based on the principle that reality is one at bottom. The same divinity is present everywhere and in everyone, explicitly and implicitly. It is precisely for this reason that the mind of each student should be consulted in its growth through education. We find an echo of this view in a beautiful song by Rabindranath Tagore, a contemporary of Sri Aurobindo. There, the poet says that he intently listens to his heart from where a secret dweller sends him messages which he keeps trying to decipher.[21] What is implicit in this song is explicitly present in Sri Aurobindo's philosophy. He says,

> . . . the true central being is the soul, but this being stands back and in most human natures is only the secret witness

---

20. Sri Aurobindo, *Integral Education*, compiled by Indra Sen, Pondicherry: Sri Aurobindo International Society, 1952, p. 4.
21. Rabindranath, Tagore, *Rabindra Rachanabali*, Chaturtha Khanda, Song no. 1197, Paschimbanga Sarkar, 1987, p. 475.

> or, one might say, a constitutional ruler who allows his ministers to rule from him, delegates to them his empire, silently assents to their decisions and only now and then puts in a word which they cannot at any moment override and act otherwise. But this is so long as the soul personality put forward by the psychic entity is not yet sufficiently developed; when this is strong enough for the inner entity to impose itself through it, then the soul can come forward and control the nature. It is by the coming forward of this true monarch and his taking up of the reins of government that there can take place a real harmonisation of our being and our life.[22]

It is only through a proper education that the human can aspire to have a divine life here on earth. "Everyone has in him something divine, something his own, of perfection and strength in however small a sphere which God offers him to take or refuse. The task is to find it, develop it and use it."[23] Ultimately, the true development of an individual is achieved when both his outer being and his inner being are transformed. This will ultimately lead man to a spiritual freedom that is based on the realisation of a divine brotherhood among human beings across cultures and beyond national boundaries.

22. *SABCL*, vol. 19, *The Triple Transformation*, p. 900.
23. *SABCL*, vol. 17, *A System of National Education*, p. 204.

2

Sri Aurobindo's Views on Education and Its Relevance

Sushmita Bhowmik

EDUCATION constitutes the primary basis that lays down the foundation of a civilised society. By nurturing the inner as well as the outer lives of the individual beings, it leads to the development of man and society. It shapes human sentiments, moulds man's social behaviour and thereby enriches the society's institution, customs, culture and social life as a whole. Thus from the very beginning of human civilisation the great sages, the intellectuals, social thinkers and the social reformers have tried to determine the nature and the aim of such education that can satisfy individuals' needs and interests and help them to evolve into ideal human beings.

During the end of the nineteenth and the beginning of the twentieth century, India has also witnessed the rise of many such great thinkers who in their mission to rebuild the nation devoted themselves to the task of reforming the then education system. The most prominent amongst them were Rabindranath Tagore, Swamī Vivekananda, Mahatma Gandhi and Sri Aurobindo. Each of their views on education had some distinct and significant ideals and aims in view, but they essentially aimed at the uplift of humanity and the wholesome growth of human personality. In the present article it is not possible to discuss the illuminating thoughts of all those men of wisdom. This article seeks to focus upon Sri Aurobindo's views on education and wants to explore their relevance in the educational system of the present society.

Sri Aurobindo has been one of the greatest spiritual seekers of India, a *yogī*, whose aim was to bring about the good of the entire mankind through the awakening of spirituality within it. He tried to determine a spiritual purpose of human life and activities on this earth and firmly believed that in their attempts to fulfil that purpose human beings can transform and transmute their inner as well as outer lives and thus realise eternal peace and harmony for which they have been yearning for ages. However, it is interesting to note that during the early period of his life, from 1893-1910, Sri Aurobindo was actively involved in the political activities related to the freedom struggle of India and emerged as one of the greatest nationalist leaders. But after 1910, he gradually detached himself from political activities and dedicated the rest of his life and activities to the search and realisation of the spiritual meaning of life. Now during the initial period of his career, from 1897 to the early part of 1906, Sri Aurobindo taught French and English in the Baroda College and eventually became its principal. Later he also became the principal of the Bengal National College which later came to be known as the National Council of Education. During those days Sri Aurobindo had an experience of the dismal condition of India that made him feel the acute need for a true national education. He then wrote many articles on education in the *Karmayogin* and in the *Arya* which reveal the deeper philosophical thoughts of Sri Aurobindo regarding education.

While determining the principles of national education, the first and foremost concern of the great visionary was to build up India as a great nation. Sri Aurobindo explained,

> National education cannot be defined briefly in one or two sentences, but we may describe it tentatively as the education which, starting with the past and making full use of the present, builds up a great nation.[1]

The primary aim of Sri Aurobindo was to make the youths of the nation conscious of their own culture and heritage and develop them as self-reliant human beings. While explaining the purpose of national education, Sri Aurobindo discussed about the fundamental aim and significance of true education. According to him, there are three things which are to be taken into consideration in a true and living education. They are, "the man, the individual in his commonness and in his uniqueness, the nation or people and universal humanity."[2] The growth and development of the individual should be the primary objective of an ideal education. The individual has some unique qualities of his own. The aim of education should be to help the individual for the complete development of those qualities so that he may realise the full purpose of his life and activities. Again he has some qualities which he shares in common with the other members of the society. Through the proper nurture of those propensities education should help him to become an ideal member of the nation who may gradually unite with the entire humanity. Thus true education should bring harmony between the man, the nation or people and the universal humanity.

In this connection it may be noted that Sri Aurobindo conceived some distinct ideas regarding the nature of man, the nation and the world, which were deeply spiritual in nature and gave his educational thoughts a spiritual orientation.

---

1. Sri Aurobindo, *Out of the Ruins of the West . . . India's Rebirth*, Paris: Institut De Researches Evolutives, p. 36.
2. Sri Aurobindo, and The Mother, *On Education*, Pondicherry: Sri Aurobindo Ashram, 1st edn., 1956, p. 7.

Sri Aurobindo explained that man is not merely a living body developed by physical nature and characterised by certain vital propensities, an ego, a mind and a reason; nor is he only a reasoning animal possessing thinking, feeling and willing. It would not be right to define man either as a political, social and economic being. According to Sri Aurobindo all these are no doubt different aspects of the human being but they constitute his outer being and do not represent his true nature. Then what is the real nature of man? Here, we need to make a brief discussion on the metaphysical thoughts and principles that underlie Sri Aurobindo's vision of the life and the world and form the basis of his entire philosophy.

Sri Aurobindo considered the Supreme Spirit or the Self as the highest truth and described it as the one eternal and all-pervading *Brahman* or the *Saccidānanda* which is of the nature of pure consciousness. He argued that since the divine reality is all-pervading, it is already present within us as well as in the external material world. The aim of human life is to realise its unity with the divine truth and then to work for its manifestation in his own life, in the life of the entire humanity and thereby in the entire material world. This would result in a radical transformation of the entire nature and the physical existence of man. A divine life characterised by peace and harmony would then emerge on earth. According to Sri Aurobindo this transformation towards the emergence of divine life would become possible through a gradual process of evolution of consciousness. The evolution of the world has so far reached the level of mind passing through the stages of matter and life. Time has now come when evolution must take a leap into the next higher spiritual realm that is into the Supermind or the Supreme-Truth-Consciousness. As a result of this the "mental man" would be able to overcome all forms of ignorance from which he suffers at the level of mind and thereby step into the realm of knowledge. But for this, man would have to put his conscious effort. Through the practice of integral yoga, he would have to bring transformation within his inner being and thus help in the manifestation of the divine reality on this earth.

In this connection Sri Aurobindo conceived man as a soul, a portion of the divinity enwrapped in mind and body, a conscious manifestation in Nature of the universal self and spirit. He has a mental, an intellectual, an ethical, a dynamic and practical, an aesthetic and hedonistic, a vital and physical being. Sri Aurobindo regarded all these aspects of the soul as the powers of the soul or the psychic being which manifests through them and grows with their growth. But they do not represent the soul as a whole, for, the soul is essentially a spiritual being whose ultimate objective is to realise its unity with the divine reality and thereby manifest the divine consciousness in the entire physical existence.

Similarly Sri Aurobindo explained that the nation is not an organised state or an armed and efficient community well prepared for the struggle of life and putting all at the service of the national ego. On the other hand, the nation is a great communal soul and life that has manifested a nature of its own revealed through its intellectual, aesthetic, ethical, dynamic, social and political forms and culture.

Sri Aurobindo himself said that such an account of the human or the national being maintained by him may not be accepted by all as a true account. But if it is once admitted as a true description of the man and the nation, then considering it, the central motive of education should be to help the individual in the growth of the soul and its powers and possibilities. In case of the nation, education should ensure the preservation, strengthening and enrichment of the nation-soul and its *dharma*. Education should help both the individual and the nation to develop into powers of the life, as well as to ascend the mind and soul of humanity. And its highest objective would obviously be the awakening and development of the spiritual being of man so that he may work as an instrument of divine manifestation and transform this physical existence into a divine life.

Hence, for Sri Aurobindo, the spiritual purpose of human life, namely the establishment of the divine life on earth, has been the ultimate guiding principle in determining the ideals of true education. Now, to fulfil that divine purpose and become an ideal instrument for the manifestation of the universal spirit on this earth, the individuals need the development and attainment of perfection of all the aspects of their beings — the physical, the vital as well as the mental, the psychic and the spiritual. Hence, in his scheme of education, Sri Aurobindo emphasised upon education related to all these aspects of man — the body, the mind and the soul. The Mother of Sri Aurobindo Ashram whom Sri Aurobindo regarded as the personification of Spirit, called such forms of education as integral education.

Sri Aurobindo said that, "If our seeking is for a total perfection of the being, the physical part of it cannot be left aside; for the body is the material basis, the body is the instrument which we have to use."[3] For the development of the body he prescribed such activities like sports and physical exercises in childhood and adolescence which should bring out the actual and latent possibilities of the child to their fullest development.

Sri Aurobindo also asked for the training of the sense organs. This constitutes the education of the vital aspect of the human being. This part of the individual being lies at the root of his various feelings, sentiments, desires and impulses and determines his character. That is why the child's education

3. Sri Aurobindo, and The Mother, *On Education*, Pondicherry: Sri Aurobindo Ashram, I[st] edn 1956, p.36.

of the vital is essentially important. According to the Mother, for such education, it is necessary to develop and utilise the sense organs. Secondly, one must become conscious and gradually acquire mastery over his character so that one may bring about its transformation. Sri Aurobindo thus regarded the perfection of the senses as ministers to thought as one of the first duties of the teacher. These senses include the five external sense organs — eye, ear, nose, skin and palate and one internal sense organ — the mind or the *citta*. In this connection the Mother felt that proper nurture and refinement of the sense organs would lead to the cultivation of nobility and generosity in the individual which would gradually have its expression in his behaviour.

One of the most important parts of education is the development of the mind, for, "The instrument of the educationist is the mind or *antaḥkaraṇa*."[4] Regarding the training of the mental faculties Sri Aurobindo suggested that the teacher should help the pupil to enhance his ability to concentrate as well as to sharpen his memory, the power of judgement and imagination. He also emphasised upon the training of the logical faculty. But the process of Sri Aurobindo's education does not end with the development of the intellect alone. The individual must also understand the true motive of life and the reason of his existence upon earth through the discovery of the eternal principle that constitutes the truth of his existence, i.e. the soul or the psychic being. Thus Sri Aurobindo admitted psychic education. Finally, for the transformation of the nature of man and his ascent towards the Supermind there is need for spiritual and supramental education.

Thus the primary objective of education in Sri Aurobindo's view is the wholesome development of human personality

---

4. Sri Aurobindo, and The Mother, *On Education*, Pondicherry: Sri Aurobindo Ashram, I[st] edn 1956, p. 14.

and a spiritual transformation of the present nature of man and thereby a gradual evolution of consciousness. However, an account of Sri Aurobindo's philosophy of education cannot be complete without mentioning the three principles of education recognised by him.

According to Sri Aurobindo, the first principle of true teaching is that "nothing can be taught."[5] The task of a teacher is not to train the pupil's mind by putting lots of information into it. Every individual possesses some innate propensities. The teacher is to help him by showing him the ways by which he can himself arouse and cultivate his inner potentialities. In the second principle of education, Sri Aurobindo insisted that education should always be in accordance with the nature and growth of the mind which is receiving it. In this connection he warned us against a mistake that people generally make. "There can be no greater error than for the parent to arrange beforehand that his son shall develop particular qualities, capacities, ideas, virtues, or be prepared for a prearranged career."[6] Thus, the parent and the teacher must give the child the freedom to nurture those innate qualities in his own way and should guide him so that he can make them perfect.

The third principle as stated by Sri Aurobindo is, "to work from the near to the far, from that which is to that which shall be."[7] According to him, man's nature, besides his soul's part, is determined by his heredity, his surroundings, his nationality, his country, the soil from which he draws sustenance, the air which he breathes, the sights, sounds and habits to which he is familiar. Since all these constitute the natural environment which moulds the nature of the child, true education should

5. Sri Aurobindo, and The Mother, *On Education*, p. 12.
6. Ibid.
7. Ibid., p. 13.

not separate the child from that natural environment; rather it should help him in his free growth and development.

It may be noted that Sri Aurobindo's views and principles regarding the nature of true education, which we have discussed so far, have some important implications and are very much relevant in relation to the present education system. In the present society we notice that due to excessive competition coupled with the tendency to treat education largely as a means to get a good job and earn as much money as possible, education is losing its true essence. It is unable to fulfil its primary objective, namely a balanced development of human personality and thus we find that anxiety, depression and different other forms of mental illness are gradually increasing within the student community. Being unable to cope with the excessive pressure and failing to achieve their desired results in the examination students are often committing suicides. Further, in spite of achieving success in the academic fields as well as in professional lives, individuals fail to meet the different other crises of their social lives. Students are even found to have engaged themselves in different anti-social activities. Altogether, there is an unrest, indiscipline and lack of peace and harmony within the student community. Thus, although the present education system has been able to equip the students with advanced information in science, technology and other fields, it has failed to pay an equal effort to nurture and develop their inner souls. It is in this regard that Sri Aurobindo's thoughts and ways towards the development of the individual soul become significant and relevant.

The most important part of the educational thoughts of the great visionary lies in its spiritual approach towards the nurture of the human soul. Such an approach can at least give a humanistic turn to the present education system and prevent it from being entirely materialistic. Money is undoubtedly one of the most important and basic necessities for the sustenance of human life and society. But it cannot be the sole determinant of the aims and the ways of the individuals' lives. For, there are different other needs and interests pertaining to the inner life of man. Sri Aurobindo rightly pointed out that if we want the individuals to cope with the real situations in life, to realise the true purpose of life and make a proper evaluation of it, then there is need for the arousal of a greater consciousness that lies hidden within them. It is the consciousness that governs one's life, that makes one think and act in his own particular way — it is the self or the soul wherein lies one's true strength and the truth of one's existence. The realisation of that truth is the true goal of life and such education like psychic education, spiritual education and supramental education would help the individual in the discovery of that truth and thereby prepare him to adjust with the difficult situations in life. As an essential part of such education the Mother proposed the practice of several introspective exercises, like self-observation and self-analysis which would gradually make the child aware of the nature of his innermost being. Overcoming the barriers of egoism, selfishness and personal attachments one would gradually learn to identify himself with others resulting in the cultivation of the values of unity and harmony. The individual would learn to overcome the excessive demands of the material life and acquire the abilities to bear the pains and sorrows pertaining to the phenomenal life.

The remarkable aspect of Sri Aurobindo's views on education is that they centre around the child's mind, nature and the soul and emphasise upon its free growth and development. The application of the principles recognised by him can make the present education system more flexible. It would allow the students to think freely and to widen the horizon of their interests. By enabling the students to realise and nurture their potentialities in their own ways, those principles would help to enhance their self-confidence. The students would be able to identify the goals of their lives according to the areas of their interests. All these would help the present student community to strengthen their mental qualities and to channelise their energies in the right direction.

However, such forms of education like psychic education, spiritual education and supramental education do not come among the recognised subjects of education. Education guided by such a spiritual ideal which hopes to transform human nature and existence into a newer and higher form of life may be regarded as unrealisable and utopian by many. But that does not in anyway diminish the value and significance of the ideas themselves. It may not be possible for us to follow the principles exactly in the way laid down by Sri Aurobindo but we should not remain indifferent to them. Rather we have to reconsider the illuminating thoughts of Sri Aurobindo and evaluate them in the light of our present education system and invent ways to implement them in our lives. We must always bear in mind the basic message that we receive from the philosophy of Sri Aurobindo and that is we can transform and uplift our lives and societies through the realisation of the strength that lies within us. We can thus fulfil the dream of the great visionary to rebuild India as a great nation and make her people self-reliant human beings.

Bibliography

Aurobindo, Sri, *Out of the Ruins of the West . . . India's Rebirth*, Paris: Institut De Researches Evolutives.

Aurobindo, Sri, *The Life Divine*, Pondicherry: Sri Aurobindo Ashram, 1st edn., 1939-40.

Sri Aurobindo, and The Mother, On Education, Pondicherry: Sri Aurobindo Ashram, 1st edn. 1956.

3

Physical Education
An Essential item of Integral Education

Indrani Sanyal

EDUCATION, understood as integral education in the light of Sri Aurobindo's thought, has some very definite and irrevocable normative suggestions. To understand Sri Aurobindo's perspective on education, we may begin by recapitulating his statement regarding man, his existence and the world process: to quote Sri Aurobindo,

> Man is there to affirm himself in the universe, that is his first business, but also to evolve and finally to exceed himself: he has to change his partial being into a complete being, his partial consciousness into integral consciousness.[1]

Man, according to Sri Aurobindo, is a developing being and education is conceived as a process for bringing about that development or transformation in man.

True education in the eyes of Sri Aurobindo, integrates individual soul, nation or people and the universal consciousness.[2] According to him, any education to be a complete education must aim at developing the main sheaths

1. *Sri Aurobindo Birth Centenary Library*, vol. 19, p. 684.
2. "What It Is to be Educated? In the light of Sri Aurobindo's Philosophy", Indrani Sanyal, in *Understanding Thoughts of Sri Aurobindo*, 2007.

of human existence — its physical, vital, mental, psychic, supramental and spiritual aspect. True education, as a process of development through physical education, vital education and mental education may be the goal of all ordinary men. In the present essay, I would like to concentrate on the very basal aspect of human existence, i.e. the physical level and would like to elaborate the nature of physical education, its objective in the whole scheme of Sri Aurobindo's view on education. I would also like to emphasise the relevance and importance of his views in the context of the contemporary thought on education. Before proceeding directly into his views on physical education,[3] it would not be out of place to refer to the different principles enacted and the various strategies adopted with regard to physical education in the twentieth century throughout the world. I would begin by referring to the International Charter of Physical Education and Sport released by UNESCO expressing its conviction that:

> One of the essential conditions for the effective exercise of human rights is that everyone should be free to develop and preserve his or her physical, intellectual and moral powers, and that access to physical education and sport should consequently be assured and guaranteed for all human beings.[4]

Concern about the insufficient amount of appropriate physical activity by young people has been expressed in statements of several major organisations including WHO, UNESCO, IOC, ICSSPE and by many other international bodies in their international health promotion meetings and conferences. In the WHO policy statement it has been said:

---

3. "Message", "Perfection of the Body", "The Divine Body", "Haṭhayoga", "The Power of the Instruments", "The Body-Mind" in *Sri Aurobindo and the Mother on Physical Education*, 2002.
4. Adopted by the General Conference at its Twentieth Session, Paris, 21 November, 1978.

> Physical activity is an essential lifelong stimulus for every individual to reach his or her full potential of growth and development, as well as to maintain optimal health and functional capacity. It also counteracts disabilities and diseases common to ageing. Regular practice of physical activity helps children and young people to develop strong muscles and bones, normal body weight and efficient function of the heart and lungs and to learn to master the skills of movement.
>
> Engagement in play and sports gives young people opportunities for natural self-expression, relief of tension, achievement, social interaction and integration as well as for learning the spirit and the rules of fair play in human relations. These positive effects are important to counteract the risks and harm caused by the demanding, competitive, stressful and sedentary way of life that is so common in present society.[5]

WHO has taken programmes for implementing Global Initiative on Active Living, wherein the term "active living/ physical activity" is explained as follows:

> The term "active living/physical activity" is considered in its broadest sense and refers to the entire spectrum of "bodily movements" resulting in energy expenditure that each person can undertake in daily life, ranging from normal active living conditions to "intentional" moderate physical activities, physical exercises, physical fitness and training sessions and sport for all activities, especially leisure and recreational sports.[6]

The programme of WHO pronouncing Health and Development Through Physical Activity specifically states,

---

5. WHO Policy Statement on Promoting Physical Activity, part I.
6. "Promoting Active Living in and Through Schools — Policy Statement and Guidelines for Action, Report of a WHO Meeting Esbjerg, Denmark, 25-27 May 1998.

Physical activity and healthy sports are essential for our health and well-being.[7]

Thus, we find that the world recognises the right to physical education as a human right and its violation has been considered as a heinous offence. But still today in many quarters the common misconception prevails that physical education is an "extra," "burdensome," "not-so-necessary" part of school curriculum. On 6 November 2010 issue of *The Telegraph* newspaper in its Metro section begins with the caption, "Wonder Years Without Outdoors", specifically referring to the plight of present-day urban kids who are thus victims of great deprivation. It is relieving, however, to read from the same issue of the newspaper that the Central Board of Secondary Education has made from the session 2010-11 the outdoor activities compulsory for students from class I to XII.

In the classical Indian tradition and the classical Western tradition the concept of integral education received enormous recognition and in the total scheme, physical education was one of the important constituents. It was Greece that made an institution of the Olympiad and through the re-establishment of the Olympic Games internationally in our times, the importance of physical culture has been reasserted. In the ancient texts like Vedas and Upaniṣads, the body has been held with great esteem and has been considered as the receptacle of strength (*bala*), for strength was one of the commendable physical qualities:

balena lokostiṣṭhati balamupasveti[8]

The existence of the world is dependent on strength. Be devoted to strength.[9]

---

7. For a detail information on related programmes and WHO documents see Bibliography.
8. *Chāndogya Upaniṣad*, 7.8.1.
9. Translation from "Physical Education in Ancient India", in *Mystery and Excellence of the Human Body*.

In the *Ṛgveda*, Indra, one of the Vedic gods, is associated with strength, and prayers are offered to him for providing strength to an individual's body, to his animals (bulls), to his descendants.[10] In the *Taittirīya Upaniṣad*, we find the teacher and the students are joining together in their prayer for strength:

> Together may we make ourselves strong[11]

In the same Upaniṣad, we find the following *mantra*:[12]

> O God, may I become a vessel of immortality. May my body be swift to all works, may my tongue drop pure honey.

Again in the *Īśopaniṣad* the *mantra* saying "Doing verily works in this world should wish to live hundred years" suggests the importance and immense potentiality of physical body. The *Sāmaveda* echoes the same yearning for a perfect physical body, when it says,

> May my limbs, speech, vitality, eyes, ears, strengthen and senses receive ample nourishment, and attain to their full development.[13]

In Sri Aurobindo's views about education a remarkable influence of Upaniṣads and other classical Indian views is observed, though his unparalleled contribution to philosophy of education is undeniable. Sri Aurobindo's views on education in general presuppose his metaphysics of *The Life Divine*. However, it would not be correct to think that Sri Aurobindo was interested in working out only certain abstruse theories about education. His interest was in offering a sort of, so to say, productive philosophy which would enrich human

---

10. *Ṛgveda*, III.53.18.
11. *saha vīryam karavāvahai* — *Taittirīya Upaniṣad*, 2.1.
12. *Taittirīya Upaniṣad*, 1.4.
13. "Physical Education in Ancient India", p. 270.

existence and life. Sri Aurobindo was very much impressed by the practical contribution of philosophy for he considered it as a matter of realisation as well. Sri Aurobindo was a complete philosopher who has interpreted and reinterpreted the Vedas and the Upaniṣads both from a theoretical perspective and an "experiential" perspective. His philosophy of education and its practice as suggested by him need to be perceived from this specific perspective. In the recent Indian context, the widespread suspicion about the very meaning and purpose of education has become so acute as the system of education has been mostly reduced to mechanical procedures for churning out degrees, diplomas and certificates without the least concern for the temperament, potentiality, quality and development of the pupils. The voices of dissension against these practices are not yet sufficiently loud to be heard. But time is quite ripe to rethink about the role of education in our life and society and this establishes the need for discussing Sri Aurobindo's philosophy of education from various perspectives. In the present essay I would like to concentrate more on his views on physical education. To vindicate Sri Aurobindo's demand for physical education in the life of a human being and his society, I have already referred to different resolutions and proposals mooted by international organisations as eye-opener. The need for physical education has been recognised by the whole world and there seems to be no doubt about its utility. Compared to Sri Aurobindo's immensely substantial approach to education, we shall see subsequently, most of the commonly accepted views, however, lack deeper insight.

Basic Philosophical Presuppositions

Sri Aurobindo in whose opinion the objective of education is spiritual self-building and self-finding states categorically, that there is a supreme Divine Consciousness and we want to manifest this Consciousness in our physical life. This is Sri

Aurobindo's answer to the question regarding the meaning of human life and existence. He believed in the existence of *Saccidānanda* (the Existence-Bliss-Consciousness). Human existence is the transformation of *Saccidānanda,* and in his opinion human beings are transitional beings, they are spirits encased in living bodies, they are spirits bound up with physical, vital and mental levels of existence. Man is looked upon as containing potentiality for some wonderful future happening. Many would acknowledge that it is really difficult to turn a deaf ear to Sri Aurobindo's frequent reminder that a great possibility awaits man, that there is something beyond, something that mankind shall be. Sri Aurobindo reminds us that a man's greatness is not to be evaluated on the basis of what he is, but in terms of what he would make possible. He glorifies human beings as secret workshops for making ready supermanhood. He has convincingly argued for the existence of a supreme Divine Consciousness and the aspirations of human beings lie in manifesting this Consciousness in physical life.

It is clear that to reach the goal envisioned by Sri Aurobindo, the total perfection of human being is essential. He makes it clear further:

> If our seeking is for the total perfection of the being, the physical part of it cannot be left aside; for the body is the material basis, the body is the instrument which we have.[14]

The ancient Sanskrit proverb, *śarīram khalu dharmasādhanam,* i.e. the body is the means for the fulfilment of *dharma,* explicitly provides support to Sri Aurobindo's requirement for the perfection of the body. He says in *Letters on Yoga,*

> It is a mistake to neglect the body and let it waste away; the body is the means of the *sādhanā* and should be maintained in good order.[15]

---

14. "Perfection of the Body", p. 7.
15. Vol. III, p. 1468.

The transformation of the body is the necessary prerequisite for establishing Divine Life upon earth.

> That cannot be unless the body too undergoes transformation, unless its action and functioning attain to a supreme capacity and the perfection which is possible to it or which can be made possible.[16]

In the pursuit of perfection an individual may proceed from both the ends of his being, that is, from the higher yogic spiritual and psychic levels or from the lower physical being of existence. Whatever may be the course of action, the importance of the body, and the need for perfection of the body cannot be denied. Sri Aurobindo does not have any sympathy for the viewpoint that always denigrates body looking upon it as an impediment to human transformation and progress. In his integral yoga since Matter is the foundation of all evolutionary process, our body obviously assumes great importance. The other perspectives like that of the materialist Cārvākas, or *śūnyvādin* Buddhists or *māyāvādin* Vedāntins are all rejected by Sri Aurobindo as partial viewpoints. He admits that the body belongs to inconscience matter and as such must be subjected to the limitations and imperfections of Matter. The energy of life is the governing principle of human life, hence its limitations and physical activities are also present here. Grossness of physical body cannot be overlooked. He did not fail to notice these limitations of the physical body. While describing the physical level of existence, he says, "This nature is in itself full of low and obscure desires, it is the most animal part of the human existence."[17] He explains the feature of physical consciousness as follows:

> It is inert, conservative, does not want to move, to change —

16. Vol. III, p. 7.
17. *Letters on Yoga*, vol. 3, part IV, p. 1423.

> it clings to its habits (what people call their character) or its habits (habitual movements) cling to it and repeat themselves like a clock working in a persistent mechanical way.[18]

But he felt in the pursuit of perfection, in whichever way the agent proceeds, the physical body has some crucial role to play. The agent may seek perfection of the vital, he may seek perfection of the mental, he may seek perfection of the psychic, or he may seek spiritual end. In each of these pursuits, the agent needs to depend upon the body.

> In yoga, the process is spiritual and psychic; even its vital and physical processes are given a spiritual or psychic turn. . . .[19]

But this requires a previous preparation of the mind, life and body to be

> fit for the reception of the spiritual energy and organisation of psychic forces and methods, but this too is given a special turn proper to the yoga.[20]

Sri Aurobindo draws our attention to the principle of self-exceeding: if the individual begins from the lower being of existence, the body, life, mind — all need to be familiar with the principle of self-exceeding. Sri Aurobindo, in his whole metaphysical scheme, always had great regard for body.

> No need to despise the physical being — it is part of the intended manifestation.[21]

When he talks about physical education he is not offering a blanket prescription for everybody to enter into spiritual life.

---

18. *Letters on Yoga*, vol. 3, p. 1426.
19. "Perfection of the Body", p. 9.
20. Ibid.
21. "Transformation of the Physical", p. 1424.

Physical education has some mundane objectives as well. The training of the body, as well as the development of certain parts of the mind and character are also desirable goals. These can achieve human perfection up to a certain limit. These would improve general conditions of life and would improve the base level of human existence. If anybody is sceptical about the higher levels of being, by achieving development of the base level of being he may be at least able to taste the benefit of good life. The development that is achieved within the human boundaries is worthy of consideration. Character traits like courage, refusal to succumb under physical suffering are results of bodily development. The body can acquire skill; the mind can attain dexterity within human boundaries to meet the challenges of the most difficult and discouraging situations of life.

To educate means to bring out latent possibilities to their fullest development; and the means and methods adopted relative to the power and capacities of the body, and those of the powers of mind, will, character, and action. Sri Aurobindo provided certain suggestions as to how the body may be made more perfect.

Sri Aurobindo on Physical Health and Scope of Physical Education

To attain development of the body is to make the body healthy. Naturally the question as to how to characterise health would arise. In our common sense, health of the body is understood in terms of its muscular strength, i.e. solid strengths of limbs and physical stamina. We are reminded of the classics like the *Rāmāyaṇa* and the *Mahābhārata* where we have witnessed the celebration of physical strength. In the very beginning of the *Rāmāyaṇa*, the author Vālmīki introduces Rāma as one who has intelligence, bears good moral character, has the skill of oration and has a perfect physique. In the *Rāmāyaṇa*, Rāma has been described as one who has high broad shoulders and whose neck is marked with three auspicious conch shell lines.

He has mighty arms reaching to his knees, well-formed head, graceful forehead, strongest jaws and deeply embedded collarbones and his eyes are large, his body is symmetrical and the colour of his body is soothing.[22] In the Āyurveda, we come across concepts like *samahanana, saṁhati* and *saṁyojana* meaning thereby compactness of the body. A compact body is characterised by the symmetry and well-divided bones, well-knit joints and well-bound muscles and proper circulation of blood. An individual who possesses such a compact body is regarded as very strong; in the absence of this, he is considered to be weak.

The person who has the capacity to adapt to different circumstances, to respond to situations with alertness is regarded as healthy. A healthy body is supposed to develop skilfulness and stability in all kinds of activity like that of a soldier, a sailor, a traveller or a explorer. Some other features of a healthy body consist in the development of individual will, skill of mind, quick perception, forcefulness of subtle physical impulsion. Thus, so far what Sri Aurobindo has said about a healthy body does not seem to be controversial at all. From a young age children should be taught respect for physical health, strength and balance. The great importance of beauty must also be insisted upon.

> A young child should aspire for beauty, not for the sake of pleasing others, or gaining fame, but for the love of beauty itself; for beauty is the ideal which physical life has to realise.[23]

What is meant by beauty?

> The human body that undergoes a rational method of physical culture from the beginning of its existence can

22. *Physical Education in Ancient India,* S.H. Deshpande, New Delhi: Bharatiya Vidya Prakashan.
23. *Physical Education — The Mother,* p. 432.

> realise its own harmony and thus be fit to express beauty.[24]

The Mother maintains that a good many bodily defects and malformations can be avoided by enlightened physical education given at the proper time. Healthy body in order to be healthy depends on various factors like the types of food consumed, the types of activities to which the body is subjected to, the rest and sleep provided to the body. The normal adult body has its own physiological demands for its normal growth and development. Sri Aurobindo also acknowledges sex energy in its real nature as a fundamental energy of life.

All the important constituents of a healthy body, their natural limitations and also ways of overcoming those limitations have been elaborately discussed by Sri Aurobindo mostly in his *Letters on Yoga*. The question of food to be taken is also a very important lesson to be learnt. Foods serve many roles in the whole of our being. We need to comprehend the concept of food in its holistic sense rather than as just something to eat, lust after and satiate our hunger.

> . . . from one's very childhood, one should know that one eats in order to give to the body strength and health, and not to enjoy the pleasures of the palate.[25]
>
> The child should be given the food that suits his temperament, prepared with all care and hygiene and cleanliness, pleasant to the taste and yet very simple: and this food should be chosen and measured out according to the age of the child, and his regular activities; it must contain all the chemical and dynamic elements that are necessary for the development and the balanced growth of all the parts of the body.[26]

24. *Physical Education — The Mother*, p. 432.
25. Ibid., p. 428.
26. Ibid.

> . . . the child will be given only the food needed for maintaining health and supplying necessary energy.[27]

No doubt, nowadays nutrition has become one of the important subjects. Culinary education for vitality and energy and also nutritional consultation are common. Everybody is aware of the menacing effects of both the underfeds and the overfeds. The Ethiopian-type ill-nourished, famine-starved emaciation on the one hand and obesity on the other have become dominating newspaper headlines in recent times and are becoming increasingly serious problems. The modern science has definitely taught us to relook at food and nutrition from newer angles.

Sri Aurobindo is very much clear about the importance of food; he reinterprets the *Gītā* concept of food as tāmasic food, rājasic food and sāttvic food as follows:

> . . . tāmasic food, it seems to say, is what is stale or rotten with the virtue gone out of it, rājasic food is that which is too acrid, pungent, etc., heats the blood and spoils the health, sāttvic food is what is pleasing, healthy, etc.[28]

Sri Aurobindo's injunction on food eating does not always sound too esoteric. Rather his advice sounds quite contemporaneous with recent advices of the nutritionist.

> Too much eating makes the body material and heavy, eating too little makes it weak and nervous — one has to find the true harmony and balance between the body's need and the food taken.[29]

Sri Aurobindo does not say that food is not necessary for the body, rather he warns about the disadvantages of pursuing that course. He frequently says that his kind of education does

27. *Physical Education — The Mother*, p. 428.
28. "Words of the Master", p. 55.
29. "Transformation of the Physical", p. 1467.

not need total suppression of *rasa* or taste but to get rid of greed of food. To quote from Sri Aurobindo,

> It is the attachment to food, the greed and eagerness for it making it an unduly important thing in the life, that is contrary to the spirit of yoga. To be aware that something is pleasant to the palate is not wrong; only one must have no desire or hankering for it, no exultation in getting it, no displeasure or regret at not getting it. One must be calm and equal , not getting upset or dissatisfied when the food is not tasty or not in abundance — eating the fixed amount that is necessary, not less or more. There should be neither eagerness nor repugnance.[30]

Sri Aurobindo does not, however, take the common-sense perception about food and body to be satisfactory and decisive. In his view body's dependence on food may also undergo change: the spiritual seeker may be able to free himself from the gross physical instincts for consumption, from the desires of palate and from the greed of food. These are the things that would happen not on the surface level of physical education, but on the higher planes of physical education. He cites the instances of the Jaina ascetics who take the course of fasting which at least temporarily relieves them from the clutches of the body's demands. Instead of fasting, Sri Aurobindo emphasises upon the development of the capacity of the body to draw upon the universal energy to sustain its vital part of physicality without relying upon sustenance from any outside substance of matter. The power of yoga, to which Sri Aurobindo refers, may enable one in course of his long fasting hours to think deeply, write day and night, walk eight hours at a stretch and carry on many other activities without feeling any loss of strength, fatigue, any kind of failure and decadence. Subsequently, food may be taken to replenish lost

30. "Words of the Master", *Sri Aurobindo and the Mother on Physical Education*, p. 55.

energy. However, it may be asked: Does not this cause waste of material tissues of the body, its flesh and substance? Sri Aurobindo did not avoid answering this question. He was in search of some practicable solution to avoid this wastage. His answer seems to be that the evolved being might acquire the power "to draw those means from above rather than draw them up or pull them in from the environment around, all about it and below it."[31] Until something like this has been achieved one has to depend on food, the already accepted material forces of nature. Thus, it is clear that Sri Aurobindo is not oblivious or unaware about the limitations and requirements imposed by the physical part of the body.

The Mother substantiates Sri Aurobindo's claim for a healthy body as a stepping stone to a perfect body and she herself also does not endorse the belief that brilliant minds have weak bodies. The Mother says,

> it is a delusion and has no basis. There was perhaps epoch when a romantic and morbid taste for physical unbalance prevailed; but fortunately that tendency has disappeared.[32]
>
> Nowadays a well-built, solid, muscular, strong and perfectly balanced body is appreciated at its true value.[33]
>
> Children should be taught that to be ill is a sign of failing and inferiority, not of a virtue or a sacrifice. Sri Aurobindo teaches everybody to take care of his body and to maintain good condition of the body through proper food, rest, sleep and sufficient exercise. He never supported prolongation of ill health.

In dealing with physical body, the discussion about sex impulse cannot be avoided, for it is natural for a matured physical body and all human beings as physical beings are naturally

31. "Words of the Master", p. 30.
32. Ibid., p. 429.
33. Ibid., p. 428.

predisposed towards it. Sri Aurobindo draws a clear-cut distinction between sex-principle and the gross physical indulgence of sex impulse. He was never blind to the importance of sex-principle in the life of an individual. Sex-principle, on the other hand, has been admitted to be an integral aspect of life; hence it is not supposed to be something to be banished from life. Sri Aurobindo discovers a link between the sex-principle and the divine or cosmic principle. He does not consider sex-principle to be an undivine principle. For Sri Aurobindo, sex is not wholly a tabooed subject to be completely banished from life. Like the rigid ascetics, Sri Aurobindo would not say that banishment of sex should be the cardinal principle of a spiritual life. But, he would strongly reject one's falling prey to gross instincts of body, sexual impulses and desires. He writes quite categorically,

> All gross animal indulgence of sex-desire and impulse would have to be eliminated.[34]

His advice for the spiritual seeker is that sex will have to be refined, to be submitted to the spiritual or psychic impulse and to be placed under the control of the higher mind and higher vital. The nature of love will also attain refinement. The love of man and woman would also undergo elevation and consummation. He admits great power of sex energy with two distinct functions, one meant for procreation — i.e. in its function as a physical energy, which is called as *retas* in classical literature and the other for spiritual realisation, i.e. in its function as a spiritual energy of the body, and called as *ojas*. The Mother also speaks about liberation in action. According to the Mother, "Continence therefore is the rule for all who aspire for progress." But this statement needs further elucidation. According to the Mother those who are aspiring for super-mental manifestation this continence must be

34. "The Divine Body", p. 28.

substituted by abstinence. But this substitution of continence by abstinence is not to be achieved by coercion or suppression. This is to be achieved by a kind of inner alchemy through which the energies usually used in the act of procreation are transmuted into energies for progress and integral transformation.[35]

Sri Aurobindo also found a close connection between sports and spirituality. He did not turn a blind eye to other aspects of sports and exercises related to amusement and entertainment. Apart from providing amusement to people, he was in search of something deeper behind these uses. Sports gives an opportunity to vent energy of the body. Sri Aurobindo says that sports enable us to develop habits, capacities and qualities which are necessary in our life. He speaks with great admiration the contribution of ancient Greece that made an institution of Olympiad which survives till today as an international institution. He thinks physically fit people are the assets for any country whatsoever since these people are storehouses of energy. Basically, physical education is considered necessary for enabling one to acquire health, strength and physical fitness. But Sri Aurobindo also focuses upon some other contribution of physical education as well:

> But of a higher import . . . is the development of discipline and morale and sound and strong character towards which these activities can help.[36]

Sri Aurobindo very meticulously observes some of the good qualities of character that a person can acquire through sports. Among some of the valued traits of character we may include qualities of courage, energetic action and initiative, firmness of will, rapid decision and action, ability to cope with emergency, which are all learnt through sporting activities.

---

35. *Physical Education — The Mother*, p. 438.
36. *Bulletin of Physical Education*, February, 1949.

The awakening of the essential and instinctive body consciousness is also another gift derived from practising sports. Sri Aurobindo believes body to be conscious also and awakening of body consciousness is something different for him from mental consciousness. This instinctive body consciousness enables one to see and do what is to be done without being accompanied by any mental thought. Physical education is an attempt to educate one about the physical body and it also forms the capacity for the harmonious and right movements of all parts of the body. Another contribution of sports is the development of the sporting spirit in an individual.

> That includes good humour and tolerance and consideration for all, a right attitude and friendliness to competitors and rivals, self-control and scrupulous observance of the laws of the game, fair play and avoidance of the use of foul means, an equal acceptance of victory or defeat without bad humour, resentment or ill will towards successful competitors, loyal acceptance of the decisions of the appointed judge, umpire or referee.[37]

He also speaks about enormous contribution of some other games in developing discipline, team spirit, habit of team work which are considered essential for many spheres of our life. Sri Aurobindo thinks that sports and participation in sports are laboratories for the preparation of leaders and also for the followers both alike. This strictness of training does not imply curtailment of human freedom. In his opinion it is rather teaching one to make right use of freedom. In the national life of India he considered sports as one of the necessary instruments for character building. But Sri Aurobindo also harps on some further advantages of training in sports and games in an individual spiritual pursuit.

---

37. *Bulletin of Physical Education*, February, 1949, p. 424.

> In all kinds of concerted action this rule is indispensable; orchestration becomes necessary and there could be no success for an orchestra in which individual musicians played according to their own fancy and refused to follow the indications of the conductor.[38]
>
> In spiritual things also the same rule holds; a *sādhaka* who disregarded the guidance of the guru and preferred the untrained inspirations of the novice could hardly escape the stumbles or even the disasters which so often lie thick around the path to spiritual realisation.[39]

It was quite undoubtedly accepted under the influence of Sri Aurobindo and the Mother in the general programme of education for children at Pondicherry Ashram, that sports and outdoor games should be given a fair place; that, more than all the medicines of the world, will assure them good health.

But in any case a child should have a sufficient number of hours for sleep. This number will vary with age. But till the adult age the number should not be less than eight hours and that in a quiet and well-ventilated place. To know how to relax the muscles and nerves is an art which should be taught to children even when they are very young. All these practices are to be covered under physical education.

The Mother also makes it very clear that to pursue an integral education for attainment of supramental realisation four types of austerities need to be practised. In this connection it should not be supposed that the Mother is going against the teaching of Sri Aurobindo. The austerity of the ascetic which has been disparaged by Sri Aurobindo has also been disparaged by the Mother. There are some ascetics who in their search for spirituality consider body to be an obstacle, body to be an impediment in achieving their goal. There are some ascetics who do not care to spiritualise the physical

---

38. *Bulletin of Physical Education*, February, 1949, p. 424.
39. Ibid.

existence. Sri Aurobindo and the Mother would never agree with the ascetics who maintain that the body is a useless burden, a bondage fettering all spiritual progress. The underlying message of physical education is to do away with the presumption that body is a thing that cannot be made perfect and is a burden that has to be borne till death.

Sri Aurobindo never considered our present bodily existence merely as a means for reaching some other higher goal. His philosophy is to achieve the Life Divine upon earth. We hear the same philosophy is being echoed by his ablest collaborator Mother when she says,

> Life on earth is not a passage nor a means merely; it must become through transformation, a goal, a realisation. When we speak of austerity, it is not out of contempt for the body, with a view to dissociating ourselves from it, but because of the need of self-control and self-mastery.[40]

In fact, the Mother was very much aware about the abuses of asceticism and like Sri Aurobindo she would also never encourage any kind of perverse needs for suffering. The *sādhu*'s bed of nails and the Christian anchorite's whip and sack cloth are according to the Mother results of sadism.

> In reality these things are very far from the spiritual life; for they are ugly and low, dark and diseased; spiritual life on the contrary, is a life of light and balance, beauty and joy.[41]

The basic programme of physical education as viewed by Sri Aurobindo and the Mother, is to build a body, beautiful in form, harmonious in posture, supple and agile in its movements, powerful in its activities and resistant in its health and organic functions. Again all these have to be achieved not for the sake of the body. This physical education as the forerunner of physical culture, aims at building a body fit for

40. *Bulletin of Physical Education*, February, 1949, p. 434.
41. Ibid.

the demands of higher consciousness. To get these results it will be good to form habits and utilise them as a help in organising material life. The Mother suggested the observance of a fourfold austerity regarding food, sleep, work activities, depending on the needs of one's body — for needs may vary from one body to another. To quote Mother,

> The all-absorbing interest that men, without exception, even the most intellectual, take in food, in its preparation and consumption, should be replaced by an almost chemical knowledge of the needs of the body.[42]

One must also have adequate hours of sleep and neither it should be without any sleep nor it should be only hours after hours of sleep. Again sleep is not just falling into unconsciousness. It has been very explicitly made clear that it is not quantity but the quality of sleep that matters. The effective sleep provides the body the required rest and repose.

The Mother says about physical *tapasyā* which is nothing but doing regular exercises according to the needs of the body under the supervision of able supervisors.

> The body of each one, with regard to its perfection or simply improvement, is a problem to be solved and the solution demands much patience, perseverance and regularity.[43]
>
> Similarly, in the field of work one should learn to work with interest any work that has been allotted to him.
>
> For the man who wishes to perfect himself, there is nothing like small or big work, important work or unimportant.
>
> Whatever be the occupation or task must be done with an earnestness to do it better and better in a constant drive to perfection. In this way all things become interesting from the material labour to the most artistic and intellectual work.

---

42. *Physical Education — The Mother, p. 435.*
43. Ibid., p. 436.

Sri Aurobindo's Philosophy of Physical Education

Thus we see for Sri Aurobindo along with his collaborator Mother, physical education is to be pursued to make physical bodies perfect. But in their philosophy this is not the goal of physical education; perfection of body is a prerequisite for awakening the body consciousness. Sri Aurobindo views body as nothing but consciousness concealed within itself. According to him, in all forms in the world, there is a force at work, but it may remain unconsciously active or oppressed by inertia in its lower formulations. In human beings conscious force is conscious from the first, with its potentialities partly awakened partly latent or in sleep. Sri Aurobindo advises to work for making the awakened consciousness fully conscious, to arouse or set to work the sleeping consciousness and to evoke and educate what is latent in the physical body. His observation about two aspects of the body consciousness is comparable to the belief regarding the functioning of the body. When the automatic functioning of the body is taken into consideration, the large part of our body appears to function like a machine as if functioning without any intervention of the mind. This sort of functioning of the body without any intervention of the mind, does not only imply the actual functioning without any intervention of the mind but also suggests functioning without any possibility of the direct intervention by the mind whatsoever. But Sri Aurobindo believes that mind can exert control over the body.

> The mind pre-eminently is man, he is a mental being and his human perfection grows the more he fulfils the description of the Upaniṣad, a mental being, *puruṣa*, leader of the life and the body. If the mind can take up and control the instincts and automatisms of the life-energy and the subtle physical consciousness and the body, if it can enter into them, consciously use and as we may say, fully mentalise their instinctive or spontaneous action, the

> perfection of these energies, their action too become conscious and more aware of itself and more perfect.[44]

Sri Aurobindo speaks about the evolution of the mind as well for mind must also grow in perfection and must depend less on the fallible physical body.

> Even within the limits of its present evolution it is difficult to measure the degree to which the mind is able to extend its control or its use of the body's powers and capacities and when the mind rises to higher powers still and pushes back its human boundaries, it becomes impossible to fix any limits.[45]
>
> Wherever limitations recede and in proportion as they recede, the body becomes more plastic and responsive and in that measure a more fit and perfect instrument of the action of the spirit.[46]

This is Sri Aurobindo's reason for seeking perfection of the body. One who does not believe in his philosophy, may not agree fully with his views. But that does not minimize the importance of physical education. For if the body fails to attain perfection then the insufficiency of the body stands in the way of its being responsive to the vibration of the brain and its openness as a channel for the power of thought and vision. Sri Aurobindo has a definite sense of human progress. The consciousness with its greater awakening and its climbing to higher and wider domains are the conditions of its progress. In the process of achieving progress there need to have some transformation of the mind, life and body.

> . . . the body itself a conscious vessel of the truth and part of the means of its self-effectuation and a form of its self-aware-existence.[47]

44. "Perfection of the Body", p. 15.
45. Ibid.
46. Ibid., p. 16.
47. "The Divine Body", p. 20.

The question may be raised as to why our body needs to be perfected at all. Sri Aurobindo would say,

> As an instrument the body would acquire a fullness of capacity, a totality of fitness for all uses which the inhabitant would demand of it far beyond anything now possible.[48]

Generally, the total perfection of the spiritualised body does not come all at once. But at times, so to say very uncommonly, this may happen at once when divine Power, Light and Ānanda situate themselves in the life of the being. Sri Aurobindo makes clear the implication of divine life on earth by saying,

> A Divine Life in a divine body is the ideal.[49]

To speak about a divine body requires some parameters against which it is distinguished from the undivinely body. Host of questions arise as to the nature of the divine body, its structure, the principle of its activity, the conditions and operations of that sought-after physicality. Sri Aurobindo depends on the philosophy of evolution — "an evolution out of our human imperfection and ignorance into a greater truth of spirit and nature." But he also searches for the process to bring about a rapid transformation. The process for evolution upon earth has been slow and tardy — what principle must intervene if there is to be a transformation — a progressive or sudden change?

Sri Aurobindo's philosophy spreads optimism by spreading the message for evolution into a greater truth of spirit and nature out of our human imperfection and ignorance. He does not say that imperfection and ignorance are the final human destiny and human beings are doomed to such imperfection and ignorance for ever. But the very pertinent question remains: What must intervene between imperfection

48. "The Divine Body", p. 20.
49. Ibid., p. 21.

and ignorance on the one hand and truth of spirit on the other? Sri Aurobindo's yogic vision also corroborates various scientific observations regarding the different steps to be envisaged in between the coming of Matter, Life and Mind in Nature. It is Nature which has evolved beyond Matter and manifested Life. It is Nature which has evolved beyond Life and manifested Mind. This perennial seeking of Nature consists in, as situated in a particular plane of existence, always for manifestation in a higher plane; that is the essence of Nature. Sri Aurobindo argued that Nature must evolve beyond Mind and manifest consciousness and power free from imperfection. The process of evolution has been slow and tardy upon the earth and the process would remain so till the Nature grows into truth-consciousness. But once the Mind evolves to the level of supramental the process of evolution need not be slow and tardy as before. The supramental truth consciousness has the "native powers" to transform mind, life and body upon earth into a manifestation of the truth-conscious spirit. The supramental consciousness can bring into the earth enough of the omniscient light and omnipotent force of the spirit to conquer. All earthly things need to respond to this supramental light and force to receive the omniscient light and omnipotent force of the spirit to be conquered by it. The earthly things can respond by opening up to the fullness of its light and power. No doubt the very idea of "opening up" as proposed by Sri Aurobindo may evoke various images. Is the "opening up" like keeping windows ajar to receive sunrays? Is it like "opening up" to newer ideas? Sri Aurobindo maintains, "whatever does open must to that extent undergo change." Whoever opens up, as it appears from Sri Aurobindo, participates in the process of give and take. This has been referred to as the principle of transformation. Thus, it is clear that this opening up presupposes a certain change, or transformation. What is the sort or type of change that Sri Aurobindo is speaking about? He speaks of psychological change and also of bodily change. He refers to that sort of psychological change that would establish divine life upon earth. The psychological change that he talks about is meant for elevation from the brute humanly existence to supramental plane. Throughout his different writings, we find Sri Aurobindo's craving for divine life. But he pointed out, this bringing about supramental living, i.e. transformation would not be complete if the body remains untransformed. The untransformed body would impose its inevitable limitations of its untransformed form. Now, if our goal is the total transformation of the being, a transformation of the body must be an indispensable part of it. Without the transformation of the body, no divine life would be possible.

> A transformation of the body must be the condition for a total transformation of the nature.[50]

Another misgiving about transformation is that all humanity would rise in a block into the supermind. Sri Aurobindo does not make any such extravagant claim. He makes it quite clear that transformation would result in stages. The question remains as to how far can such physical transformation be carried on? Or, in other words, what are the limits within which body must remain to be consistent with life upon earth and without carrying that life beyond the earthly sphere? So long as a man is considered as an embodied being, the limitation of his body and obstacles created thereby would be there. Sri Aurobindo had admitted that language, brain, heart, senses — all these bring bondage to the spirit. Physical body when bound to the earthly nature fails to respond to the call of the spirit to climb higher. This is the perennial problem of tug-of-war between body and spirit to outdo the other and maintain dominance of one over the other. The bodily mechanisms, its need, food, the pre-occupation with

---

50. "The Divine Body", p. 22.

the means of getting it, storing it, fatigue and sleep, satisfaction of bodily desire, etc. limit the scope of its large ambitions and longings. These bodily obstacles are taken to be insurmountable. Rather, we find Sri Aurobindo speaks with great optimism when he says,

> These obstacles can be overcome, the denials and resistance of the body surmounted, its transformation is possible.[51]

The important question then arises as to why do we need education. The answer seems to be this: in order to make the inconscient animal part in us illumined and capable of manifesting the god-nature. Sri Aurobindo never thinks this to be an absurd dream. He is always in favour of achieving that goal. He suggests that what seems to us to be supramental truth consciousness of the divinity can be transformed into a reality. But he reminds, that is possible on a condition. He says,

> The obligation and compulsion of its animality must cease to be obligatory and purification of its materiality by which that very materiality can be turned into a material solidity of the manifestation of the divine nature.[52]

Thus physical education is needed so that "Matter itself can be turned into a means of revelation of the spiritual reality, the Divine."

The Mother also gives due importance to physical education. The physical domain of consciousness as elaborately explained by the Mother has some additional advantages than other domains of consciousness. The Mother has rightly observed some basic characteristics of the physical domain of consciousness. Physical consciousness is akin to matter and like Matter it may lack plasticity or receptivity. But it is not

51. "The Divine Body", p. 27.
52. Ibid.

difficult to change these features. Material domain is more governed by method, order, discipline and procedure. For that reason often we find Matter is regarded as the best field for scientific work. The physical education to be effective must be rigorous and disciplined. All education of the body must begin from the birth and it must go on till the end of life.

On Physical Consciousness and its Transformation

The important thing that Sri Aurobindo reiterates about physical existence is that it has to be transformed. In fact, he does not agree with the view of those who aspire to rise into the spiritual or psychic realms and leave the physical part as it is without attempting to transform it. But at the same time he does not consider the physicality of the being to be easily transformable. He says,

> . . . but practically it is found that the physical impurity is strong enough to bar the inner progress and limit rigidly the inner experience to some passive peace.[53]

In his yogic experience he must have got clear understanding about the nature of physical consciousness. His description of physical consciousness is as follows:

> It is inert, conservative, does not want to move, to change — it clings to its habits (what people call their character, habitual movements) which repeat themselves like a clock working in a persistent mechanical way.[54]

A few pages later he also says,

> It is obscure, stupid, indolent, full of ignorance and inertia, darkness and slowness of *tamas*.[55]

---

53. "Transformation of the Physical", p. 1423.
54. Ibid., p. 1426.
55. Ibid., p. 1429.

Sri Aurobindo says:

> *Tamas*, inertia, ignorance, stupidity, littleness, obstruction to the true movement are universal characteristics of the material consciousness, so long as it is not enlightened, regenerated and transformed from above. . . .[56]
>
> . . . when one gets fully or exclusively into it, one feels it to be like that of an animal, either obscure and restless or inert and stupid and in either condition not open to the Divine.[57]

Sri Aurobindo variously describes physical consciousness in terms of persistent obstinacy, with a massive force of negation and inertia.

> The inertia of the physical consciousness is always a difficult thing to eliminate.[58]
>
> The physical's tendency to inertia is very great; even after the habit of living in the higher consciousness is there, some part may feel the pressure of the inertia.[59]
>
> A certain inertia, tendency to sleep, indolence, unwillingness or inability to be strong to work or spiritual effort for long at a time, is in the nature of human physical consciousness.[60]
>
> In dealing with the physical and subconscient the working is always slower than when it acts on the mind and vital because the resistance of physical stuff is always heavier and less intelligent and adaptable; but as a compensation the work done in the being by this slower movement is in the end more complete, solid and durable.[61]
>
> The main difficulty of the physical consciousness is that it is unable, before it is transformed, of maintaining any

56. "Transformation of the Physical", p. 1430.
57. Ibid.
58. Ibid., p. 1436.
59. Ibid.
60. Ibid., p. 1461.
61. Ibid., p. 1437.

> tension of *tapasyā* — it wants periods of assimilation, sinking back into the ordinary consciousness to rest. . . .[62]
>
> The physical is the slave of certain forces which create a habit and drive it through the mechanical power of the habit.[63]

If we turn to the pages of *Letters on Yoga,* we find the notion of education is quite replaceable by the notion of transformation. He has suggested a good definition of transformation. In his opinion, the transformation that he is talking about applies to each part of the being including physical, vital and others. In Sri Aurobindo's opinion, transformation means, by overcoming the obstacles that are peculiar to each part of being, gaining capability to respond to the demands of the higher part of being. However, Sri Aurobindo would not say that is the full change as understood by him, because in his scheme, the full change comes by the ascent to the above and the descent from the above. For that yoga and *sādhanā* are essential. The yoga that he advocates has to be regarded as a living thing, not a mental principle or a set of methods. A lazy body is certainly not a proper instrument for yoga. According to Sri Aurobindo it is a mistake to neglect the body and let it waste away; the body is the means of *sādhanā* and should be maintained in good order. In Sri Aurobindo's yoga the aim is not only the union with the higher consciousness but the transformation (by its power) of the lower including the physical nature.[64]

The *Gītā* says yoga is not for one who eats too much or sleeps too much, neither is it for one who does not eat or does not sleep, but if one eats and sleeps suitably — *yuktaharī yuktanidrāḥ* — then one can do it best.[65]

62. "Transformation of the Physical", p. 1439.
63. Ibid., p. 1443.
64. Ibid., p. 1468.
65. Ibid., p. 1470.

To Earth, to Cosmos, to Supracosmos and Towards their Integration

Finally, I would like to address the allegation that Sri Aurobindo does not give importance to life. One of the very superficial ways of reading Sri Aurobindo's philosophy is to bring the accusation of denigrating life. In the whole scheme of integral education as proposed by Sri Aurobindo, as I have already discussed,[66] there are different levels through which education proceeds, viz. physical, vital, mental, psychic and supramental. In this article, I have specifically dealt with physical education to vindicate Sri Aurobindo's concern for what is very much mundane, material, physical and close to common sense. Sri Aurobindo's Integral Vision of reality and the world process does not leave body out of its scope for it assigns a very distinctive role to body, its physicality to bring about divine life upon earth. Hence he neither does deny life or its material basis nor could he deny the worth of the physical body. To cite a quotation from Sri Aurobindo,

> Neither neglect this turn of the nature (food-desire) nor make too much of it; it has to be dealt with, purified and mastered but without giving it too much importance.[67]

In the domain of metaphysics we come across different theories about the nature of existence and these theories are mostly partisan in their attitude towards the body. The explanation of existence in terms of cosmic terrestrial, view that makes this mutable terrestrial, physical, vital existence the sole truth, according to Sri Aurobindo is really providing us half truth. The following oft-quoted jargon of the materialist Cārvāka sums up succinctly their attitude to life and body.

---

66. "What It Is to be Educated? In the Light of Sri Aurobindo's Philosophy", pp. 96-122.
67. "Transformation of the Physical", p. 1468.

> Live merrily so long as you live; partake of butter even if by borrowing. Whence is the possibility of our coming back, once the body is reduced to ashes?[68]

On the other hand, the other extreme viewpoint of the supracosmic theorists is not acceptable to Sri Aurobindo either. Since in the view of supracosmic theorist the sole reality is some transcendental reality, hence the world or human existence and his life do not have any meaning. Sri Aurobindo argues very strongly that an explanation that deprives worldly existence and individual life cannot give whole explanation of human existence. The material plane in which our natural life flourishes, of which our very body is a product, needs to be duly accommodated in any explanation of human existence. The third view Sri Aurobindo discards is the supraterrestrial view of existence according to which the true abode of human spirit or soul lies beyond the earth in some supraterrestrial world. According to him all these urges are truly human, urge towards earthly life, urge towards cosmos and urge towards supracosmos. The integral philosophy of Sri Aurobindo which is the very basis of his integral education, rests on the assumption:

> the lower consciousness of mind, life and body cannot arrive at its full meaning until it is taken up, restated, transformed by the light and power and joy of the higher spiritual consciousness, while the higher too does not stand in its full right in relation to the lower by mere rejection, but by this assumption and domination, this taking up of its unfulfilled values, this restatement and transformation — a spiritualising and supramentalising of the mental, vital and physical nature.[69]

---

68. *yāvat jivet sukham jivet, ṛṇam kṛtvā ghṛtam pivet* | *bhasmibhūtasya dehasya punargamanam kutaḥ?*

69. *The Life Divine*, pp. 677-78.

Bibliography

Deshpande, S.H., *Physical Education in Ancient India*, New Delhi: Bharatiya Vidya Prakashan.

Gambhirananda, ed., *Upaniṣad Granthabali*, Calcutta: Udbodhan Karyalaya, 2005.

"Health and Development through Physical Activity and Sports", World Health Organization, WHO/NMH/NPH/PAH/03.2, 2003, http:/ www.ucalgary.ca/lib-old/ssportsite/biblio.html

Joshi, Kireet, *Mystery and Excellence of the Human Body*, Pondicherry: Indian Council of Philosophical Research, Auroville Press, 2003.

Mukherjee, Jugal Kishore, *The Destiny of the Body*, Pondicherry: Sri Aurobindo International Centre of Education, 1st edn., 1975, 3rd impression.

"Promoting Active Living in and through School — Policy Statement and Guidelines for Action", Report of a WHO Meeting, Esbjerg, Denmark, 25-27 May 1998.

Sanyal, Indrani, "What It Is to be Educated? In the Light of Sri Aurobindo's Philosophy", in *Understanding Thoughts of Sri Aurobindo*, eds. Indrani Sanyal and Krishna Roy, New Delhi: D.K. Printworld, (P) Ltd. and Jadavpur University, 2007.

Sri Aurobindo, *Sri Aurobindo Birth Centenary Library*, vol. 19, Pondicherry: Sri Aurobindo Ashram.

———, *The Life Divine*, Pondicherry: Sri Aurobindo Ashram, 1st edn. 1939-1940, 6th edn., 2001.

———, *Letters On Yoga*, vol. III, Pondicherry: Sri Aurobindo Ashram, 1st edn., 1958, 7th impression, 2000.

———, "Message", "Perfection of the Body", "The Divine Body", "Haṭhayoga", "The Power of the Instruments", "The Body-Mind", in *Sri Aurobindo and the Mother on Physical Education*, Pondicherry: Sri Aurobindo Ashram, 2002.

4

Roots of Violence
Insights from Education

Anirban Ganguly

Some Initial Thoughts: Prologue

WRITING "A Preface on National Education" in his philosophical monthly *Arya* nearly nine decades ago Sri Aurobindo formulated a definition of what he perceived to be a "true and living education." Such an education according to him had to definitely take into consideration and work out certain fundamental perspectives; it had to take into account "the individual in his commonness and in his uniqueness, the nation or people and universal humanity."[1] He further continued defining a "true and living education" by stating that such an education must ensure a full scope of the inherent potential in the individual to develop and at the same time it ought to help the individual enter into a "right relation with the life, mind and soul of the people to which he belongs and [also] with that great total life, mind and soul of humanity of which he himself is a unit and his people or nation a living, a separate and yet inseparable member."[2]

1. Sri Aurobindo and The Mother, *On Education* (henceforth *On Education*), 2004, p. 13.
2. *On Education*, p. 14.

A dual aspect emerges from these observations, one, that the individual ought to be treated as what he is, i.e. as "an individual." Sri Aurobindo opposes here the concept of an industrial-education mindset which merely looks at the pupil as a uniform entity and encourages him to undergo the rigours of an uniform syllabus, following a routine method, to achieve a routine objective neglecting the individual's propensities, inclinations and needs. Treating him as a product to be tailor-made to market requirements and brands — overlooking what has been termed as the individual's *svadharma* — "truth of one's inner movement." This approach therefore obstructs the right working out of one's own law of action — *svadharma su-anuṣṭhitaḥ*[3] providing little space for variations and innovations and introduces at an early stage an element of stress in the educational ambience because of this inability of the system to often appreciate the true needs of the individual. What is encouraged is a superficial sense of competition at every stage — instilling the notion that "a competitive spirit will bring glory to the school" and as a result the legitimising of personal aggrandisement "in the name of institutional goals"[4] — thus pushing the learner to evolve his relationships on concepts of self-aggrandisement and acquisitiveness. These eventually express themselve in forms of opposing ideologies, mutual-distrust and ill-will, encouraging manifestations of differences in violent forms. In fact, and it may perhaps sound too harsh, as educators and parents we have a hand, to a certain extent, in incubating the seeds of such violent outbursts or despairing depression. When Sri Aurobindo observes "that the business of both parent and teacher is to enable and to help the child to educate himself, to develop his own intellectual, moral, aesthetic and practical capacities and to grow freely as an

3. *Sri Aurobindo Birth Centenary Library* (*SABCL*), vol. 30, 1976, p. 350.
4. Krishna Kumar, *What is Worth Teaching*, 2004, p. 48.

organic being, not to be kneaded and pressured into form like an inert plastic material"[5] he was perhaps pointing to the origins of this expression of violence and was advocating the freedom of growth that every child needs and which the present system of education denies to a great extent. It is this pressure, this kneading of the child-nature in pre-determined moulds under the influence of a fixed hierarchical system — "a mechanical forcing of the child's nature into arbitrary grooves of training and knowledge in which his individual subjectivity [is] the last thing considered . . ."[6] — that, apart from other causes, creates a potential for violence in young

5. Sri Aurobindo, *The Human Cycle*, 2005, p. 333. Sri Aurobindo was discussing the "new ideas about the education and upbringing of the child that became strongly current in the pre-war era." To set in perspective Sri Aurobindo's views one may recall that the pre-war years in the West witnessed a growing interest in educational thoughts and experiments of, among others, Maria Montessori (1870-1952) who working since 1907 when she founded the "Casa Dei Bambini," Children's House in Rome — began talking of the child as a "spiritual embryo". It was a formulation that reflected her belief that "the growing human being [was] not simply a biological or psychological entity, but a spiritual energy seeking expression in the form of a human body within the physical and cultural world." A guiding principle of Montessori's pedagogy was the concept of the "sensitive period" that envisaged children as moving through different growth periods during which they are specially "attuned to particular characteristic in their environment" such as when they wished to learn languages they would fast absorb it from the spoken word around them, they would similarly tackle the development of motor skills from their surrounding. What Montessori emphasised was that the role of the parent and educator during these active periods was to "provide the stimulation and resources" to the child and recognise that it was a compelling spiritual need that was driving the child to form its personality; careless parenting or over-education stunted this spontaneous process and lead to various negative manifestations. [Ron Miller, *Nourishing the Spiritual Embryo: Educational Vision of Maria Montessori*, 2002, accessed at www.pathsoflearning.net; and Maria Montessori, *The Secret of Childhood*, Orient Longman, rpt., 2006].

6. Sri Aurobindo, *The Human Cycle*, p. 32.

minds. Modern psychologists [have attributed] the destructive tendencies of young people to a repression and deviation of their creative urge.[7] Such is the price we pay for ignoring the uniqueness of the individual and assisting instead in his *"commoditisation."*[8]

The second aspect that emerges from such a definition and one that is also extremely contemporary to our age and to the concept of education for international living is the view that the commonness of the individual — i.e. the individual as a part of the collectivity — must be taken care of; a true and living education ought to capacitate the individual to evolve a method of balanced living *vis-à-vis* his surrounding. It ought to generate the perception in him that while retaining his distinct identity, his individual and collective existence,

---

7. Pavitra (P.B. Saint-Hilaire), *Education and the Aim of Human Life*, 1999, p. 93. Pavitra, the first Director of the International Centre of Education at Pondicherry, while discussing the needs of the child in the light of the integral education also points out that boisterous and unruly behaviour in children are to be attributed to periods of forced immobility during class-work and "lack of outlet for their plentiful energies." The incapacity for sustained activity in children, he points out, may be attributed to the parents' ignoring the child's needs and disturbing him frequently in his play or work — play for the child he observes is work.
8. Similar to the "spiritual embryo" Sri Aurobindo's metaphysical presupposition regarding the individual refuses to see man as simply a mechanical element or commodity but instead as "a portion of the Divinity enwrapped in mind and body, a conscious manifestation in Nature of the universal self and spirit [and] at the summit of his ascent man is bound to rise to something greater than his physical, vital and mental personalities, to his spiritual being. And therein lies the supreme manifestation of the soul of man . . ." his ultimate *raison d'être* "his real *paramārtha* and highest *puruṣārtha*" [Jugal Kishore Mukherjee, *Principles and Goals of Integral Education*, 2005, p. 10]. Education, Sri Aurobindo contends, must give the individual that scope for self-fulfilment. He was also in a sense anticipating the present-day human rights discourse albeit from a different perspective and stressing the aspect of a cooperative-fulfilment as opposed to a competitive one.

he can yet emerge as an inseparable part of a global collectivity.[9] It is this aspect of education that is most acutely needed at present times and which, if given adequate scope of expression, shall proceed to mitigate divisions and conflicts. For, the failure to see oneself as such a unit of the whole perpetuates division, conflict and intolerance and engineers a trend of violent competition "against each other over scarce resources in rigid win-lose situations."[10] But this aspect of creating a vision for global citizenship among young minds is absent from the curricula of our schools because of a "false perception that it clashes with the ideas of national citizenship, patriotism and national autonomy ignoring the Indian perception of a world citizen based on world ethics encoura[ging the] peaceful coexistence of a sane and legitimate patriotism and wider loyalty, a love of humanity as a whole."[11] There is a total neglect in understanding the individual's role and place as an important constituent in an era of global living.

My intention is to show, first, that classical Indian education thought contained in it the concepts of respect for the individual and his needs and inclination and thus provided space for the learner's self-expansion in terms of developing

9. It would be appropriate to point out here that eight decades after Sri Aurobindo had written this the Earth Charter-2000 while placing as one of the principal demands the need to "promote a culture of tolerance, non-violence and peace" emphasised that it was necessary to "Recognise that peace is the wholeness created by right relationships with oneself, other persons, other cultures, other life, Earth, and the larger whole of which all are a part" (16.f). This then is to be the initiating vision for developing a culture of peace through education and of an education that recognises the intrinsic worth of the individual. [Source: http://www.earthcharterinaction.org/2000/10/ the_earth_charter.html]

10. "What is the Culture of Schooling" in *The Dark Side Literacy*, 2003, p. 74.

11. Indra Nath Choudhuri, "Education for Global Citizenship — Challenges of the Twenty-first Century", 2006, p. 115, in *School Society Nation: Popular Essays in Education*, eds. Rajni Kumar, Anil Sethi, Shalini Sikka.

his character in a holistic manner and gave him scope to nurture greater linkage, reciprocity and unity of purpose with his fellow-beings and his environment. It recognised the right of the individual's self-determination — "the right to direct one's own education" — by allowing him a spontaneous and non-coercive process of growth and placed before him ideals whose fulfilment would bring about a culture of greater mutuality, harmony, "tolerance, self-respect, love for human dignity, respect and compassion for others, individual freedom and human rights, internationalism, rejection of cruelty, [and] the practice of non-violence."[12] All qualities that are much in need today but which the present-day education system neglects to consciously cultivate by negating the individual's right for free growth, by standardising him, by refusing to recognise his special inclinations and by compelling him to undergo a system of competitive survival and triumph. It is these suppressions, I agree, that prepare the ground for future manifestations of violence.

In the second part I wish to read some of Sri Aurobindo's thoughts on self-determination *vis-à-vis* the individual and some of his thoughts on education dwelling on the individual and the violation of his rights by the system and would like to point out how the wider inculcation of such a perspective in the present education system is an imperative if the system is to be ultimately rid of the propensity of neglecting the individual. An understanding of such a perspective may also help in understanding the origins of violence in the minds of men.

Expansion of the Individual, Growth of Mutuality — Negation of Violence: Classical Indian Concept of Education: Some Pointers

Education in classical Indian thought was integrative in nature

12. Bikash C. Sanyal, *Need for Value-Based Education in the Twenty-First Century*, International Institute for Educational Planning, Paris.

and remained conscious of the individual, the environment, as well as the collectivity.[13] Like modern thinkers of the "progressive education movement" who insisted that education be understood as the "art of cultivating the moral, emotional, physical, psychological, artistic, and spiritual — as well as intellectual — dimensions of the developing child" and held a holistic vision of education which believed in facilitating the "students to identity, meaning, and purpose in life through connections to the community, to the natural world, and to spiritual values such as compassion and peace" and believed in doing this through a "passionate love of learning and reverence for life" through a "direct engagement with the environment" instead of a rigid curriculum and "instructional packages,"[14] education in classical India sought to harmonise man with his "own subjective being" sought to develop "a harmony between individual and individual, a harmony between an individual and the group or groups of which [the individual] is a part and finally [attempted to establish] a harmony between the different groups."[15] It is this concept of education that ought to be included as a core principle of education and it is this that can act as pointers in efforts for creating a space for peace in education and the tackling of violence in growing minds. The present competitive educational culture ignores this fundamental truth. In fact, education in the classical context was never "equated with learning of books by heart"; it did not have the creation of a career or the amassing of material wealth as principal aims;

---

13. The following is not a comprehensive treatment but a brief analysis of the core vision and goals of classical Indian educational thought.
14. C. Panduranga Bhatta, *Holistic Development through Education: Ancient Indian Cultural Experience*, 2007, p. 22.
15. Jugal Kishore Mukherjee, *Principles and Goals of Integral Education*, 2005, p. 7.

instead its goal was a "desire for knowledge"[16] and thus it avoided giving rise to unbridled and violent competition and stress. It rather proposed a very interesting goal, that of creating the *śreṣṭha* (the best). This was consciously placed as the goal because it was "consciously recognised that people tend to follow the best and distribution of the best qualities among people at large [could] be effected only by encouraging and fostering the best." It encouraged the developing of qualities of heart — benevolence, compassion, altruism, long suffering, liberality, patience, etc., of character — courage, heroism, energy, loyalty, truth, honour, justice, reverence, etc. It encouraged the *śreṣṭha* to develop in his mind wisdom, intelligence, love of learning, openness to beauty, art and a dedicated capacity and skill in works. It encouraged the individual aspiring to *śreṣṭhatva* to develop his inner life by urging him to seek after the highest perfection and truth. In short the *śreṣṭha* was an ideal that education had to strive after, transforming the learner into one possessing in himself balance, and a capacity at an integrated existence.[17] The *śreṣṭha* had to grow not through competition but through emulation.

The learner in classical Indian thought retained an exalted position, he was considered to be a seeker, one "not to be silenced by dogmatic answers, but to be uplifted in higher processes of thought," his *utsāha* (enthusiasm) was of utmost importance and was unreservedly encouraged and nothing was imposed upon him except the willing acceptance of discipline.[18] The learner was not treated as a mere automaton nor did the teacher demand an unthinking adherence, the approach to

16. For a detailed analysis of the classical concept of "what it is to be educated" *vis-à-vis* the present contours of education see, e.g. Indrani Sanyal, "What it is to be Educated" in *Understanding Thoughts of Sri Aurobindo,* eds. Indrani Sanyal & Krishna Roy, Kolkata: Centre for Sri Aurobindo Studies, Jadavpur University, 2007.

17. Kireet Joshi, *Education at Crossroads,* 2007, p. 131.

18. Ibid., pp. 126, 135, 151.

education was in the manner of a quest and was dialogic in nature and ensured a process of "connect from within" as opposed to an imposition from external agencies. Learning was sought as the means of salvation or self-realisation, emancipation, or *mukti*. The Upaniṣads exhorted the learner to be *śānta* (unmoved, self-possessed), and be possessed of qualities such as *dāma* (regulation of the inner impulse), *dāna* (altruism), *dayā* (compassion), *śraddhā* (faith), *satyam* (truth) — the essential virtues. It imparted the vision of unity through identification, "not for love of all is all dear, but for love of the Self, all is dear" it envisioned and asked the pupil to grow such a feeling through the instrument of *dhyāna* (meditation) an intense contemplation and concentration for positive self-expansion.[19] The learner therefore retained respect and had a distinctly unique role to be worked out for a balanced living and growth. These qualities continue to remain relevant for us in our quest of realising a peace-based culture through education and in understanding the origins of violence in the present-day education system and learner-treatment. It may be said that education in the classical Indian thought did not possess a suppressive, coercive or competitive character but rather supported a process of gradual unfolding, respected the individual's needs and constantly sought to integrate him with his surrounding — immediate and distant. It did seek to develop the individual but not in a separative sense — ego-based sense with self-aggrandisement and acquisitiveness as principle aims.

It is this approach that is most often absent in the present system and it is still this approach which may provide indicaters in attempts to develop a vision of peace and global living through education and in arresting the cycle of violence in young minds.[20]

---

19. Radha Kumud Mookerji, *Ancient Indian Education*, 1998, pp. xxi, 157, 264.

20. Pointing out an intervention by Mahatma Gandhi in favour of →

The Negation of the Individual's Scope of Growth in Education and the Seeds of Violence: Some Thoughts

Most of Sri Aurobindo's writings on education were done a century back while he was still active in Bengal. His ideas have been extensively discussed and I am not going to take

---

→ indigenous Indian education may not be out of place here. The Mahatma observed that India by the very fact of her long established and elaborate civilisation had once the advantage of an educational system of her own. The only thing entitled to be called 'national' he perceived this education to be 'fundamentally distinct from the Anglo-Indian type and from the pseudo-national type' a descendant of the former. Talking about the then prevailing colonial system of education he observed that it had "broken up the continuity of our existence." He then defined a sound education as one that is "meant to fit one generation to take up the burden of the previous and to keep up the life of the community without breach or disaster. The burden of social life is continuous, and if at any stage one generation gets completely out of touch with the efforts of its predecessors or in anyway gets ashamed of itself or its culture, it is lost." This is what according to the Mahatma was being done by colonial education. He identified a series of high loyalties, loyalty to faith, calling, parents, family and *dharma* as forces that maintain society together, and argued that the ancient educational system maintained those forces in the growth and sustenance of society. He finally made a demand that "enquiry must be made promptly as to what constituted the elements of education before Indian universities were constituted, before Lord Macaulay wrote his fatal minutes." In short his exhortation for enquiry may perhaps be said to be an attempt in trying to sift elements from the ancient educational framework that could contribute to cohesion, integration — individual and collective — in the present system. [*Young India*, 20 March 1924, in *Towards New Education* by M.K. Gandhi, ed. by Bharatan Kumarappa, 2007, pp. 30-31.] Later researches in the indigenous Indian system of education by the late Shri Dharampal, J.P. Naik and others have proved the truth of the Mahatma's observation on the existence of a widespread indigenous system of education. But that is an altogether a separate area of study — to see how the colonial system instead of absorbing the indigenous one gradually decimated it in all its aspects.

them up in detail. I would like to indicate, however, in spite of repeating myself, that the individual's primacy is evident in these formulations of his. He anticipated the whole New Education movement which began by working for the growth of a "new attitude towards the child. An attitude of understanding and love, and above all an attitude of respect" and for development of convictions that "a child must be happy and that the educator's first task is to make sure that he is happy . . . and that [adults have] everything to gain by leaving a child as long as possible in [an] age of primal innocence . . . instead of trying to shape him at any cost into [their] own image." The New Education vision also held the belief that the child had within him everything that allowed a process of true education to unfold and this happened through "ceaseless activity, incessantly revived, in which [the child] is totally engrossed" and in this the educators and parents must simply help the child and not imposingly direct him.[21] It is such a space that the learner must be given to avoid repression, a

21. Pavitra (P.B. Saint-Hilaire) op. cit., p. 45. Pavitra quotes here the exposition on *L'education nouvelle* (New Education) by one of its pioneers Roger Cousinet (1881-1973). Cousinet's lifelong experiment and work with learners convinced him of a new approach to child-learning which had to provide the right space for the child to evolve. "Education can no longer be an action exerted by a master on his pupils, for such action has proved futile," observed Cousinet. "It is, in fact, an activity whereby the child works towards his own development, in a favourable environment and with the help of an educator who is now available for merely consultative capacity. It follows that *active methods are not teaching but learning tools,* that they must be placed in the hands of the pupils alone and that any teacher introducing them into his or her class will be prepared not to use them, and so doing will refrain from teaching." According to Cousinet the introduction of the New Education method in schools "implied first and foremost a radical change in the educational attitude of the teacher in his relationship with his pupil." [*PROSPECTS: The Quarterly Review of Comparative Education*, vol. 23, nos. 1 / 2, 1993, UNESCO: International Bureau of Education, Paris.]

mutilated growth and its negative expressions.

Education thinkers have dwelt on this aspect — the origins of violence in young minds — and their views based on direct experiments with and observations of the child have been somewhat similar. "Life has an inner dynamism of its own; it tends to grow, to be expressed, to be lived. The amount of destructiveness in a child is proportionate to the amount to which the expansiveness of his life has been curtailed. Destructiveness is the outcome of the unlived life,"[22] observed Erich Fromm (1900-80), the German social psychologist and humanistic philosopher. That "coercion [is] the worst teaching method" was a basic precept of education with Jean Piaget (1896-1980), Swiss philosopher, natural scientist and long-time Director of the International Bureau of Education.[23] He enunciated the ideal of "a school without coercion . . . where pupils actively experiment with a view to reconstructing for themselves what is to be learnt." Piaget's experiments convinced him that "learning takes its own time; that it may be destructive to speed up learning or development."[24] But this freedom and joy of discovering are aspects that the

---

22. Quoted by Sylvia Ashton-Warner in her *Teacher*, 2008, pp. 101-2.
23. Piaget observed that example rather than coercion must play a more important role in the field of education. The pupil's active participation was another of his fundamental precept. "A truth learnt is only a half-truth," he argued, "the whole truth is reconquered, reconstructed and rediscovered by the pupil himself/herself. . ." [*PROSPECTS*, vol. 24, nos. 1/2, 1994, International Bureau of Education, Paris.] It may be pointed out here that the Mother (1878-1973) Sri Aurobindo's principal spiritual collaborator who gave shape to his Ashram and later set up the Sri Aurobindo International Centre of Education made uncoerced teaching the norm at the Centre of Education and pioneered a number of educational experiments that would allow the child to grow in a free ambience. The Centre of Education revolting against the established system of examinations and syllabus does not follow a set pattern of examination or an externally prescribed syllabus.
24. Krishna Kumar, op. cit., p. 49.

majority of our schools ignore or are unable to work out. It is this reduction or negation of the individual's self-expansion, this refusal to treat him as an autonomous and free entity and instead handle him "as raw material to be moulded after stale preconceptions" of adults[25] that remains, apart from other factors, the root of early negative expressions.

Similarly, let me point at two areas where, as Sri Aurobindo observes, mishandling or coercion may have permanent negative manifestations. While enunciating his second principle of teaching he pointed out that a lack of free expansion and growth occurs due to the attitude of the parent or the teacher of "hammering the child into a shape" decided upon by them. He calls this a "barbarous and ignorant superstition" that "permanently harms or mutilates the nature of the child" and forces it to abandon its naturally ordained direction in life. Is it not natural then that this mutilation retains its scars?[26] Again

---

25. Krishna Kumar, op. cit., p. 48.
26. *On Education*, pp. 20-21. This hammering also often finds expression in child abuse in schools and also at homes. Pressure of completing a syllabus, compulsions of imposing an external discipline, the exhaustion induced by trying to maintain cohesion among a large number of students under poor infrastructural conditions and education ambience often lead to these outbursts among teachers. Corporal punishment is an outdated notion but a study conducted by the Indian Ministry of Women and Child Development reveals that 69 per cent children still reported abuse including corporal punishment and 62 per cent of the corporal punishment were in government and municipal schools — which are schools still availed by the mass of "non-privileged" in our country — it thus reveals the shocking continuation of a mutilating practice which inflicts permanent scratches on the growing psyche. [Sakshi Khattar, "An Effort to Tackle Violence in Schools", The *Times of India*, 25 November 2008.] Another factor for growth of violence may be pointed out here, it relates to violence at homes. Parents who want conformist children often get into the abusive mode when they find them non-pliant and wishing to pursue their course of growth and interests. The NCERT Position Paper of the National Focus Group on Education for Peace observes that one of the factors in

→

he reasserts the individuality of the learner by saying that each one "has in him something divine, something his own, a

→ quantum leap of violence in schools is the violence children witness at home. This creates emotional alienation resulting in the "erosion of togetherness and the virtual death of communication at home" — such a situation it terms as "the substance of [the child's] silent suffering" that threatens to assume epidemic proportions. Alienation according to the paper "is the seed of violence." It also observes that the absence of a strong experiential and relational aspect in the learning process which is mainly individual achievement-oriented makes the young learner unable to develop reciprocity, sensitiveness and responsibility towards his mates. This "lopsided development" makes the child vulnerable to violence." [*Position Paper, National Focus Group on Education for Peace*, 2006, pp. 2-3.] All the above factors are detrimental to the child's *need for security* — the necessity for the child to be sure that his growth will not be hampered or prevented. [Pavitra, op. cit., p. 100.] This blow at his security needs further strengthens the possibilities of negative manifestations. One must also draw attention here to a nearly forgotten feature of education for wise parenthood in the scheme of the Nai Talim or Basic Education as propounded by Mahatma Gandhi. All parents are educators because it is they who shall provide for the child in the most material as well as emotional sense, and because they are "responsible for the environment of the home where the child grows up, and for its first social contacts the Nai Talim scheme placed much emphasis on their integrated training. One important aspect of this education was "to help the parents realise how much their own character, habits and behaviour influence their children" because "almost all the young child's first impressions of life are received from his parents and other adults in the home. Constant petty disputes and quarrels destroy the child's sense of security and do a great deal of harm. A child who feels happy and secure is eager to explore and experiment with his surroundings. . . ." [Marjorie Sykes, *The Story of Nai Talim, Fifty Years of Education at Sevagram: 1937-1987*, 1998, pp. 63-64, see this monograph for a detailed exposition of theme.] The concept of education for wise parenthood had been thrown out when the dominating majority system rejected lock, stock and barrel the Gandhian Basic Education model because it required a great deal of out-of-box thinking for which the entrenched system did not have time or patience. It did not see any profit in implementing it. A reapplication of this concept, in my opinion, may go a long way in arresting the growth and spread of violence in young minds.

chance of perfection and strength in however small a sphere which God offers him to take or refuse. The task is to find it, develop it and use it."[27] The question is whether the present competitive education system compelling young minds to confront pressures and demands of various kinds has the time or inclination to look at the individual in such a manner, whether it retains the capability of halting this predetermined hammering of the child and truly understanding the origins of violence in young minds. It is seen that it does not allot the indispensable "large blocks of time in which the child can totally engross himself in activity," instead it creates pressure "to learn faster and to outshine others" and in this manner "kills all intrinsic motivation to learn"[28] and makes him live in a pressurised atmosphere of performance — reward — failure — destruction of self/others.

In the same manner, in his third principle of teaching one may perceive clues to the reasons of violence in youth. This principle is one that often continues to be ignored. Sri Aurobindo argues that it is always better in case of the mind to "work from the near to the far." He makes a case for beginning the child's education by sensitising him to his surrounding, by developing an organic link and identification with his immediate environment, by making him aware of

27. *On Education*, op. cit., pp. 20-21.

28. Krishna Kumar, op. cit., p. 49. The NCERT National Focus Group on Education for Peace in its Position Paper states that "inordinate parental ambition, in a context of intense competition" and "the approach to teaching that limits its scope to covering the syllabus makes the teacher view the syllabus as a burden" and transmit unawares that "sense of burden to the student." "The underdevelopment of personality and inner resources" on account of such an approach results in the inability [of the student] to cope with stress and strain and also magnifies them", it lists these as factors that "degrade learning into a burden." [*Position Paper, National Focus Group on Education for Peace*, National Council of Educational Research and Training, 2006, p. 20.]

factors such as heredity, surroundings, nationality, country, sustaining soil, sights, air, habits, etc., all factors, that he views to be the basis of man's growth.[29] This aspect of relating to one's surrounding environment has been highlighted by a number of educators and pedagogues. It was extremely relevant especially at the time Sri Aurobindo wrote it during the first peak of the struggle against colonial rule in India. Most Indian education reformers then found the books in use to be "suitable for boys in an English school, [but] remarkably inadequate for boys of an Indian one. For, the information on geography, productions, natural objects, etc., which was given about India, was absolutely out of all proportion in comparison with the information given about European nations" and taught the Indian boys much about England but very little about "their own country." The result was that an Indian boy could quickly give the "name of the capital of Switzerland [but hunted] confusedly in the south of India for Kashmir."[30] This demand made then was part of the national quest for the reassertion of a national identity but it contained seeds of a deeper psychological truth that later experiments in education across the world proved. To take one example, Sylvia Ashton-Warner (1908-84) the legendary "Teacher" who taught indigenous Maori children in New Zealand for over two decades and meticulously developed a unique method of teaching through the "key vocabulary" concept — where a set of special meaning words related to the child's environment and emotional life enabled her to develop a reading method for children who were otherwise "failing" in school — realised through her work the incongruity of teaching language by using English primers that had little respect for, or reference to, [the indigenous

29. *On Education*, op. cit., p. 21.

30. Annie Besant, "What Sort of a National Education is that?" in *The Dawn and the Dawn Society's Magazine, March 1905*, vol. 7, 2007, pp. 195-99.

child's] lives.[31] Mahatma Gandhi too while evolving his philosophy of the "Basic Education" recognised this problem when he wrote that almost from the beginning textbooks deal, "not with things that the boys and the girls have always to deal with in their homes, but things to which they are perfect strangers." The pupil is never taught to have pride in his surroundings and "the higher he goes, the farther he [gets] removed from his home, so that at the end of his education he becomes estranged from his surroundings."[32] Does this estrangement not nurture a perpetual state of instability somewhere? Sri Aurobindo continuing with this observation seems to point out that, "We must not take up the nature by the roots from the earth in which it must grow or surround the mind with images and ideas of a life which is alien to that in which it must physically move." He observed, "If anything has to be brought in from outside, it must be offered, not forced on the mind." It may be said that this distinction between offering and forcing is almost never made in the current syllabus-completion-examination-passing system. "A free and natural growth," feels Sri Aurobindo, "is the condition

31. A typical book would read — 'John come out, look at the boats.' They may have been relevant in an English setting but made no sense to the indigenous Maoris of New Zealand. Arvind Gupta in his Foreword to Ashton-Warner's "*Teacher*" op. cit., p. 1.

32. *Towards New Education* by M.K. Gandhi, op. cit., pp. 31-32. The NCERT Position Paper on Education for Peace points to the persistence of this problem in the present context when it observes that "a major limitation that textbook writing has to reckon with is in respect of reflecting the immediate contexts of students in their specificities." Textbook writers "usually hail from urban privileged background" and are therefore in most cases insensitive to the rural user and his surroundings and situations. [*NCERT Position Paper on Education for Peace*, op. cit., p. 21] The estrangement of the learner with his surrounding therefore still continues and affects young minds; unless these core technicalities are addressed along with other factors it is futile to expect reform to be of a comprehensive nature.

of genuine development" and if this artificial imposition becomes the norm, then "the majority languish, become empty, become artificial"[33] and the first casualty of an artificial existence is reciprocity, mutuality, compassion and a genuine feeling of *ātmatva* or *ekatva* with the "other" facilitating the rise of insensitiveness and violence reflected in an alienated and delinked existence. The key is to make this possibility of a "free and natural growth" available at least in some measure.

Self-Determination of the Child and Abandoning the Notion of Right of Property in Education

Sri Aurobindo poses a fundamental question. "Life," he observes, "is self-fulfilment which moves upon a ground of mutuality; it involves a mutual use of one by the other, in the end of all by all. The whole question is whether this shall be done on the lower basis of the ego, attended by strife, friction and collision with whatever checks and controls, or whether it cannot be done by a higher law of our being which shall discover a means of reconciliation, free reciprocity and unity."[34] My contention is that the existing majority education system predominantly permeated by the competitive spirit cannot contribute positively towards evolving that "higher law" of being where reconciliation, free reciprocity and unity become fundamental laws of interactions. The present system having the market concept of individual self-possessiveness as one of the principal aims is primarily based on what Sri Aurobindo terms the ego, and the ego principally wills at "self-satisfaction" and possesses "the instinct of a double self-assertion, its self-assertion against other egos and its self-assertion by means of other egos." Sri Aurobindo elaborates the process: "in all its [ego's] expansion it is impelled to subordinate their [other egos] need to its own, to use them

33. *On Education*, op. cit., p. 21.
34. Sri Aurobindo, *War and Self-Determination*, 2005, p. 628.

for its own purpose and for that purpose to establish some kind of control or domination or property in what it uses, whether by force or dexterity, openly or covertly, by absorption or by some skilful turn of exploitation." "Human lives," Sri Aurobindo further observes, "cannot run upon free parallels," there must be intermingling, intermixing and exchange and in an ego-based life that must nearly mean always a clash."[35] The system that we witness teaches the learner early how to strengthen his ego by a process of exploitation, confrontation and competition rarely if ever through accommodation. An initial start on the way out of this morass may come about if one perhaps understands the true significance of the term self-determination.[36] In Sri Aurobindo's definition of self-determination too one perceives the primacy of the individual. According to him the principle of self-determination really means, the existence "within every living human creature, man, woman and child, and equally within every distinct human collectivity growing or grown, half developed or adult, . . . of a self, a being, which has the right to grow in its own way, to find itself, to make its life a full and satisfied instrument and image of its being."[37] But this can only start happening when there is a right idea of the self — and not an idea of the ego as the self. A re-articulation of this term *vis-à-vis* the individual therefore is a necessity not only in the socio-political context but also in the educational discourse. But to be able to truly understand this idea Sri Aurobindo proposes another shift, a travelling away from the

35. *War and Self-Determination*, op. cit., p. 627.

36. Sri Aurobindo began discussing this word after the end of the First World War when this term was indeed being intensely debated and defined. Sri Aurobindo found this word "in itself a happy discovery, a thought-sign of real usefulness. For it [helped] to make definite and manageable what was apt till [then] to be splendidly vague and nebulous." [p. 623]

37. *War and Self Determination*, op. cit., p. 626.

old notion of the "right of property of man in man" — the old notion of "the right of property of the father over the child, of the man over the woman, of the ruler or the ruling class or power over the ruled, of the State over the individual."[38] This notion of property based on domination nurtures the propensities of acquisitiveness and self-aggrandisement and contradicts liberty that is the basis of a co-operative and mutual existence.

My proposition is that the educational system too must be rid of this notion of property; the parent and the teacher dominating the child under a sense of ownership right activate a control mechanism that does much harm and sows the seeds of a future violent mode of living. Similar to his stance on the issue formulated a decade earlier in 1910 we see in this formulation of Sri Aurobindo also a strong rejection of the property concept over the child and the hammering method applied on him to get him into a "socially acceptable" shape. He points out that in the old patriarchal system the child was the "live property of the father; he was his creation, his production, his own reproduction of himself; the father, rather than God or the universal Life in place of God, stood as the author of the child's being; and the creator has every right over his creation, the producer over his manufacture."[39] This description of the parental notion of property over the child is true even in the present system in spite of the notion getting outdated in a number of areas. "He [father — creator] had the right to make of him [the child] what he willed, and not what the being of the child really was within, to train and shape and cut him according to the parental ideas and not rear him according to his own nature's deepest needs, to bind him to the paternal career or the career chosen by the parent and not that to which his nature and capacity and inclination pointed,

38. *War and Self Determination*, p. 630.

39. Ibid.

to fix for him all the critical turning-points of his life even after he has reached maturity." This notion had a crude reflection in the education system where "the child was regarded not as a soul meant to grow, but as brute psychological stuff to be shaped into a fixed mould by the teacher."[40] The education system as it is largely implemented today remains wedded to this notion of the learner — it has not been able to confer on him true self-determination — and as long as the system in general continues to treat the individual in such a dry and soulless manner it is bound to give rise to a culture of violence. Unless the basic approach to the child, unless the primacy of competition and individual triumph alters, no long-lasting reform or transformation of education is possible; reform would not be fundamental but rather temporary and piecemeal. The indispensable basic starting-point then is to begin seeing the child as a soul — or at least an entity with some unique possibilities of perfection — "with a being, a nature and capacities of his own who must be helped to find them, to find himself, to grow into their maturity, into a fullness of physical and vital energy and the utmost breadth, depth and height of his emotional, his intellectual and spiritual being."[41] Only such an approach can bring about true self-determination in our education system and thereby move towards the mitigation of violence to a great extent. A reading of some of Sri Aurobindo's key texts on education and self-determination seems to provide some direction as to the cause of one aspect of the malady — the manifestations of violence in tender minds — the remedial action though seems formidable. In spite of Sri Aurobindo pointing towards the advent of new conception of the child at least nine decades back — this conception does not seem to have as yet percolated deep and wide enough into the system (though there have been exceptional and inspiring efforts over

40. *War and Self Determination*, pp. 630-31.

41. Ibid., pp. 631.

a number of decades which have helped in keeping the idea alive) for making general the demand for a complete revamp. The Mahatma was perhaps right and indicated a future course of action when he said that the true quest for peace "shall have to begin with children" and that if they will grow up in their natural innocence then one shall not have to struggle, nor pass futile resolutions but rather "go from love to love and peace to peace until at last all corners of the world are covered with that peace."[42] A true self-determination of the child is to be found in preserving the possibility of his growing up in that state of natural innocence — the present system and other factors usually pay no heed to that essential need.

A Postscript

Thus one can extrapolate in this manner some key aspects of Sri Aurobindo's educational thought and his ideas of individual self-determination placed in an educational context and reach at some understanding of the causes of violence witnessed in the minds of young learners and also appreciate the causes for their immediate and later manifestations. This is not an exhaustive study taking into account various facets of educational and child psychology, nor is it a detailed tracing of the evolution of various thoughts in this area. Instead I have kept the study brief and limited to the school and the education system[43] and have attempted to read some features

42. Mahatma Gandhi, *Young India*, 19 November 1931, letter addressed to Maria Montessori, *Towards New Education*, op. cit., p. 36.

43. For example, a detailed exposition of parental violence on children or the effects of media violence on children — heavy viewers of violence of television become desensitised to "real world violence" because "they lose the ability to empathise, protest and become distressed when they witness real life violence," they become cynical about the feasibility, efficacy and possibility of peace and believe violence to be an acceptable way of resolving conflicts and differences [*NCERT Position Paper on Education for Peace*, op. cit., p. 26] — has not been taken up in detail.

of Sri Aurobindo's educational texts in a non-conventional manner. My intention was to try and ascertain whether some direction could be gleaned from these texts and applied to an area of crisis in education that has assumed critical proportions in recent times. Sri Aurobindo, it seems to me, does point out — though not in as many and exact words — the deeper (inner) causes of an acute affliction in our present education system — expressions of violence either at an early stage of growth or its suppression and manifestation at a later stage.

Bibliography

(Sri) Aurobindo and The Mother, *On Education*, Pondicherry: Sri Aurobindo Ashram, 13th impression, 2004.

(*Sri*) *Aurobindo Birth Centenary Library* (*SABCL*), vol. 30, Pondicherry: Sri Aurobindo Ashram, 1976.

(Sri) Aurobindo, *The Human Cycle*, Pondicherry: Sri Aurobindo Ashram, 2nd impression, 2005.

(Sri) Aurobindo, *War and Self-Determination*, Pondicherry: Sri Aurobindo Ashram, 2nd impression, 2005.

Besant, Annie, "What Sort of a National Education is that?", in *The Dawn and the Dawn Society's Magazine, March 1905*, vol. VIII, reprint volumes, ed. Madhabendra Nath Mitra, Jadavpur University & National Council of Education, Bengal, 2007.

Bhatta, C. Panduranga, *Holistic Development through Education: Ancient Indian Cultural Experience*, Calcutta: MCHV, IIM, 2007.

Choudhuri, Indra Nath, "Education for Global Citizenship : Challenges of the Twenty-first Century", in *School Society Nation: Popular Essays in Education*, eds. Rajni Kumar, Anil Sethi, Shalini Sikka, Orient Longman, rpt., 2006.

Gandhi, M.K., *Towards New Education*, ed. Bharatan Kumarappa, Ahmedabad: Navajivan Publishing House, 9th rpt., 2007.

Joshi, Kireet, *Education at Crossroads*, Delhi: The Mother's Institute of Research, 2007.

Khattar, Saskshi, "An Effort to Tackle Violence in Schools," *The Times of India*, 25 November, 2008.

Kumar, Krishna, *What is Worth Teaching*, Orient Longman, 3rd edn., 2004.

Miller, Ron, *Nourishing the Spiritual Embryo: Educational Vision of Maria Montessori*, 2002, accessed at www.pathsoflearning.net.

Montessori, Maria, *The Secret of Childhood*, Orient Longman, rpt., 2006.

Mookerjee, Radha Kumud, *Ancient Indian Education*, Delhi: Motilal Banarsidass, rpt., 1998.

Mukherjee, Jugal Kishore, *Principles and Goals of Integral Education*, Pondicherry: Sri Aurobindo Ashram, 2005.

Pavitra (P.B. Saint-Hilaire), *Education and the Aim of Human Life*, Pondicherry: Sri Aurobindo International Centre of Education, rpt., 1999.

Position Paper, National Focus Group on Education for Peace, New Delhi: National Council of Educational Research and Training, 2006.

PROSPECTS: The Quarterly Review of Comparative Education, vol. 23, nos. 1 / 2, 1993, UNESCO: International Bureau of Education, Paris.

PROSPECTS: The Quarterly Review of Comparative Education, vol. 24, nos. 1/ 2, 1994, UNESCO: International Bureau of Education, Paris.

Sanyal, Bikash C., *Need for Value-Based Education in the Twenty-First Century*, International Institute for Educational Planning, Paris. [Accessed at http://www.here-now4u.de/ENG/need_for_the_value-based_educa.htm]

Sykes, Marjorie, *The Story of Nai Talim, Fifty Years of Education at Sevagram: 1937-1987*, Wardha: Sevagram, rpt., 1998.

Warner, Sylvia Ashton, *Teacher*, Hyderabad: Otherwise Books, rpt., 2008.

"What is the Culture of Schooling" in *The Dark Side Literacy*, Udaipur: Shikshantar: The Peoples' Institute for Rethinking Education and Development, 2003.

5

Sri Aurobindo's Integral Education in Contemporary Higher Education

Debashish Banerji

Theory of Integral Education

SRI Aurobindo (1872-1950) was a modern Indian philosopher (*ṛṣi*) and spiritual personality (*yogī*) who practised and taught a neo-Vedāntic system of spiritual discipline which he termed Integral Yoga. The goal of this discipline could be thought of as an attempt to integrate the discontinuous and fragmented human personality and to exceed it through spiritual union with a higher universal and transcendental consciousness. In his words:

> Man is there to affirm himself in this universe, that is his first business, but also to evolve and finally to exceed himself: he has to change his partial being into a complete being, his partial consciousness into an integral consciousness.[1]

As may be inferred from his universalistic use of the term "man," Sri Aurobindo did not see this goal as merely an individual one, but one which pertained to the human species. Any individual effort and achievement of an integral consciousness, needs thus to be seen in the context of a social

1. Sri Aurobindo, *The Life Divine, Sri Aurobindo Birth Centenary Library*, vol. 19, Pondicherry: Sri Aurobindo Ashram, 1972, p. 684.

transformation, not merely as an esoteric practice and fulfilment.

INTEGRAL YOGA AND INTEGRAL EDUCATION

Thus Sri Aurobindo envisages the goal of human becoming as a transformed society and civilisation based on the expressions of an integral consciousness. However, in keeping with the collective dimension of this goal, a transformed society was envisaged by him not merely as the end result of individual transformations, but as the dynamically transforming life-context or field which would allow and facilitate individual transformation. Seen from this standpoint, the social discipline of education, meant to "socialise," "in-form" and inculcate the cultural, knowledge and epistemological skills of the social habitus for individual engagement takes on a changed meaning related to a new phenomenology, epistemology and teleology of human and social becoming. Integral education then becomes a socially acknowledged and authorised praxis of the integral yoga or at least the pedagogical condition for its social possibility and collective transformation.

In terms of his personal experience of higher education, Sri Aurobindo came into contact with the pedagogical structure and methodology practised at Cambridge University, England, where he took his Tripos in the Classics. Later, in India, he taught and served as Vice-Principal at the Baroda College (1899-1906) and was the Principal of the Bengal National College (1906-07). His writings on education appeared mostly as articles in the Bengali nationalist paper *Karmayogin* (1909-10) and in the serialised journal *Arya* (1920). The term "integral education," in the context of Sri Aurobindo's teaching, was used by his spiritual collaborator, the Mother, in a message to the Indian Education Commission (1964) and there connoted an education which integrated Spirit and Matter, redressing the lopsided materialistic basis of modern education.[2] The Mother's directorship of the Sri Aurobindo International Centre for Education and her conversations and talks relating to the founding and operations of this institution along with Sri Aurobindo's writings referred to above have become the bases for our present understanding of integral education and the principles for its implementation.

In a nutshell, integral education envisages an emphasis in the development of the faculties and inner psychological conditions of knowledge acquisition and expression and the development of the skills to engage with and transform society. The human personality is seen as a mental-vital-physical complex which needs integration around the soul or psychic being and this integrated instrument then put to the use of the spiritual and supramental consciousness. One may see this as identical in scope with the integral yoga, but attempted through the social facilitation process of education. The training of each of the parts of the being, as expressive instruments, with an emphasis on the emergence of the soul as the central evolving principle in human beings is the heart of this form of education. This is accomplished through an appropriate mentorship process, and through what has been termed a "free progress" system of individualised curriculum selection and self-paced learning.

PRINCIPLES OF A "TRUE EDUCATION"

The roots of Sri Aurobindo's theory of integral education go back to his writings on national education in the first decade of the twentieth century. The foundations of educational practice articulated by him during this period and seen as the cornerstone of his integral education by later proponents are

2. The Mother, *Collected Works of the Mother*, vol. 12, Pondicherry: Sri Aurobindo Ashram, 1972, p. 25.

what he calls the three principles of a true and living education. A perusal of these principles reveals the social and psychological bases of his conception. The first of these three principles is perhaps the most radical. It says: "The first principle of true teaching is that nothing can be taught."[3] Here Sri Aurobindo presents the teacher's role as that of a mentor helping the student to learn how to acquire knowledge for himself or herself. But what is more radical is that the source of knowledge is indicated as being "within" the student. The teacher should help the student to perfect his instruments of knowledge and show him how he can draw on this knowledge within at will, so it can be "habituated to rise to the surface."[4] A few questions rise immediately from the statement of this principle: What is the nature or mode of this knowledge? What are the instruments of knowledge? What is the inner location of knowledge and what is the process by which it is acquired?

PHENOMENOLOGY OF NON-DUALISM

The Vedāntic basis of this theory of knowledge is easy to discern. By the time Sri Aurobindo was writing these nationalistic articles on education, he had already passed through major ontological shifts which may be characterised as spiritual and cosmic. Thus he was familiar in more than a theoretical way with the Upaniṣadic difference between knowledge (*vidyā*) and ignorance (*avidyā*) or between "higher" (*parā*) and "lower" (*aparā*) forms of knowledge. These distinctions are central to the epistemology of the Upaniṣads. They arise from a phenomenology of non-dualism as the foundation for "knowledge" (*vidyā*), sometimes known as

---

3. Sri Aurobindo, "A System of National Education", *Sri Aurobindo Birth Centenary Library*, vol. 17, Pondicherry: Sri Aurobindo Ashram, 1972, p. 204.
4. Ibid.

"higher knowledge" (*parā vidyā*) as opposed to the dualism of the "normal" human structure of knowing, which can only provide an indirect knowledge or a form of ignorance (*avidyā*), also sometimes known in Vedāntic literature as "lower knowledge" (*aparā vidyā*). Thus a normative distinction was established between two forms of knowledge and knowledge acquisition — one derived by mental processes acting on the evidence of the senses and the other acquired through identity of consciousness.

Sri Aurobindo would later characterise these forms of knowledge by their means of acquisition as knowledge by outer or "indirect contact" and "knowledge by identity."[5] These have also been called forms of indirect and direct knowledge (*parokṣa* and *pratyakṣa*). In *The Life Divine,* where he presents this distinction, Sri Aurobindo introduces also a third and intermediate kind of knowledge, which he terms knowledge by inner or "direct contact."[6] Evidently, the support for the statement that nothing can be taught comes from this distinction. Analogous to Plato's understanding of human representation as one of "making copies of copies," teaching in the established pedagogical sense, can be seen in this light to be a second level of indirection — representations and interpretations of a reality and its constituents that will remain in themselves unknowable to us by dint of their ontologically transcendental status.

To Enlightenment philosophers like Kant in the Western academy, there was no alternative to this basis of knowledge. While acknowledging the unbridgeable division between

5. Sri Aurobindo, "Knowledge by Identity and Separative Knowledge" in *The Life Divine, Sri Aurobindo Birth Centenary Library* vol. 18, pp. 524-25.

6. Ibid. Here, he actually identifies two such degrees of "direct" or subliminal knowledge.

subject and object that this implied, it affirmed the universality of human reason as the human property of making a reasonable home for itself and its kind in an unknowable world. But to Sri Aurobindo, there was an alternative. As part of the revisioning of a post-colonial India, Sri Aurobindo's educational theory needs to be understood as a critique of the episteme of modernity based in an alternate Vedāntic epistemology and personal experience affirming this cultural knowledge. And as befits the incipient globalism of (colonial) modernity, this critique is not innocent of its post-colonial intent being also a postmodern potential — a revisioning of the basis of "Enlightenment" in the Age of Enlightenment. Thus, Sri Aurobindo's "nothing can be taught" addresses at once the hubris of colonialism, Western civilisational superiority and its "white man's burden" of "teaching" the non-Western native the enlightened ways of reason; and its replacement by the Vedāntic norm of acceptable knowledge as that alone which can be known by identity of consciousness from within.

The *Śāṇḍilya Upaniṣad* offers a statement of the ubiquity of this non-dual knowledge: *yasmin vijñate sarvam idam vijñātam* (that knowing which all this/here may be known).[7] Knowledge of *Brahman* through identity of consciousness is the knowledge of the One Reality without a second — that which knows all things as forms of itself. Thus acquisition of the double knowledge, *parā vidyā*, knowledge of the *Brahman* and *aparā vidyā*, knowledge of the world and its objects, becomes a project reducible to a primary knowledge by identity of consciousness of *Brahman* and a secondary knowledge by extension of consciousness to the infinite forms or formulations of *Brahman*. This could also be called the primary root of integrality in Sri

7. *Śāṇḍilya Upaniṣad*, 2.2; cf. *Muṇḍaka Upaniṣad*, 1.1.3.

Aurobindo's theory of integral education — identification in consciousness with the One Reality which knows itself and all things reductively as itself (*advaita*) and non-reductively as forms of itself extended for relational enjoyment (*dvaita*). The simultaneity of these forms of knowledge as a mode of non-dual knowledge belongs to a *Brahman*-consciousness Sri Aurobindo would call the Supermind and equate with the plane of consciousness called *vijñāna* in the Upaniṣads.

But though we may say this is the Vedāntic basis or support for Sri Aurobindo's statement that "nothing can be taught," his explanation does not explicitly reference this basis. Instead, his language indicates a process of inner contact — something within which "awakens" and "rises to the surface."[8] Such a process of transformation in the basis of knowing, implies a developed applied psychology, with its specialised vocabulary of the forms and instruments of knowledge and their relative qualities and valuation. Sri Aurobindo would later develop this theory of praxis, drawing on the terminology of different schools of Indian psychology and adding his own observations in the formulation of a phenomenology of transcendence. The elaboration of this theory is beyond the scope of this paper but for an approach to integral education, it may suffice to draw from this that its primary goal is a change in the form and source of knowledge and the method and instruments of its acquisition. Put simply, it implies a transition from the knowledge acquired by reasoning on the evidence of the senses and built piecemeal as an edifice of specialised interlocking systems (knowledge by indirect contact) to a non-dual and integral direct knowledge which is at once temporal and ahistorical (knowledge by identity) — through a process of transformation mediated by a stabilisation of forms of intuitive

8. Sri Aurobindo, "A System of National Education", *Sri Aurobindo Birth Centenary Library*, vol. 17, p. 204.

knowledge (knowledge by inner contact). What are these forms of intuitive knowledge and how can they be fostered? We can see a more complete development of this question in the educational teachings of the Mother, in her practical formulation for the Sri Aurobindo International Centre for Education (SAICE).

IMMANENT ROOTS OF INTEGRALITY

Sri Aurobindo's second principle of education addresses the internal or immanent roots of integrality. It says: "The second principle is that the mind has to be consulted in its growth."[9] On the face of it, this looks like an obvious precept, which modern views of idealistic education and developmental psychology consider to be self-evident. But his description points to Vedāntic roots once more. In his elaboration here: "To force the nature to abandon its own *dharma* is to do it permanent harm, mutilate its growth and deface its perfection. It is a selfish tyranny over a human soul and a wound to the nation. . . ."[10] The use of the term *dharma* relates to the teaching of the *Bhagavad-Gītā*, as Sri Aurobindo knew and developed it both in his implication for the individual (*svadharma*) and the nation. *Dharma* is an ubiquitous term in the *Gītā*, and in Sri Aurobindo's interpretation, has to do less with duty and moral righteousness than with the dynamic principle of cosmic unity as it unfolds in every individualised consciousness. It is thus closely related to the notion of soul (as he states explicitly in the description) both of the individual and the nation. Once again, we see both the psychological and nationalist bases of Sri Aurobindo's educational text and once again, this nationalism must be understood as an alternate cultural psychology presenting a transformative post-colonial and

9. Sri Aurobindo, "A System of National Education", *Sri Aurobindo Birth Centenary Library*, vol. 17, p. 204.

10. Ibid.

postmodern critique of colonialism and modernity. The consultation of the mind itself here implies an art of mentoring, where the various levels and forms of human consciousness are penetrated through dialogic engagement in an attempt to arrive at the irreducible kernel of personality, the true person within. The process of "consulting the mind" itself is thus not a static but a dynamic and transformative process, conducted through a desireless warmth and compassion in the teacher attempting to aid the inner integration and expression of the student's drives for knowledge and experience through an insight of personal quintessence and proportional representation. Here, again, the forms of inner knowledge related to the soul come into question as in the previous principle.

In Sri Aurobindo and the Mother's teaching, the soul or psychic being is the core of the human person, persisting from life to life and carrying in itself the law of personal expression. It is wrapped in the subtle forms of mental, vital and physical consciousness and expresses through these modalities in the human life. Each of these other sheaths of consciousness are independent and discontinuous in human beings, representing the evolutionary breaks in earthly consciousness — life appearing as a new principle with independent properties in matter and mind appearing as a further unprecedented principle in life. Each of these have their independent lives within us, with their own interests, preferences, priorities and forms of understanding. It is the soul or psychic being within which can integrate this inner psychology and utilise their specificities proportionately for the evolution of consciousness in the person. The psychic being is the evolving entity within the human, and the educational enterprise, from one angle, can be seen as the facilitation of the growth and expression of the psychic being in itself and through the instruments of mind, life and body.[11] The "consultation of the mind" thus aids in the development of a customised curriculum for the student, enabling the emergence of the soul and giving the proper proportionate emphases to the soul-qualities as expressed in the aspirations of the physical, vital (pertaining to emotion and will) and mental beings. It would also address the soul's aspiration for universality experienced in a variety of specific ways as its doors of realisation of spiritual consciousness.

SOCIAL AND CULTURAL FOUNDATIONS

But, as one can see in the nationalistic sensitivity of the statement, this principle addresses not only an ideal of psychological development based on a human soul essence but envisages a group or national soul as well. Today, following the excesses of nationalism in a post-Second World War era, ideas such as that of nation soul are likely to look more suspicious than they would have in an era of anti-colonial resistance. Nevertheless, Sri Aurobindo's idea of the nation soul needs to be understood not as a chauvinistic or ahistorical essence but more properly as a cultural palimpsest, an accumulated subjectivity forming the intimate discursive basis of a living culture and seeded with its invisible preferential forms and questions of communication, expression and growth.[12] The seemingly psychological bias of integral education here reveals its social and cultural foundations. To engage with the world from a culturally situated perspective is to preserve the living marks of cultural history, not necessarily as unchanged forms, but as creatively adapting choices.[13]

11. The Mother, "The Science of Living", *Collected Works of the Mother*, vol. 12, Pondicherry: Sri Aurobindo Ashram, pp. 3-8.
12. See Sri Aurobindo, "True and False Subjectivism" in *Social and Political Thought: Sri Aurobindo Birth Centenary Library*, vol. 15, pp. 37-47.
13. The Mother, "An International University Centre" in *On Education: Collected Works of the Mother*, vol. 12, pp. 39-47.

Sri Aurobindo's third principle of education continues to address this socially constituted subject of education. It is also and perhaps more primarily, a statement of spiritual pragmatism. The principle states: "The third principle of education is to work from the near to the far, from that which is to that which shall be."[14] The description addresses more explicitly the place of local and cultural traditions as educational groundings, skills and ideals with which to move towards universality. Just as the psychological transcendence of habitus is implied and indicated in the first and part of the second principles, the importance of cultural embeddedness is brought to the fore here. Our physical and a good part of our vital existence is formed through unconscious intangible assimilations of culture and habitus and the refinement and upliftment of these parts through exposure to ideals present within them is among the foundations of this aspect of education. However, the ability to have a part of the being which is not subject to parochialism and can creatively engage with wider cultural forms and ideals of a more universal kind is also part of this third principle, which acknowledges a progressive role in education. The vantage of a transcendent consciousness brought into engagement with a firmly acculturated tradition so as to subject it to transformative forces in keeping with the needs of historical advance, without compromising the highest ideals present in it, is the offering of this principle.

VEDĀNTIC EPISTEMOLOGY

Since the epistemology of integral education, in its holistic view of the human person and personality, addresses what it sees as distinct modalities of knowledge, in its curriculum,

14. Sri Aurobindo, "A System of National Education", op. cit., pp. 204-5.

training and assessment, it would be fruitful to consider briefly the Vedāntic and consciousness bases of these knowledge modalities. If, following Vedānta, knowledge (*jñāna*) is the self-consciousness of infinite Conscious Being, in its active emergence into a manifest form of an interacting and evolving multiplicity, self-contained as space and ever-developing as time, stages and forms in the operation of this self-consciousness may be formulated. This is done in the *Aitareya Upaniṣad*, where the foundational and inexpressible knowledge as identity, *jñāna*, is expressed in the forms or stages of *vijñāna*, *prajñāna*, *saṁjñāna* and *ājñāna*.[15] In Sri Aurobindo's interpretations of these terms, *vijñāna* refers to the self-consciousness of the One — a comprehensive knowledge; *prajñāna* refers to the knowledge of its parts in themselves and in their relations — an apprehensive knowledge; *saṁjñāna* refers to a knowledge of the essence of the One in its parts — a contactual knowledge; and *ājñāna* refers to a knowledge of control and unfoldment of the parts by the One — a practical knowledge.[16] Thus *vijñāna* can be thought of as the identification with *Brahman* in consciousness (yoga); *prajñāna* as the perception of *Brahman* in all things (*darśana*); *saṁjñāna* as the sense-experience of the *Brahman* (essence) in all things (*ānanda, bhāva*); and *ājñāna* as the will, instrumental knowledge, creative skill or technology of unfoldment of *Brahman* in all things (*tapas, kauśalaḥ*).[17] This succession of knowledge modalities can also be seen as emergent and expressive grades in a manifestation of the inexpressible knowledge by identity — *vijñāna* and *prajñāna* as more properly the knowledge by the One of itself and of the Many; and *saṁjñāna* and *ājñāna* as

15. *Aitareya Upaniṣad*, III.2.
16. Sri Aurobindo, "The Upaniṣads", *Sri Aurobindo Birth Centenary Library*, vol. 12, pp. 188-89.
17. Compare *Bhagavad-Gītā*, II:50, *yogaḥ karmasu kauśalam*.

more properly the knowledge by the Many of the One in itself and in the Many. According to Sri Aurobindo, these forms of knowledge coexist in Supermind, the conceptive and creative faculty of *Brahman* for manifestation, and in all of them the knowledge of the Oneness of *Brahman* is primordially present, either as singular or as foreground or as background. This is the nature of knowledge in the modality of manifestation known as the knowledge (*vidyā*).[18]

In the modality of manifestation in which we find ourselves, also known as the ignorance (*avidyā*), these same forms and grades of knowledge are operational, but with the two differences: (1) they operate not in conjunction and unison but separately or independently; and (2) the knowledge of Oneness of *Brahman* is everywhere absent or suppressed and knowledge in all these four forms is that of the Many by the Many.[19] A little reflection will bring home the correspondences of these forms of knowledge in the human experience in the ignorance. Firstly, *vijñāna* as the knowledge of identification with *Brahman* is absent. Next, *prajñāna* can be seen as external knowledge by observation and measurement (perception). Then, *saṁjñāna* can be understood as affective knowledge arising out of sense contact, or the knowledge of others attained through the experiences and apparatus of senses, sensations, feelings, moods, sentiments, emotions and affections, marked by the dualities of pleasure and pain, attraction and repulsion. Finally, *ājñāna* can be seen as practical or technical knowledge, inclusive of the knowledge of will and skill. The identification of these forms of knowledge in the human being with the instrumental sheaths of mind (*manaḥ*), life (*prāṇaḥ*) and body (*śarīra*) respectively can also be

18. Sri Aurobindo, "The Upaniṣads", op. cit., p. 190.
19. Ibid., p. 189.

seen. Mental or cognitive knowledge would relate to *prajñāna*; affective vital experience would relate to *saṁjñāna*; and a knowledge operating in the physical domain, as skill in the body, will in the vital, and technical understanding of process and practice in the mind would relate to *ājñāna*. As we have touched on earlier, Sri Aurobindo points out that the evolutionary discontinuities in the appearance of each of these modalities of consciousness on earth renders these forms of knowledge and experience distinct and independent in the human being. They are subject in their operation to the exclusivity of aims of their corresponding beings, the mental, vital and physical and suffer therefore from disunity of intent and interference or immixture of understanding.[20] The ultimate correction of these errors of knowledge in the ignorance is only to be found by a discovery of and identification with the sources of these forms of knowledge in the knowledge — i.e. a dwelling in Supermind and conversion of the sheaths and instruments of knowledge to their supramental counterparts.[21] But this distant goal has to be approached through a gradual process of preparation by the third precept of Sri Aurobindo's principles of teaching — i.e. moving from the near to the far. This would imply an attention to developing the factors lacking in these operational forms of knowledge — i.e. attempting to activate the root of knowledge by identity within these forms of separative knowledge; and attempting to discover a root of integrality which would harmonise the activities of these different modalities under a single intent and co-ordinated action. In Sri Aurobindo's phenomenology, this root of

20. Sri Aurobindo, "The Synthesis of Yoga", Chapter III, *Sri Aurobindo Birth Centenary Library*, vol. 20, pp. 15-25.

21. Sri Aurobindo, "The Triple Transformation", *The Life Divine* Chapter XXV, *Sri Aurobindo Birth Centenary Library*, vol. 19, pp. 889-918.

integrality within us is the psychic being. In its emergence and occupation of a leading role in the human personality and life, a harmonious development of the different forms of knowledge, each in its dynamic and proportional development in the individual, becomes possible.[22] But even prior to this emergence, each of the independent beings in us, the mental, vital and physical, can receive its intimations from within in the form of intuitions of the inner or subliminal mental, vital or physical beings. A receptivity to and development of these intuitions of identity in the forms of psychic or spiritual knowledge then, would form the direction of training of the different instruments of human knowledge. This would form the development of the intermediate form of knowledge, knowledge by inner contact.[23]

At the mental level — of *prajñāna*, an openness to intuition to bring direct intimations of conclusions otherwise deduced from the evidence of the senses, could then form part of this training. In science, it is known as a practical fact that hypothesis formation (and often leaps in deductive processes) is often arrived at by inexplicable and intuitive means. Similarly, in metaphysical thinking, large schema are often "seen" all at once in the minds of the philosophers who have made important contributions to our views of reality — and often worked out in their details afterwards. To be made aware of such processes and encouraged to apply them to cognitive thought would be an underlying approach to the method of mental education. Similarly, a vital education, would take up the life of the senses through the sublimation of the aesthetic sense and its development in the inner perception of forms of beauty and affective delight connecting us in all things to the

22. Sri Aurobindo, "The Triple Transformation", pp. 889-918.
23. Sri Aurobindo, "Knowledge by Identity and Separative Knowledge", op. cit.

self-existent and causeless Delight (*ānanda*) of *Brahman*. In all contacts, the intuitional experience and articulation of degrees and varieties of the One Being of Love in the universe, veiled or unveiled, would be encouraged. In terms of will, an intuition of power in its works of production and organisation in the world — not the animal instinct of personal survival and possession, but the intuition of the enhancement of unity and consciousness through works, would be the direction of the growth of this form of knowledge; and in terms of the body, an openness to physical intuition in its harmonious and healthy maintenance and instrumentality and in its instinctual skill in action, would form important elements of the progress of the physical being.

INTEGRAL EDUCATION AND MAINSTREAM HIGHER EDUCATION

In mainstream higher education, it is cognitive knowledge that is mainly addressed. In professional forms of higher education, such as engineering or business administration, we find some degree of practical knowledge, mostly oriented towards theoretical consideration, though contemporary business management schools have increasingly addressed other modalities of knowledge. In idealistic education and in postmodern critiques of contemporary civilisation, this lopsided equation of education and even consciousness with rationality has been brought to the front. For example, thinkers such as Michel Foucault have called for an acknowledgement of different forms of rationality.[24] Contemporary workshops (mostly extra-curricular and professional) to enhance the health of different forms of knowing and an openness to intuition have been in the ascendant. A pluralist approach to

---

24. Michel Foucault, *Power/Knowledge: Selected Interviews and Other Writings 1972-1977*, Harvester Press, 1980, p. 47.

knowledge, evidenced in the currency of such terms as multiple intelligences, emotional intelligence or social intelligence is growing in importance, though hardly yet mainstream in academia. On the other hand, contemporary globalism is best understood as a late-Enlightenment phenomenon in which a kind of omnipotence, omnipresence and omniscience has been achieved for humanity in general but at the cost of individual insignificance through the cascading torrent of technological progress. This has made for a civilisational crisis erupting from every direction — ecological, cultural and financial. In this volatile environment, fraught with danger, Sri Aurobindo's revisionary approach to knowledge, its instruments, sources and forms of acquisition and establishment merit consideration, for the coherence and integrality of its vision and realisation.

Integral Education: Its Original Implementation

In terms of the implementation of integral education, the original form was laid by the Mother and the founding teachers of the Sri Aurobindo International Centre of Education in the ashram at Pondicherry, India. The higher educational wing of this ashram, known as Knowledge, has attempted to give form to these ideas in terms of higher education. The salient features of these forms include a customised curriculum closely co-created through the interaction of the student with a mentor, attention paid to the physical, vital, mental, psychic and spiritual forms of consciousness and their growth and expression, and a facility for languages — both indigenous and international: most students know Sanskrit and at least one other Indian language plus English and French. The social location of this experiment in an ashram composed of residents practising the integral yoga makes many features of the integral education practically effective. The teachers are familiar with the epistemology and terminology of Sri Aurobindo's teaching as lived and experienced or at least intimately intuited realities and as aspects of their life practice, and translate these realities into education as part of a seamless habitus. Such a close community could run the danger of unconscious religious cultism in its pedagogy, and in spite of the Mother's insistence on freedom of choice for the students, the conventionalised forms of address and practice relating to Sri Aurobindo, the Mother and the integral yoga, seem indeed to have subsumed the educational habitus. Moreover, the mentorship practice has not gone deep or far enough either in pushing the boundaries of the faculties of knowledge or of an integrally expressive engagement in the curriculum or of a penetrating and informed assimilation and questioning of tradition and its engagement with aspects of contemporary global culture or civilisational values and lifestyles.

CONTINUOUS LEARNING HABITUS

Students entering this higher educational stage do so as part of an integrated programme which begins at childhood, so that the principles of integral education have to be seen as a continuous application through school and in college. Thus, the development of the faculties of the mind, of concentration and reasoning and synthesising ability, of the development of the imagination and the openness to inspiration and finally, of the replacement of the mental activity by intuitive sources of knowledge, are meant to be introduced at the school level. However, they could in general be given more importance or made an independent part of the education, since the critical transformation in the definition of knowledge in Sri Aurobindo's teaching rests on this training. At the higher educational level, training of the mental faculties is assumed to have been achieved and generally not exercised in any principled manner. Though Sri Aurobindo, in his writings, outlines some methods of meditation and the Mother provides some guidelines on the ways in which the mental faculties may be developed, these have been left as general as possible, so that the inner process of learning in each student be given its full creative possibility as knowledge from within. But this then makes the mentorship process all the more critical and it is doubtful whether the isolated teaching community has risen to the occasion.

Given that all the teachers are practitioners of the integral yoga, the convergence of that practice with the mentorship process provides a greater likelihood of success in this area. The "free progress system" devised by the Mother is the structure through which students arrive at their curriculum for study in consultation with a mentor.[25] This process is initiated from the high school level and continues in higher education. "Classes" are usually conducted in an informal setting with the teacher surrounded by a small group of students interacting through an intimate dialogical participation. Evaluation of success in course completion is usually measured through student-chosen research projects. No degrees or certificates are provided at course or programme completion, and a student is allowed to take his or her time to progress through the curriculum chosen.[26]

INTEGRALITY OF THE CURRICULUM

The question of the comprehensiveness or integrality of the curriculum needs next to be considered. Is the integral education being practised at the Sri Aurobindo Ashram meeting in higher education its own set criteria for the development of the five areas of human consciousness — mental, vital, physical, psychic and spiritual? Are these being chosen for each student in keeping with the needs of the

25. See "Sri Aurobindo International Centre of Education" in *On Education: Collected Works of the Mother*, vol. 12, pp. 109-10.

26. Ibid.

growth of the soul through these modalities? And is the curriculum sufficiently cognisant of the engagement of the individual with tradition on the one hand, and the concerns of a global modernity on the other? Again, the education of the five areas of consciousness begins from high school. In terms of content, mental education encompasses the areas of science, mathematics, philosophy and other cognitive disciplines. Vital education, in terms of skill and faculty development, concerns itself with the training of the senses, sensations, feelings and aesthetic judgements on the one hand and the development of character, will and practical effectiveness in work and organisation on the other. In terms of content, this encompasses the areas of the creative arts — literature, art, music and theatre and of history, biography, ethics, social and political theory and administration/ management. All these fields of study are potentially represented in the ashram education at both elementary, secondary and post-secondary levels, but as mentioned before, their place in a student's curriculum and specific implementation is left to the mentor and the student. Here the role of the mentor cannot be overemphasised. Unfortunately, the ideal of "free progress" has become largely interpreted as a *laissez-faire* attitude towards students' choices, which, without proper exposure and inspiration, tends to be determined by environmental conditionings. The extended community of the ashram could also be said to represent expertise in all these areas, but such expertise is hardly well utilised. At the practical and expressive level, the community life at the ashram provides ample opportunity for the expression and display of creativity and work/administrative skills through theatre, art exhibitions, publications and collective work projects. Particularly in the arts and in physical culture, this has yielded an aspect of cultural interest, but this tends to exist in isolation without a sufficiently creative and critical acknowledgement of contemporary world culture.

Physical education, which is hardly addressed in traditional higher education, except as an extra-curricular activity, is among the exemplary contributions of integral education at the Sri Aurobindo Ashram. In one of his last writings, Sri Aurobindo draws out the importance of physical culture in an integral education.[27] In the far reaches of Sri Aurobindo's yoga philosophy, the physical body is meant to be made fully conscious and awakened to its identity as a material form of divine consciousness, translating its eternity to immortality.[28] Physical education as part of an integral education is a preparation of the physical consciousness, enhancing its inner capacities for health, longevity, co-ordination, harmony, endurance, stamina, capacity for intensity of experience (*dhāraṇa sāmarthyam*) and the direct intuitive skill of a working physical instrument. Physical culture at the Sri Aurobindo Ashram, in the form of a choice of exercises, group activities and sports is mandatory at all levels of education and is voluntarily continued by a large proportion of ashram residents well into advanced age. What is encouraged through the physical exercises is the recognition and cultivation of an independent consciousness of the body, a cultivation through awareness more than through an insistence on any particular form or tradition of physical culture. So, for example, though Indian *haṭha-yoga* has been known to have developed an approach to physical culture which enhances the limits of physical capacity in every way, this is not the only or even "suggested" form of physical culture at the Ashram. People

27. Sri Aurobindo, "Perfection of the Body", *The Supramental Manifestation and Other Writings, Sri Aurobindo Birth Centenary Library,* vol. 16, pp. 5-19.

28. "The Divine Body", op. cit., pp. 20-40.

take their choice of callisthenics, long distance running and other individual activities along with co-ordinated group activities of a variety of forms.

The two other forms of education, special to the integral education at the ashram are Psychic Education and Spiritual Education. These are the forms meant specially to bring the individual directly into contact with an aspect of *vijñāna* (knowledge by identity), either as an immanent (psychic) or a transcendental and cosmic source (spirit). At the higher educational level, these forms are addressed mainly through a study of Sri Aurobindo and the Mother's works on these forms of consciousness and comparative study, and contemplation of these teachings applied to one's own life and experience. Again, a more systematic attention to addressing an understanding and experience of these forms of knowledge/consciousness can be facilitated than what is offered presently at the ashram. Sri Auorbindo's works of *dārśanika* phenomenology (*The Life Divine*) or of applied integral psychology (*The Synthesis of Yoga*) are introduced as texts, but seldom with a specialised consideration or application of the bases of a Vedāntic epistemology or of the instruments of knowledge and their transformation. Moreover, at the higher educational level, cross-traditional and cross-epochal researches into spiritual experience and trans-egoic methods with a view to internal understanding and assimilation can be fruitfully facilitated.

Apart from these psychological bases of integral education, the question of curriculum must answer to what degree the content of the education addresses cultural knowledge of habitus and tradition and global forms of contemporary culture as forms of assimilation and critical engagement. As mentioned before, one powerful tool in this direction is the expanded language awareness within the ashram curriculum.

For the most part, science subjects are taught in French, while the humanities are taught in English.[29] This makes for a cultural expansion through two of the major languages of modern Europe and with it, an enhanced appreciation of the different gifts of perception and expression held by these cultures. Along with this, most students learn Sanskrit, and through it, are exposed to the roots of ancient and medieval Indian culture. Finally, they are also encouraged to study formally their mother tongue or some other modern language of their liking. This helps both in an informed acceptance and appreciation of the ideals in one's culture and in a universalisation of one's local cultural roots, bringing many of the unconscious assumptions of social behaviour into awareness as choices. However, again, in this area, I feel the curriculum stays largely insulated from the problems of contemporary Indian or global culture. Though Sri Aurobindo's profound works on social and political theory, *The Human Cycle* and *The Ideal of Human Unity* are taken up for study, the contemporary rethinking of civilisation launched by postmodern and post-colonial thinkers is hardly brought into alignment or engagement with Sri Aurobindo's vision and critical thinking, leaving it static and ahistorical in its reception and interpretation. The same can be said about the introduction to Indian culture and history, where a nationalistic idealism traces its continuity with early twentieth century approaches but ignores more contemporary cross-cultural or subaltern studies or critical historiographies opening vistas on the future.

GURUKULA AND THE ROLE OF THE TEACHER

In its implementation, as mentioned earlier, this model of education is highly dependent on a mentorship process. Of course, higher education in the modern academy also

---

29. "Sri Aurobindo International Centre of Education", op. cit.

recognises the need for customised mentorship, with its research guide and committee at the thesis or dissertation stage. But with integral education at the ashram, mentorship and personal awareness are the bases of the pedagogy, and determine the students' curriculum planning and scheduling, assessment and determination of progress. In a way, this is a translation into a quasi-modern academic form of the pre-modern Indian *gurukula*, where the student stayed in the home of the teacher and was guided and taught through all aspects of daily living. The principle of pedagogy being primarily one of the integral development and expression of faculties and thus methodological, this closeness of relation with someone who has practised and experienced the psychological bases of integral education, is indispensable. As mentioned above, at the ashram, this is possible, because it provides a habitus of residential practice, where the education merges seamlessly into individual and collective life. The relationship between student and mentor or student and teacher in the small groups which study together, is however, different from that of the unconditional obedience and surrender on the part of the student and the unquestioned privilege on the part of the guru demanded in the pre-modern *gurukula*. Student and teacher are related here more as a fraternity of co-travellers, sharing knowledge and experience in a process of mutual growth. The high teacher to student ratio is also made possible by the economics of the ashram, where teachers whose living needs are taken care of by the community, offer their educational services free of cost. Thus, a translation of this model to settings other than that of a residential community committed exclusively to a change of consciousness and seeing education as part of the means to this end, poses serious difficulties which only implementation can measure in terms of success or failure. Again, though the factors mentioned above make the ashram habitus ideal for the social practice of Sri Aurobindo's and the Mother's integral education, the insular and insulated nature of such a setting tends to distance the faculty from contemporary currents in thinking, having an effect of making the courses anachronistic and ahistorical, thus diluting the potential for students emerging from such a system to become creative agents for civilisational change in the contemporary world. An informed critique of modernity and its discontents, of neo-liberalism, neo-colonialism, technology and culture, globalisation or post-national capitalism, patriarchies, superpower politics and ecological imbalance in the light of the revolutionary vision and teaching of Sri Aurobindo and the Mother and the power to offer and shape solutions to the critical evolutionary crisis of our times is not much in evidence among the alumni of this institute.

Some Contemporary Attempts and Approximations

THE CALIFORNIA INSTITUTE OF INTEGRAL STUDIES AND INTEGRAL THEORY

Outside of Pondicherry, numerous schools throughout India and some abroad today claim to follow the principles of integral education, attempting to replicate the principles and forms found in the school at the Sri Aurobindo Ashram. However, implementation of integral education at the higher educational level is not easy to come across. An example worth considering by dint of its founder's inspiration in the teaching of Sri Aurobindo and its explicit reference to integralism in its title, is the California Institute of Integral Studies (CIIS) at San Francisco (http://ciis.edu). Founded in 1968, this institute was shaped under the leadership of Haridas Chaudhuri, a disciple of Sri Aurobindo, and succeeded the American Academy of Asian Studies, co-founded by Chaudhuri in 1951. The CIIS fields undergraduate and graduate programmes under its two main schools of Professional Psychology and of Consciousness and Transformation. In its institutional description of the term "integral education" as implied in its title as a methodological focus, it mixes a large variety of definitions:

(1) a need to synthesise the fragmentary aspects of contemporary thought and culture into a meaningful whole;

(2) a creative synthesis of the highest values of East and West;

(3) encompass[ing] all aspects of learning: the intellectual, the experiential, and the applied;

(4) integrat[ing] knowledge beyond the confines of traditional academic disciplines — viz. cultural diversity, multiple ways of knowing, spirituality, a sense of community, emancipatory ideals, and ecological sustainability;

(5) connect[ing] the spiritual and practical dimensions of intellectual life; and

(6) integrat[ing] the wisdom traditions.[30]

While some of these definitions may be more properly called creative or synthetic, some spiritually universalist and others cross-cultural, a loose mapping of this locus to Sri Aurobindo's foundations of integral education may be sensed. But no direct reference to an integral consciousness or knowledge and its forms, modalities and processes, as elucidated by Sri Aurobindo, whether psychological or social, is to be found here. The pedagogical bases of the institute are also largely mainstream, as in most institutes of higher learning. There is no demand on the faculty members to practise

30. California Institute of Integral Studies website: http://www.ciis.edu

any alternate form of consciousness or knowledge acquisition or transformation or teach or foster any such methods or realisations. The model of the individual as an evolving soul with its nature sheaths and instruments is not explicitly affirmed, though a relative acceptance of a variety of psychological models including the Aurobindonian are to be found in some of its courses and programmes. The cosmic extrapolation of this evolutionary perspective at the ecological and social level is also not directly assumed, though again a variety of evolutionary perspectives are not absent. All in all, the California Institute of Integral Studies may be seen as an interesting experiment providing an intermediate possibility of integralism located somewhere between contemporary social ethics, mind-body therapeutics and cultural/spiritual universalism. The possibility of the understanding, contemplation and practice of an Integral Philosophy and Psychology or a consciousness-based theory of social and cultural critique and unity as taught by Sri Aurobindo is not absent in this mix, though rendered dilute and compromised by mixture with other relativist paradigms. Though interesting in its eclecticism and experimental creativity, a critique of this approach from the viewpoint of Sri Aurobindo's teaching, would be that an integral consciousness and knowledge cannot be synthesised from relative and speculative perspectives with their roots in the ignorance (*avidyā*). An experiential foundation in an integral consciousness, as claimed by Sri Aurobindo and backgrounded by a history of Vedāntic practice, can alone be the vantage (as in the image of the cosmic *aśvattha* tree from the *Gītā* with its roots above and branches below)[31] from which partial approaches can be put in place. To overcome this limitation, of course, is to challenge the very foundations of

31. *Bhagavad-Gītā*, XV.1.

epistemology in the Western academy, which is intrinsically relativist and lacks the history of social practice to accept an independent basis in Integral Knowledge. Postmodern critiques of modern pedagogy have made it possible to open up alternate epistemologies, including those based on phenomenologies of spiritual experience (*darśana*), what Michel Foucault has called "an insurrection of subjugated knowledges."[32] From a certain viewpoint, instead of a rationally limited relativism, this implies a hyper-relativism, but one which allows for a staging and testing of various non-rational bases and claims for truth. The institutional bastions of educational standardisation (e.g. accrediting agencies) are not likely to look kindly on theories and approaches which lack verifiability by reason, so within this disciplinary topography, the California Institute of Integral Studies may be seen as an institution of higher education which has certainly been active in pushing the boundaries of the modern academy in the direction of an integral education within permissible bounds. However, an important distinction and danger here should not be overlooked. Integral education, as taught by Sri Aurobindo and the Mother, is envisaged as an aspect of culture serving a vision of consciousness change in the individual and society. As such, its method and content is meant to prepare for and subserve such a change of consciousness. In this, it follows a Vedāntic cultural epistemology, where theory (*darśana*) cannot be separated from practice (yoga), and the former takes a supporting and clarifying role for the latter, which is considered primary. At the CIIS (and elsewhere in the modern academy, such as in the work of Ken Wilber), following an Aristotelian primacy of logocentrism, metaphysical edifices of "Integral Theory"

32. Michel Foucault, *"Society Must Be Defended": Lectures at the Collége de France, 1975-1976*, tr. David Macey, New York: Picador, 2003, p. 7.

with orthodox social potentialities are in the making. Such "theoretical" dogmas, of course, are not absent among the followers of Sri Aurobindo, but there this must be seen as aberrations of the intent of Integral Philosophy, which is best understood not as metaphysics but as a (supra-)rationally mediated phenomenology (*darśana*), companioning an Integral Yoga, not as a statement of social fundamentalism but as an orientation and instrument of discrimination and intuitive awakening in individual practice. If this includes a social dimension, it is clear that such a society must emerge intentionally through a collective accumulation of experience arising out of engagement with these texts and thus validating their "truth," "universality" and "freedom."

CIVILISATIONAL IMPERATIVE OF INTEGRAL EDUCATION

To wrap up this discussion on contemporary implementations of integral education, I would like to touch on a higher educational endeavour which is in its formative stages as a further model for the future. This is also inspired by the educational philosophy and pedagogical intent and methods of Sri Aurobindo and the Mother and differs from the examples dealt with earlier, in being a distance learning school. Though this may make certain aspects of integral education, e.g. the physical and the social/collective dimension harder to realise, it offers a greater reach and through a combination of onsite and online activities, facilitates, in my belief, a more introspective and creative engagement with the educational contents. The term "integral" here is understood as (a) an integration of the personality; (b) an integration of modalities of knowledge; and (c) an integration of cultures. The core offering in the initial phase will be a graduate programme in Integral Culture, where students will choose a mix of courses representing cognitive, creative, ethical, administrative and hands-on (practicum) courses taken from the disciplines of Indian, postmodern and integral philosophy and psychology, consciousness approaches to the creative arts, eco-communities and civilisation studies. The majority of the teachers (facilitators) will be selected from practitioners of the Integral Yoga so that they may be able to share their experience of inner growth with the students and guide their inner and outer educational progress. The specific curriculum for a student will be arrived at through a process of mentorship and interaction between the student and a faculty member s/he develops a bond with and will take into account the student's inner needs in terms of mental, vital, physical, psychic and spiritual growth. Courses on the yoga philosophy and psychology of Sri Aurobindo will include studies of the instruments and stages of knowledge and processes of transformation as well as of forms of consciousness and their progress. These understandings will be brought into a comparative frame with traditional spiritual paradigms as well as contemporary approaches to epistemology and transpersonal culture. An orientation towards future society and civilisational ideals and values will be fostered through holistic studies in history, eco-communities, organisational development and through the acquisition of postmodern tools of analysis and critique. The programme implementation will be largely through the use of an online classroom management system, allowing rapid interaction between students and facilitators and including teleconferencing. Assignments will be geared to an introspective assimilation of and identification with the ideas introduced by seeding course materials with reflective questions pertaining to one's inner engagement with the material covered. This approach is modelled after the Vedāntic learning progression of *śravaṇa* (audition/reception), *manana* (reflection/contemplation) and *nididhyāsana* (meditation/identification in consciousness) mediated by the facilitator/mentor. It is hoped that the accumulation of practice and expression arising from such processes of engagement will constitute a field and an archive of experience continuously deepening the inner contributions of education, both in terms of the sources and instruments of knowledge and in the power of individual and social transformation.

Conclusion: Integral Education and a Post-Secular Social Consciousness

In conclusion, Sri Aurobindo and the Mother's principles and implementations of integral education belong to a post-secular social consciousness which embraces a universal spirituality based on an integral model of reality and personality and an openness to a transformation in the source and instrumentation of human knowledge. It also envisages a transformed society with new ideals and goals leading towards an optimistic and holistic vision of the future based on experiences of relational and cosmic identity. This is fundamentally an optimistic vision, and in a time of global crisis, sectarian fundamentalism, techno-capitalistic conditioning and spiritual bankruptcy, an epic hopefulness in the human capacity to rise to its full potential of the stewardship of the earth and the ushering of an era of peace and harmony based on consciousness and creativity.

6

Education for a Faith in the Future[1]

Manoj Das

Of Roots and Branches

WITH the proliferation of newspapers and news magazines as well as the gradual increase in the number of their pages, reports and essays on important issues and topics, sometimes through special supplements, have become a regular feature and one such recurrent topic, no doubt, is Education. Also several volumes on the subject have been published, including a series by the UNESCO, during the past three decades than ever before. This shows on one hand that public interest in the subject has grown wider, but on the other hand, if I can be pardoned, the situation provokes one to wonder about the quality and character of this wider interest, for a wider interest alone is not a sure sign of a serious or deeper interest. The interest the media has cultivated among an even wider readership in a category of news that are billed out as art,

---

1. The National Council of Educational Research and Training (NCERT), the apex organisation assisting and advising the central and state governments on school education, recently instituted a scheme entitled *Sri Aurobindo Memorial Lecture*. The first lecture under this scheme was delivered by Manoj Das at the Presidency College auditorium, the University of Calcutta, on 2 July 2008. This version of his talk is supplemented with a few illustrations. By courtesy: *The Statesman Festival Number 2008.*

culture and literature is rarely anything more than in entertainment, glamour and items for titillation.

No doubt, the level to which the concept of education can be diluted has a limit, unlike topics of culture such as art or literature. But the danger in the case of education is less perceptible. When something ugly or vulgar is offered as art or music or dance, we can shut our eyes or ears to it, we can very well do without them, but when education is presented as a discipline entirely devoted to external accomplishments, mastering ever new inventions in technology, promotion of career and prosperity, we may not find anything amiss in it because we need such opportunities; there is nothing vulgar or apparently degrading in them. The worldwide challenge of competitions and the demands of what is often termed as fast life does not give us respite enough to reflect on the question if what we accept as education today is the genuine stuff, if education did not have some greater role to play in our life than obtaining to us the aforesaid accomplishments and vocational facilities.

That brings to mind a brief dialogue, but a significant one. Thoreau and Emerson both had been students at Harvard. Once while the two celebrated alumni were reminiscing over their days in that famous university, Emerson said that by now their alma mater had several branches of education. Thoreau, who was better acquainted with the ground realities, observed, "Yes, indeed, prolific branches there are; but what about the roots?"

With the passage of time things like lifestyle, fashion, communications and social and political structures are bound to change; but certain things do not change — a mother's love for the child, the need of faith in our communion with one another in our daily life or our need for peace and progress, for example. The same applies to our basic trust in the necessity of honesty. We exclaim with appreciation, "What a wonderfully honest man is he!" We do not exclaim with the same emotion "What a wonderfully dishonest man is he!" We instinctively recognise the indispensability of such qualities for our collective survival. Maybe, it is even more subtle than instinctive, for according to a study (2007) published in the journal *Nature,* infants as young as six months can differentiate between good and bad elements, outdating the theory that children developed that sense along with their knowledge of language when they were about two years of age. A team of psychologists including Prof. Karen Wynn of Yale University, Connecticut, carried out a study on two groups of babies, the first aged six months and the second aged ten months, showing to them a climber trying to ascend a hill who was helped by one blob and hindered by another. Offered a choice between the two, the babies chose the blob helping the ascent.

Like these values that had not changed just as the Himalayas had not ceased to be overwhelming or a flower had not stopped being beautiful despite prevailing for millennia, the original role of education had not changed despite our ignoring it and that role could not have been more precisely stated than what the ancient Indian scriptures said, *sa vidyā yā vimuktaye* — education is that what liberates.

Life, it was agreed, was the greatest university, but a certain outlook was required to be cultivated in the young to transform their transient experiences in the world into lasting lessons. From its very indeterminable beginning, education in its classical sense had two aspects: first it cultivated in the student a quest for knowledge and next trained him or developed in him a skill for supporting himself in the existential sense as well as for playing a purposeful role in the community. Innumerable testimonies are there in the Indian tradition of literature and philosophy to suggest that the teachers of yore tried — and they must have succeeded in many cases if not in all — in striking a balance between these two ideals of education for a considerable length of time. They studied the *pravṛtti* — the inherent inclination — of the student and accordingly helped him to choose his *vṛtti* or vocation. If the vocation was already fixed by heredity, the pupil was taught the way of taking equal care, if not more, of his *pravṛtti,* that was generally in consonance with his *svadharma,* the inner law of his being.

It will take long to identify the historical forces that disrupted this balance, resulting in those who cared for only their inner self breaking away from the so-called worldly life and those who led the typical life as social beings distancing themselves from their inner self. This unfortunate development, by now, had reached its culmination. We rarely remember that beneath our surface, self-dominated by our senses, craving for pleasure and pride and given over entirely to satisfaction of ambitions and desires, we had an inner self thirsting for truth and the knowledge of a different order — that liberates us from our bondage of ignorance.

But, such is the constitution of man that the satisfaction his surface self seeks does not come through a mere preoccupation with desires and ambitions. Hence the multiple innovations in the means of enjoyment and search for pastures new for pleasure.

This is the psychological state of affairs that had inevitably given a diabolical boost to consumerism. As a thinker observed, once we knew necessity to be the mother of invention whereas today it is the invention that is the mother of necessity. Our illusory needs, illusory hopes for joy are continuously whetted by the militant intelligence behind consumerism manipulating our taste and dreams. By and by it is the culture of hedonism that dominates and blinds us. "Modern man is drinking and drugging himself out of awareness, or he spends his time shopping, which is the same thing," says Earnest Becker, in his *Denial of Death.*

A Confession and a Question

May I be allowed to bring in here the confession of a gentleman, as a representative illustration of the pattern at work. This is from one who was once a successful scholar, about 10 years senior to this author, who as an entrepreneur proved equally successful but had just stopped short of reducing himself to a complete android. Let me put briefly his lengthy moaning.

> You know, like many other youths of the immediate post-Independence decade I carried in me the residues of idealism that had inspired the best among my preceding generation, inspiring them to make so much sacrifice for the country. In the changed circumstance, I had two ideal ways open before me: either I become an element in the bureaucracy and serve the country honestly or contribute to the economic progress of my country through some independent enterprise. I chose the latter, for I had some dynamism in me. I do not know at which point of time I forgot my mission. It was, I'm afraid, a gradual but rapid process of decline that my mind was not alert enough to detect, or I could be deceiving myself, for the lure of affluence is irresistible for the average man, as I have seen. I found myself amidst a corrupt gang of associates and rivals and I could not have competed with them without being corrupt myself. To my amazement my college-day friends who were once equally idealistic like me and some of whom were by then either in politics and power or in the administrative service and whose help naturally I needed from time to time, seemed to have subjected their minds to the same brand of morphine.
>
> Thus together we continued to slip farther and farther down the path of moral paralysis. But there was still that puny substance called conscience somewhere deep in the self and at times it would hum a sad song; there was somewhere in me that forgotten love for silence and serenity that would nostalgically remind me of the poet Davies we studied in our High School: *"What is this life, if full of care; we have no*

time to stand and stare?" But the demand of exigency, of strike in the factory, of betrayal by a distributor, blackmail by hoodlums, sudden fall in export, to mention a few, would push those precious moments down into oblivion. My children grew up amidst affluence and in their show of loyalty to me shouldered the burden both of my wealth and my worries, but without the idealism that had launched me into the adventure or the knowledge of the struggle I had put into it.

My grandchildren grew up amidst a new culture, or call it a want of culture if you please, looking upon luxuries and the arrogance they breed as their birthright and divided their time between pleasure on one hand and the care of their early diabetes, blood pressure, etc. on the other hand. I was condemned to look on as one of my grandsons, in his early thirties, was dying in the intensive care ward of a star hospital, suffering from a heart ailment. He had returned from the West, with the highest training available in management. Poor boy! The last query he made, before closing his eyes finally, was regarding the very first export deal he was handling. What was even greater pity, later I was confided to by his most intimate friend that the young man, already father of a kid, frequented an exclusive private club where he had been ensnared by a vamp whose pretensions to love — even a promise to marry him — my unfortunate heir took seriously. She exploited him thoroughly and by the time he grew suspicious of her loyalty, snubbed him as she had done to so many stupid opulent chaps. My grandson, unknown to us, was down in the dumps. This susceptibility to depression, I suppose, was probably the perverse leftover of the one meaningful trait he had inherited from me — the feeling of guilt for any unethical propensity, while his colleagues in the club were uninhibited in their amours.

You can imagine my agony when I found in his life and death nothing more worthwhile than the theme for a shoddy

> sentimental novelette. While the family wept, I only wondered, what was the use of all his super-specialisation in management if he could not manage his own petite mind and heart? What is the education we imparted to him if the very last question he must ask, even if it were to hide his real cause of anguish, should be nothing nobler than a routine export? What was the meaning of our having inspired him to study more and more, do better and better when it led to his forgetting that there were more worthy issues for reflection at that moment than an export humdrum? Now, in my eighties, I wonder what the meaning of my own life was either. In search of happiness I made my whole life a span of tension. I read the other day, what I had read fifty years ago, that a cosy bedroom costing a million is no guarantee for even a minute's sound sleep. The truth overwhelms me now; but why had it no effect on me fifty years ago? I tell you, my friend, something was grotesquely wrong in the education we received. True, colleges in our time, unlike now, had not been cursed with careerism, but as I deeply reflect on what went amiss, I find that nothing in our system told us that life was not all that we lived on the surface, that there was an inner life, that there was an element called soul, that our true happiness or a true sense of contentment depended on it.

Consumerism thrives on keeping us forgetful of the inner life. Glamour and dazzle constitute the life consumerism would like us to live; momentary sense-satisfaction, through power or pleasure, is the *raison d'être* of our existence. Parents are grooming their children for realising this ideal. This even could pass, but the problem is it is proving to be more and more frustrating. There are some well-researched studies in this regard and I refer to one of them, *The Price of Privilege*, by psychologist Dr Madeline Levin. She observes that students today are much more smart and intelligent. As their parents have more resources to spend, they buy them cellphones, cars, other luxuries and provide them with enough money to spend at will. But they don't give them love or intimate company. They have greater expectations from their children in terms of social and economic success. They drive the kids into the race for excellence, not excellence as human beings, but as status-achievers. And what is the result? I quote a few lines from Dr Levin's study:

> We know that this group of kids has three times the rate of depression and anxiety disorders as ordinary teenagers, as well as substantially higher rates of substance abuse, cutting and suicide. The most dangerous feelings a child can have are of self-hatred; yet middle-class parents are unwittingly instilling those feelings by expecting so much.

How much different is the situation in India? "In this age of instant gratification, fewer children and greater resources mean that kids are indulged as never before," says a report highlighting a study by the Mumbai clinical psychologist Narendra Kinger, who observes,

> In such cases kids are unable to handle the occasional refusal and treat it as rejection. At times they may show anger and hatred by running away from home or withdrawing to their room, or even refuse to eat, or display negative behaviour. In extreme cases it may lead to suicide.

The conclusion is, the child must be taught to live with refusals to half of their demands. "Tough" love of parents can do that.

Indulgence was never the Indian way of love; a genuine concern could transmit to the child the necessary conviction that the love is the basis for refusal. One remembers that beautiful story of Mulk Raj Anand, *The Lost Child*. On his way to a fair and then passing through the festive fair with his parents the child is fascinated by so many objects and wishes his father to buy them for him. But the father refuses to oblige the child. Somehow the parents and the child are separated from each other in the jostling crowd and the crying child is found by a sympathetic soul. Eager to console the child he offers to buy him the very stuff he craved for a while ago, one after another. But the child now has only one need, "I want my mother, I want my father!"

An Associated Press report says that one-third of America's younger children — babies through age 6 — live in home where the television is on almost all the time. Almost one child in five under 2 has a set, despite the American Academy of Paediatrics announcing serious warnings against this practice. The parents are not only apathetic to it, but also are proud about it. The report quotes a mom laughing and narrating how her "15-month-old sang the McDonald's jingle, *ba, ba, boppa, ba* every time they drove past the golden arches."

Ignorance of the devastating consequence apart, the reason the parents encourage their little ones to fall in love with this monster is obvious: they are exempted from devoting their attention to them. What is the situation in India? "Television viewing has become the Indian drug of choice. As the drug suppliers, offering more and more channels and inane programmes to fill them, celebrate the mass addiction, cautionary voices warning of the dangers tend to be lost in the self-congratulatory cacophony of the pushers and users," says psychoanalyst Sudhir Kakar. He says further,

> Over the past two decades studies from many parts of the world have established the harmful consequences of television viewing. They find little mention in our popular discourse although their validity is no less than of studies which link smoking to various health problems. I am not even talking of the psychological impact of the content of television programmes. For instance, the relation between violence shown on television and the increase of actual violence is now clear-cut. Only someone who is ignorant of facts can continue to doubt that television increases the propensity to violence.

At the present rate of superfluity and affluence and its unholy but unavoidable ally, hedonism, today's child is going to be the victim of unsuspected killers as he grows up. The report of the World Health Organisation, released in June 2010, warns that as the people get richer, smoke, drive and eat more, non-communicable diseases will become bigger killers during the next two decades than the infectious ones. Dr Ties Boerma, Director of Health Statistics for the WHO says that he sees more obese people and more smokers in capitals around the developing world. It should be mentioned here that TV watching and obesity among middle-class Indian children has been already asserted by survey.

But for the campaign against smoking that has lately gathered some momentum, greater addiction to that habit was inevitable. That is because a major temptation for smoking before it becomes an addiction is the urgency for a momentary diversion from nervous and worrisome mental preoccupations — and such preoccupations have multiplied.

The situation conjures up in my mind a comical scene: At the middle of a road there is a boulder, obstructing smooth passage. Atop the boulder rests a lamp. If you ask why is the boulder there, the answer is, to uphold the lamp. Should you ask why is the lamp there, the answer is so that the pedestrians or drivers avoid dashing against the boulder. We embrace tension in order to live, and we must live in order to go on experiencing tension. The illusion is, both justify each other; the reality is, both cancel each other, thereby rendering the whole phenomenon absurd. Alas, the list of factors adding to this condition of absurdity is long.

Values: Then and Now

Philosophers and thinkers have identified many a sign that differentiate man from the other creatures on our planet. One of them is, be he conscious of it or not, man lives by some values. Not that the value had to be necessarily lofty. The noted social reformer of Gujarat, Ravishankar Maharaj, devoted years to change the life of a tribe of hereditary burglars. One day, as he talked to a young practitioner of the tradition, the latter said with disarming frankness,

> Maharaj, if you ask me to give up my practice, I will do so. But the fact is, Goddess Lakṣmī, buried under the floors of some householders, shouts out to me as I pass by, asking me to liberate Her. Only then I dig a hole through the wall and enter the house and coup out the treasure.

Alas! the values in which the masses believed have faded out one by one. Once men were ready to die for their kings; the culture is a distant memory. Religion was the most powerful, the most meaningful and satisfying value people upheld in their life and with which they justified their sorrows and sufferings — even their very existence. But today the tradition is kept alive more for political and egotistic purposes and for collective assertion of selfishness than for true faith, barring rare exceptions. If gods and goddesses are worshipped with greater hullabaloo than ever, it is not for devotion, but for festivity and competition among the local islands of communal ego. Not long ago we read that in a city that had been the home of some of the greatest intellectuals and spiritual giants not only of India but also of the world, a film actor's image was ritualistically worshipped as a deity, making the devaluation of religious divinities complete. I also read a headline that the actor was shocked at this. For a moment I was consoled under the impression that at least he was sensible enough to feel shocked, until I read the text under it saying that he was shocked with delight.

If the age of institutional religion is past, spirituality, the only alternative that could play with greater effect the role the religion at its best played, had not yet made a bold debut, not to speak of filling up the vacuum. Fake and pseudo-mystic cults, selling "cosmic cushions" for instant cosmic experience, or offering *nirvāṇa* through telephone, have usurped quite a vast space.

We all know how Curzon's move for partition of Bengal created such an upheaval that the British rulers had to agree to "unsettle the settled fact." But later developments brought about not only the partition of Bengal, but also the partition of India, thereby planting the most damaging blow to our value of nationalism and patriotism.

There was a time when the wealthy was looked upon as blessed by divinities and hence deserved respect. Today the wealthy are often hated and necessarily suspected, thanks to the notoriety earned by most of them for their greed, vainglorious exhibitionism, corruption and betrayal of the interest of the country.

Family values had broken down. This is not to say that the family relationship had vanished. That has so far survived the changing life patterns in India. But what had received the most horrendous jolt is the institution of social relationship, the trust men could have in men, particularly the reliance the masses had on those who are educated, for the fact is that most of the sophisticated criminals, swindlers of the people's treasures and saboteurs of national security and manipulators of legal provisions to serve their impish interest are people with handsome degrees and diplomas. The respect the educated commanded till the other day, the term *vidyā* associating in the popular imagination a personality like Vidyasagar, the epitome of truth and nobility, is only a memory. In other words, the moral value that went with education had been reduced to zero. That reminds me of what the late Dr Malcolm Adisesaiah, noted educationist who held an important position in the UNESCO once told us at Pondicherry: London was bombarded during the Second World War. The state of aviation being what it was, the degree of accuracy with which the pilots hit their targets was surprising. The mystery was solved when, at the end of the war, it was found out that the bombers were those German students who got their higher education in London as British Council scholarship holders.

Print media as well as the media as a whole, commands no respect, however avidly it may be consumed. The sanctity with which the printed word was associated, had cleanly evaporated.

Perhaps the harshest blow to have fallen is on the relationship between the patient and the doctor, the latter till lately seen by the common man as his godly saviour. The day the doctors of a major hospital in a state capital walked out at the call of their union literally leaving the hearts of their patients open or pulling out the oxygen masks from the unconscious trusting client at his mercy allowing them to "die like flies" as the reports said, they stabbed the most tender limb of social corpus. As if this was not enough, shortly thereafter the staff of India's first mental sanatorium walked out for the same reason one afternoon, leaving the doors of the cabins open. The gleeful inmates, totally oblivious of themselves, stepped out to the streets, several of them to be crushed under the traffic.

Each one of these protesters was probably a good parent, a good spouse and a friend to you or me. How could they all of a sudden turn so inhuman, so pitiless? Obviously the education had failed to impart to them any value more than what was instinctive and indispensable for merely self-centred survival and career.

And who must occupy the vast space vacated by such values? The answer unfortunately is not any new set of values, but wrong values. They assault intelligence, common sense and higher tastes. Their immediate preys are the students. Let me refer to one such value. Several studies have shown how pop and rock music contribute to both physical and mental problems of the young. I quote from one serious study of the problem, *The Closing of the American Mind* by Allan Bloom:

> . . . It has risen to the current heights in the education of the young on the ashes of classical music, and in an atmosphere in which there is no intellectual resistance to attempts to tap the rawest passions. Modern-day rationalists are indifferent to it and what it represents. The irrationalists are all for it. . . . But rock music has one appeal only, a barbaric appeal to sexual desire — not love, not Eros, but sexual desire undeveloped and untutored. It acknowledges the first emanations of children's emerging sensuality and addresses them seriously, eliciting them and legitimatising them, not as little sprouts that must be carefully tended in order to grow into gorgeous flowers, but as the real thing. Rock gives children, on a silver platter, with all the public authority of entertainment industry, everything their parents always used to tell them they had to wait for until they grew up and would understand later. . . .
>
> Ministering to and according with the arousing and cathartic music, the lyrics celebrate puppy love as well as polymorphous attraction, and fortify them against traditional ridicule and shame. The words implicitly and explicitly describe bodily acts that satisfy sexual desires and treat them as its only natural and routine culmination for children who do not yet have the slightest imagination of love, marriage or family. . . .

The Indian film lyrics and what is in circulation as so-called album songs are perhaps not lagging far behind in such unabashed suggestiveness, for the clever culture-vultures know that most healthy inhibitions could be eliminated through means that have some pretensions to culture. Academically sound studies have established how this process of reckless exploitation in the name of culture had found its intimate allies in drug and violence, directly related to mercenary consumerism. In an era of rapid growth of global communication and exchange, we cannot expect such developments to remain confined to any one continent. In fact it has already become a worldwide phenomenon in the absence of any bulwark against its wicked network, often enjoying the patronage of powers that be.

Factors Aggravating the Corrosion

Two prominent factors among those aggravating this process of corrosion of values are the media and the hawkers of career education. Let us briefly focus on the first factor first. As the veteran Hiranmay Karlekar, former editor of the *Hindustan Times* and co-founder of the National Union of Journalists, bluntly states,

> What is happening can only be described as the colonisation of the print media by television. The latter is imposing its culture on the former in the same way colonial powers imposed theirs on the colonised . . . they are acquiring the latter's orientation towards entertainment in a competitive market whose ethos are increasingly influenced by television. The more serious publications still involve themselves in serious discourse. They too however are changing and, in an environment in which people demand to be continuously entertained and want to avoid thinking, their role as media of critical discourse is liable to be overshadowed by their role as media of entertainment. The minority of readers who are interested in the more serious parts of newspapers like editorials, reflective editorial-page articles, book reviews and in-depth articles in Sunday magazines, are rapidly becoming fewer in relation to the total readership. The majority of readers who mainly read sports, cinema and television news and give a cursory glance at the rest of it, are growing in number. The trend is destined to gain further momentum. As the market economy has society more completely in its grip, people drained by

> the effort to hold their own in an increasingly competitive environment, are increasingly inclined to seek nothing but entertainment outside working hours.[2]

What is more unfortunate and alarming, the role of media, by and large, is not confined to that of a chic entertainer, it is playing havoc with values. Not that it is fighting old values for new and progressive ones, it has mindlessly kept itself engaged in degrading and confusing values — spearheading a lamentable trend of cultural anarchy.

In September 2006 a women's college in Chandigarh prohibits the use of cellphones during the class hours. Protests by students took an uncouth turn, the jean-clad young ladies climbing the parapet and smashing several objects, all properties of the college, but flowerpots in particular. An alert TV channel projected the scene in the evening, prominently showing the lady who was leading that vulgar spree of destruction.

We wonder what the lady's guardians at home would be thinking of their daughter's conduct. If they belong to the average sensible mentality, they would feel embarrassed if not disgusted and would probably take their ward to task; but imagine their predicament when a Mumbai film-maker rings up the lady and informs her that he had chosen her to play the lead role in his multi-crore production in the offing.

The big newspaper that had carried the picture of the chaos in the college on its front page does not think twice before claiming credit for being the courier of this silver luck to the girl. It repeats the claim, under slightly different pretexts, several times and does not forget to inform us that the girl has thanked the paper through a TV channel.

---

2. "The Media: Evolution, Role and Responsibilities" in *Looking Back: India in the Twentieth Century* by N.N. Vohra and Sabyasachi Bhattacharya.

Whether the young lady could prove herself an artiste or not is a different issue. Maybe, there are more countable things than art for that glittery. In any case the producer got publicity worth a million, free.

Thus was rowdyism glorified and rewarded. What is remarkable, neither the newspaper, not the TV channel, nor the producer bothered to reflect on the effect of their conduct on the society; about the horrendous example they set before tens of thousands of young minds who stand on the crossroads of destiny. Alas, the newspaper also gleefully reported how the said lady is engulfed by a deluge of wannabes "all struck by glamour, all wanting fate to rewrite their ordinary scripts." What an extraordinary ambition being promoted!

Glamour is the thing. Let us read from the same newspaper extracts from a report regarding Students' Union election in a leading university in our very national capital, an event expected to be a grand opportunity for debates on issues purposeful, intelligent and intellectual:

> Candidates for the Delhi University Students' Union (DUSU) elections may be parroting the expected lines at the hustlings, but on ground there is just mascara. Lots of it as the ideal *hamārā netā aisā ho* look to woo student voters is all about looking zany. That is where Prem Studios in Kamla Market comes in. A veteran in the business of giving DUSU aspirants that dream look since 1978, this time the only brief has been, says Umesh Sabharwal, managing director of the studio, "glamour, glamour and more glamour."

The paper interviews students.

> For . . . a first year student of Economics and his friends, it is the DJ parties, free sandwiches and the cold drinks that will guide the choice. The group has so far been to three such parties, but the lack of drinks other than water was a definite let down, feels . . . of B.Com. (Hons).

This author is omitting their names, but the paper not only gives the name of the young lady thirsting for some evocative drink, but also coddles her by printing her photograph, all smiles.

What is wrong with this tide — this collective resignation to the spell of hedonism — is not its immoral and unethical character, for one can argue that concepts of morality and ethics change from time to time. The situation is bad because it is against the spirit of evolution, because it is a negative reaction to the call for an adventure in consciousness. Hedonism not only fails to deliver the promised pleasure, it drains one of one's zest for life, and leads to either self-destruction or anarchy.

Nobody can really be unaware of this situation, whether one be involved or not in the world of education. And, needless to say, what emerges is a portrait of gloom. Is there any remedial possibility involved in the spirit of education itself? Some time ago this author read a summary of the *Education for All* global monitoring report covering till year 2005. The situation might have slightly changed, but it says that approximately 103.5 million children do not go to schools. About 800 million adults are illiterate. Of this 70 per cent live in nine countries of the sub-Saharan Africa and East and South Asia, "notably India, China, Bangladesh and Pakistan." The report calls upon the governments concerned to undo the situation, but what is surprising and disheartening, those who have commented upon the report have, without exception, looked at education as technology-intensive training. One comment stresses the importance of trade among nations and wishes education in the developing countries to be accordingly oriented.

Here lies the crux of the problem. Trade and technology are indispensable, no doubt, but we seem to have forgotten that they are only parts of the external aspect of education; they must not become synonyms of education. They are designed to serve man; man is not designed to serve them. They are by no means to be shunned, for the evolutionary time-spirit has placed them at our disposal so that we become more efficient masters of our environment. But trade and technology do not constitute progress, they are external aids for progress and the true progress is a growth in consciousness. Once in a while we come across an essay on Montessori or Bernstein or Sadler and their sophisticated theories, but they are in academic magazines with meagre circulations and are like a cry in the wilderness, for no theory or doctrine could stand the sudden and powerful sway of education for sake of trade and technology.

Coming to the hawkers of career-education, here are extracts from a report from Mumbai:

> For the painfully shy Shitikanth, topping the fiercely competitive IIT entrance exam has been akin to wearing a crown of thorns. Ever since the results were declared, the bespectacled 18-year-old's life has been turned upside down. So much so that he fled his house in Patna and arrived in Mumbai on Monday a little past midnight to escape the long line of politicians, touts, coaching class tutors and other opportunists who had given him no rest since the IIT declared him the topper. Unable to bear with the constant badgering and cajoling "please endorse our class," "please appear in this ad," "please be the chief guest," — the reticent teenager did the only thing he could think of to retain his sanity. He cut and ran.[3]

An Evolutionary Crisis

How come so many sections of people, in the course of a few decades, could grow bankrupt of conscience, any capacity for circumspection, not to speak of introspection? No doubt the innate instinct of self-preservation obliges one to be self-

3. *The Times of India*, 6 June 08.

centred; but there are any number of instances to prove that there is enough in us to inspire our thoughts and actions beyond the programme of mere survival or if anything more, survival with pleasure. History presents glimpses of ages when people were spontaneously concerned about one another while taking care of their self-culture. It is not as if we are lacking in ideals; but something in us that has come to the forefront makes a caricature of the ideal in the process of its execution. All of us must be having case in point of this irony in our daily life, but let me narrate a first-hand encounter to make it clear.

It was a pleasant drive along a lonely and lengthy road flanked by a major lake and green fields. This author's car stopped amidst a large number of vehicles, from bullock-carts to trucks. I woke up to the fact that there was a *rāstā roko*, a *bandh*. No more than 20 men with flags had brought all movements at both their ends to a grinding halt. The *satyāgrahī*s (Followers of Truth!) as they called themselves, were inhabitants of the nearby village and they had a list of local grievances with which none of us taken hostage had the slightest knowledge nor anything to do. There were more policemen than the *satyāgrahī*s, but they had been instructed to stand stoic.

I had, like hundreds on both the sides of the spot under seize had imperative works to attend, but were rendered impotent by a small gossiping and smoking throng, obviously elated at discovering their own potency. It was a summer noon. I got down and surveyed the travellers, men, women and children peeping out from the rural buses on their way to the town for legal, medical or other urgencies, anxious, worried and sweating. At one side of the road, under the solitary tree, was parked a cycle-rickshaw with two passengers — an octogenarian woman supporting a teenage lady who was in an advanced stage of pregnancy and in a state of swoon. The rickshaw-puller told me that they belonged to his village and as the young lady was in a critical condition, she had volunteered to carry her to the primary health centre another few kilometres away, but had been detained there for the past two exasperating hours. "I don't think she can survive the ordeal," he murmured in a sort of soliloquy and sighed.

I walked up to the leader of the Followers of Truth and, hands folded, appealed to him to let the single rickshaw pass. His voice charged with the spirit of democracy and socialism, the leader asked me, "How can you, though you seem to be somewhat educated, advise me to be partial?"

I stood educated in the theory of equality in action. But further enlightenment awaited me — regarding the ideal of freedom. As another gentleman stepped forward and asked, "Why should you block a road that belongs to the public?" one of the leader's junior compatriots, eager to steal the thunder, retorted, "In free India every inch of place is owned by all the citizens of India."

I realised that we the Indians had reached a silent Consensus on redefining every ideal and principle our Constitution and laws have given us. But was the situation in the world basically any different? Powerful nations can redefine the principles of international relationship, snubbing any dissent; freedom of expression can be reduced by media all over the world to unabashed sensationalism and gross vulgarity. The situation can be described only as a fantastic paradox. We know what is right, we agree collectively on what is desirable, but neither as individuals nor as collective entities have we followed the right or the desirable. There is something somewhere grotesquely wrong in our consciousness. This observation no doubt applies to India more than to any other country. When a European scholar pursuing a long-term research project in India articulated his anguish before this author in the following words, he was echoing the surprise of many others:

> I know India was the country where the grand quest for the meaning of life, death, suffering and joy began. It is here that the inimitable meaningful prayers of aspiration for God, Light, Freedom, Bliss and Immortality were spelt out in Sanskrit, the mother of all the classical languages of the world. Nowhere else was the conviction that life is a progressive journey towards a sublime end, birth after birth, was so clearly formed, nowhere was the theory of *karma* so elaborately discussed, no other civilisation had assimilated lofty spiritual ideas in its rituals and daily life. How is it then one witnesses so much hypocrisy, fraud and dishonesty here?

The only observation, not an answer, that can be made is we have failed the expectations our mighty heritage legitimately aroused and have fallen as a nation. Some clues to the enigma can be found in the total loss of values already discussed. But the immediate factor responsible for the sad state of affairs is the failure of the system of our education to inspire in the young the love for truth, the faith that our total consciousness reserves much more than what only a part of it, the mind with its faculties like intelligence and intellect have unfolded so far, the truth that with the creation of mental man the process of evolution had not come to an end.

As Sri Aurobindo looks at the situation,

> At present mankind is undergoing an evolutionary crisis in which is concealed a choice of its destiny; for a stage has been reached in which the human mind has achieved in certain directions an enormous development while in others it stands arrested and bewildered and can no longer find its way.

Education can, of course, liberate us from this impasse, for it can find the greatest support in that direction in the process and power of evolution itself, for, in a sense, evolution is a gradual realisation of liberation. The manifestation of the earliest forms of life as plants out of the apparently lifeless matter was a step towards liberation of the imprisoned consciousness. A far greater degree of freedom of consciousness — and an exercise of that freedom in infinitely variant ways — was possible with the emergence of the primeval creatures, from worms and insects to the whale and the dinosaur, from the birds to the beasts of incalculable varieties. That urge for freedom inherent in nature, for releasing its possibilities and potentialities, took a new and hitherto most significant turn with the emergence of man and, needless to say, man is the only creature who had never stopped growing. With relentless zeal he had not only adapted himself to the changing environment, but also had obliged the environment to adapt to his demands. Emerging from the state of primeval nature he had created for himself new worlds of art, architecture, literature, music, philosophy and spiritual quest. His activities and achievements in all these spheres have again meant nothing but the gradual realisation of his own potentialities, a joy in the freedom of experience, adventure and expression.

If the process of evolution itself is a movement of consciousness realising its own freedom from its bondage to material and other limitations, the twentieth century we just left behind had been the witness to the most momentous events and ideas ensuring greater freedom for man in several fronts. Imperialism, colonialism, monarchy and feudalism all collapsed ensuring man's social, political and economic freedom. Revolutions and reformations, emancipation of women from social taboos and discrimination, end of apartheid, all point in the same direction. Science and technology have played their role in according a greater dignity to the individual.

But these facts of outer freedom do not come to much — they even are vulnerable to misuse — unless there is achieved the other freedom, the freedom from Ignorance. Sri Aurobindo believes that the realisation of such a freedom is not only a possibility, but also is a certainty inherent in the very nature of evolutionary developments. The true role of education is in preparing and helping man to arrive there — at a new phase of existence. Man is neither an accident nor a freak of nature. He is an evolving being, awaiting his fulfilment. No doubt he had come a long way from his primitive state via a stage dominated by vital or raw life impulses, he has been a mental creature for long and has achieved marvels with his intelligence and intellect. But proud of intellect though we may be, Einstein warns, "We should take care not to make the intellect our god; it has of course powerful muscles, but no personality."

As the Italian thinker Preme Levi stated, "Normal human beings are biologically built for an activity that is aimed towards a goal." A goal always implies a call to go farther than where we are. Till the forties of the twentieth century, so far as India was concerned, the ennobling goal of freedom from the colonial rule kept the youths inspired. Since the achievement of that goal, we have been fed with the illusion of false goals, bereft of nobler values. We must replace them with the most optimistic goal, an aspiration for transcending the present dimly lighted state of our consciousness and entering a new phase of consciousness. In his great works such as *The Life Divine, The Synthesis of Yoga, The Human Cycle* and *The Ideal of Human Unity,* Sri Aurobindo had elaborately explained this inevitable future and educators could capture from these works a thrilling new purpose for their endeavour. Once we subscribe to a sublime vision, feel inspired by an extraordinary destination, our approach to our work spontaneously receives a new impetus. It is high time we proved our intolerance of the process of drugging the youth with debauched values and phoney ideals. We must restore the true philosophy of education and reconstruct the system.

Towards an Integral Education

There are explorations and experiments, though confined to limited spheres, in evolving principles of true education and their application. I quote a few words from Prof. Kireet Joshi, an educationist who has devoted untiring decades of his life in this direction:

> In the first place the latest Indian experiments in psychic education have given us the concept of fourfold personality, — the personality of Knowledge, the personality of Power, the personality of Harmony and the personality of Skill. It is further emphasised that the fourfold personality can be integrated by the power of the psychic being as also by the powers of higher domains of the spirit. In pedagogical terms, it is affirmed that psychic education has no method and yet every method and the teacher can employ the three instruments of instruction, example and influence flexibly in every circumstance in respect of every child. This pedagogy also recognises the necessity of formulating new goals, new contents and new methods of education. It lays great stress on child-centred education and on lifelong education, recognising that early childhood is the most favoured period of psychic education and recognising that once well begun in early childhood it has to continue throughout life, since integration and harmony of personality is a lifelong process. . . .
>
> This pedagogy emphasises the combination of pursuit of Truth, austerity and harmony and joy of free creativity. It counsels us not to encumber the child with a plethora of stuff that would bury and stifle the wings and breath of the child's soul but to provide to each child the minimum programme of learning, and the basic requirements of self-education. Once the child has begun to practise the art of self-education, the teacher needs to provide each child the necessary facilities and learning materials appropriate to its inclinations, talents and actual or potential capacities,

> so that each child progresses at its own pace and according to its own natural rhythm as also according to its own judicious acceleration of progress. A time must come, sooner rather than later, when the child becomes conscious of its own living soul and guides its own processes of education. . . .[4]

The Mother founded the Sri Aurobindo International Centre of Education as a wing of Sri Aurobindo Ashram at Pondicherry to enable the student to apply to his or her life to the extent possible this vision of a new future for man. To a question why the Centre does not bestow any degree or diploma on a student, she made the following observation:

> For the last 100 years or so mankind has been suffering from a disease which seems to be spreading more and more and which has reached a climax in our times; it is what we may call "utilitarianism." People and things, circumstances and activities seem to be viewed and appreciated exclusively from this angle. Nothing has any value unless it is useful. Certainly, something that is useful is better than something that is not. But first we must agree on what we describe as useful — useful to whom, to what, for what?
>
> For, more and more, the races who consider themselves civilised describe as useful whatever can attract, procure or produce money. Everything is judged and evaluated from a monetary angle. That is what I call utilitarianism. And this disease is highly contagious, for even children are not immune to it. At an age when they should be dreaming of beauty, greatness and perfection, dreams that may be too sublime for ordinary common sense, but which are nevertheless far superior to this dull good sense, children now dream of money and worry about how to earn it.
>
> So, when they think of their studies, they think above all about what can be useful to them, so that later on when they grow up they can earn a lot of money.

---

4. Kireet Joshi, *Education at Crossroads.*

> For them study has no other purpose, no other interest.
>
> To learn for the sake of knowledge, to study in order to know the secrets of nature and life, to educate oneself in order to grow in consciousness, to discipline oneself in order to become master of oneself, to overcome one's weakness, incapacities and ignorance, to prepare oneself to advance in life towards a goal that is nobler and wiser, more generous and more true . . . they hardly give it a thought and consider it all very utopian. The only thing that matters is to be practical, to prepare themselves and learn how to earn money.

The passages tell us all what education ought to be and what education is not today. Without a collective awakening to the ignored purpose of education, the rapid corrosion of life by utilitarianism inevitably leading to hedonism, cannot be checked. It is the elite who are expected to realise this, to begin with. They can influence the authority or machinery controlling the systems of education to stop the macabre deterioration in the system we have already discussed. We must not feel helpless or too weak to do anything in this direction, for the true time-spirit will be with us. Despite the current signs to the contrary, the secret aspiration in our consciousness will guide us beyond the present imbroglio.

I conclude with a few more passages from the Mother — on her integral approach to Education:

> The education of a human being should begin at birth and continue throughout his life.
>
> Indeed, if we want this education to have its maximum result, it should begin even before birth; in this case it is the mother herself who proceeds with this education by means of a twofold action: first, upon herself for her own improvement, and secondly, upon the child whom she is forming physically. For it is certain that the nature of the child to be born depends very much upon the mother who

forms it, upon her aspiration and will as well as upon the material surroundings in which she lives. To see that her thoughts are always beautiful and pure, her feelings always noble and fine, her material surroundings as harmonious as possible and full of great simplicity — this is the part of education which should apply to the mother herself. And if she has in addition a conscious and definite will to form the child according to the highest ideal she can conceive, then the very best conditions will be realised so that the child can come into the world with the utmost potentialities. How many difficult efforts and useless complications would be avoided in this way!

Education to be complete must have five principal aspects corresponding to the five principal activities of the human being; the physical, the vital, the mental, the psychic and the spiritual. Usually these phases of education follow chronologically the growth of the individual; this, however, does not mean that one of them should replace another, but that all must continue, completing one another until the end of his life.

7

The Indian Education System and Tagore's Unmitigated Pain

Shefali Moitra

EDUCATION has all along been a primary concern for Tagore. His earliest essay on education "Siksha-r Herpher" (The Incongruity of Education) was published in *Sadhana* in 1892 (1299 *Baṅgābda*).[1] He was just 31 years old at that time. He had sent copies of this essay to Sri Bankim Chandra Chattopadhyay (1838-94), Sri Gurudas Bandyopadhyay and Sri Anandamohan Basu. All three were associated with the administration of the University of Calcutta. As a matter of fact, Gurudas Bandyopadhyay was the first Bengali Vice-Chancellor of the University of Calcutta (1890-92). Bankim was then 52 and a member of the University of Calcutta Senate. Bankim wrote back saying he agreed with every line of what Tagore had written in this article, on many occasions he had spoken to people to try and convince them of these ideas, but in vain. He writes that one day he stood up in the Senate and tried to make a point in support of Tagore's views on education, but his feeble voice was lost, it did not reach anybody's ears. Tagore comments, though Bankim's voice was silenced his pen remained powerful, and he constantly

1. Rabindranath Tagore, "Siksha-r Herpher" in *Siksha* (in Bangla), Kolkata: Visva-Bharati Granthan Bibhag, 2005 (1908).

supported Tagore's position. We shall shortly discuss Tagore's position in detail; before that we shall look further into the fate of his prescriptions.

Sri Gurudas Bandyopadhyay wrote back and said he agreed on all the major points raised in "Siksha-r Herpher," there were a few minor points on which he did not agree. Being motivated by Bandyopadhyay, some members of the Senate tabled a proposal to encourage the use of the Bengali language as a medium of instruction at the university level. In his article "Siksha-r Herpher" Tagore had strongly argued in favour of this proposal. Unfortunately, the tabled proposal was not accepted by the University of Calcutta Senate. This fact is recorded in the University of Calcutta Minutes for 1891-92, pp. 56-58. Sri Anandamohan Basu wrote back saying he had read Tagore's essay, published in *Sadhana,* with great pleasure.[2] He too had been thinking on these lines for some time. He felt that the essay should be widely publicised. The first step towards the execution of these ideas, he believed, would involve changing the examination rules relating to the use of language. Interestingly, whenever Anandamohan made such proposals the resistance came from some Bengali members of the Senate, and not from the British members. However, Anandamohan assured Tagore that he would keep on trying, and that Tagore's well-written serious essay would help in putting forth his arguments.

Tagore felt that the opposition from the Bengali members in the University Senate was understandable. They had learnt the art of opposition, irrespective of the merit of the case, they were prepared to oppose. This is a common feature of university administration even today. Instead of judging the worth of a proposal independently, there is a tendency to

---

2. The Bengali journal *Sadhana* played an important role in publishing debates on education reform during that period.

identify the power-lobby that is supporting the proposal, and deciding whether to render support or not accordingly. Tagore remarks that if the problem were one of comprehending a difficult point, within a proposal, further explanations and clarifications could be provided to simplify the point, but if the point is already simple, then there is no scope for further simplification. While arguing for the use of Bengali as the medium for instruction, Tagore could give many examples of foreign countries that have taken recourse to imparting education through the mother tongue at every level. He says it is not the case that those who are in opposition to the introduction of vernacular education at the university level do not know of these examples. This makes it all the more difficult to explain the point to them, there is nothing to be explained. They understand the need, but they have their own counter-agenda for opposition. It may be added that for contemporary India there is the glaring example of neighbouring Bangladesh, where the medium of instruction at every level is Bengali.

During the 1890s the article "Siksha-r Herpher" had received considerable attention. Sri Mohinimohan Chattopadhyay criticised Tagore's views in an article titled "Siksha-r Sankat" (The Crisis of Education). This article was serialised in three consecutive numbers in *Sadhana* in 1893. It was a scathing criticism of Tagore's article. Having read the first number Tagore wrote a rejoinder titled "Siksha-r Herpher Prabandh-er Anubritti",[3] (A Continuation of the Article Siksha-r Herpher) in which he stated that he was grossly misunderstood. He noticed that at the very outset of the critical review of his article the focus was on subsidiary points and not on the central issue. Further, instead of making an

3. Rabindranath Tagore, "Siksha-r Herpher Prabandh-er Anubritti" first published in *Sadhana*, 1893, rpt. in *Rabindra-Rachanabali*, (in Bangla), Visva-Bharati edn., vol. 12, 1960.

attempt at understanding the author, isolated points were taken up and demolished, with an aim to debunk the article. He asks to be forgiven for any isolated inaccuracy in his argument, if at all there are any; what is to be kept in mind is that the article was not aiming at providing fodder for debates, it was written out of sincere pain and a feeling of necessity.

In the 1890s, when Tagore first began writing on India's problem of education, British rule was fully entrenched in India. British education in India was geared to training competent personnel to serve the purpose of British governance. Naturally empowerment of the individual was in no way the goal. Neither was self-reliance and self-respect the cherished ideals of education. Once the British education system replaced the indigenous system the rate of literacy fell. The great historian Kali Kinkar Datta reports,

> Schools for elementary education, distinct from those meant for higher learning, were widespread in the cities and the villages and a sort of primary education was considered necessary in almost every stratum of society. Ives, a mid-eighteenth-century traveller to Bengal, wrote that there were then "many schools for the education of children".[4]

Craufurd observed a few years later, "There are schools in all the towns and principal villages."[5] "Almost all the large villages in Bengal contain common schools," wrote Ward[6] in the early nineteenth century.[7] With the introduction of the British education system the divide between the educated and the uneducated widened. The eminent Indian historian N.K. Sinha

---

4. Kali Kinkar Datta, *A Social History of Modern India*, Delhi: Macmillan, 1975, pp. 14-15.
5. Craufurd, *Sketches etc. of the Hindus*, vol. II, pp. 12-13.
6. Ward, *A View of the History of the Religion and the Mythology of the Hindoos*, vol. I, p. 119.
7. Kali Kinkar Datta, *A Social History of Modern India*, p. 15.

notes, "in 1865-66 it was admitted that the great masses of the people of Bengal, the labouring and the agricultural classes were 'scarcely touched by educational operations . . .'."[8]

Tagore fully endorsed Gopal Krishna Gokhale's call for education for all. This is evident from his Bangla article "Siksha-r Bahan"[9] (The Medium of Education) written in 1915. He reiterated his support for Gokhale's concern again in another one of his Bangla articles "Siksha-r Svangikaran"[10] (The Internalisation of Education) written in 1936. In both articles he refers to Gokhale by name, and appreciates his concern for education for all. In 1936 Tagore says he has not come to say something new, he has come to restate the urgency for universal education, and to restate the need for education through one's mother tongue. He goes on to explain that the reason he is repeating himself is that one constantly feels the need for again and again touching the site of pain. Gokhale wanted uniform compulsory education for all; he perceived this as a necessary condition for national integration. Tagore was pained by the fact that some Bengali intellectuals had opposed Gokhale. The Bengali intellectuals, like Gokhale, sought national integration, but they were not willing to give up their preference for English. Some may argue that they were right; fluency in English has given us a head start in the global context of procuring outsourced jobs today. The media keeps commenting on China's relative disadvantage in this field. This is being attributed to the dearth of English-speaking specialists in China. It is doubtful whether Tagore would see

8. N.K. Sinha, *The Historian as an Archivist*, ed. with an Introduction by Pradip Sinha, Midnapore: Vidyasagar University, 1999, p. 130.

9. Rabindranath Tagore, "Siksha-r Bahan" first published in *Sabujpatra*, 1915, rpt. in *Siksha*.

10. Rabindranath Tagore, "Siksha-r Svangikaran" first delivered as an International "New Fellowship Lecture", during the Education Week in Kolkata in 1936, rpt. in *Siksha*.

this as an advantage or as a form of further un-freedom of not being able to generate projects and jobs of one's own choice. Tagore writes,

> Until we are in a position to prove that the world has need of us and cannot afford to do without us, that we are not merely hangers-on of the world-culture — beggars who cannot repay — so long must our sole hope lie in gaining others' favours.[11]

The kind of education he envisaged could have still given a head start to the Indian worker, since, he emphasised the need for learning English thoroughly, albeit, as a second language.

Tagore held that it may be argued that our society was vibrant in the past; even today it is not totally moribund. It may further be argued that the divide between the learned and the unlearned always existed. The Sanskrit pundits with their pedantry were confined to their *tol*s and *catuspathi*s, that is, their institutes of learning. Arguably such scholarship never entered the homes of the common man. So what is the harm today, if a section of people is trained to be erudite scholars versed in British education? Tagore's response to such a possible argument is twofold. First, he is not ready to accept that Sanskrit education caused the same kind of social divide that is being caused by British education. He felt that in the past the heights of Sanskrit scholarship had a filtration effect. It percolated down to common culture, and succeeded in permeating it. Tagore uses the analogy of the forest. In a forest there is continuity between the forest-soil, the branches of the tree, and its fruit. There is a kind of cyclic continuity of

11. Rabindranath Tagore, "The Centre of Indian Culture", in *The English Writings of Rabindranath Tagore* (*EWRT*), vol. 2, ed. Sisir Kumar Das, New Delhi: Sahitya Akademi, 1996, p. 476. Sisir Kumar Das writes, "This lecture, delivered in Madras on 9 February 1919, according to Prabhat Kumar Mukhopadhyay, is the first lecture by Tagore delivered in English in India", pp. 771-72.

drawing sustenance from the soil, and giving back nutrition to the soil. In the case of British education the same kind of assimilation has not taken place; the situation is like a boat sailing against the stream. Tagore maintained that Japan over a span of 50 years was able to absorb the European science paradigm, but India did not. This paradigm is not consistent with her tradition and culture. N.K. Sinha also suggests that there was no reciprocity between Indian culture and British culture. He writes,

> there was no cultural association between Indians and Englishmen up to the eighties of the eighteenth century because the Indians, with whom Englishmen came into business contact, did not certainly represent the cultured section of the population and with some notable exceptions, Englishmen themselves had no cultural pretensions.[12]

In response to the above argument that there always was, and still is, a harmless divide in Indian society (Sanskrit/ popular, English/vernacular) Tagore makes a second point. He does think that there is a marked difference between the former and the latter type of divide instantiated above. He, however, makes it clear that he neither holds the English language or European science responsible for the British colonial schism in Indian society. He always welcomed the discoveries of science, but for him science was not an end in itself. The truths of science, like all other truths, had no geographical location. They were the common heritage of mankind. In his reply to Mohinimohan Chattopadhyay's criticism Tagore remarked that Chattopadhyay's observations were baseless; he never discarded the modern findings of science. Tagore held that it was preposterous to continue with the teaching of the Purāṇic explanation that earthquakes are caused by the movement of the snake-king Vāsukī's torso.

12. N.K. Sinha, op. cit. pp. 86-87.

Certainly the modern scientific explanations of earthquakes, received through English, need to be imparted to the students. This information needs to be made available in an easily graspable form, in a form of education that is not only affordable, but one that can easily enter the precincts of the common man's home. What could be a more appropriate vehicle for this education than the mother tongue? In this same article[13] Tagore mentions, if education is to be made permanent, deep and extensive then it has to be given in the familiar mother tongue. Otherwise the belief that the snake-king Vāsukī causes earthquakes will re-emerge, even among educated people. The language that is in the air, the language that is not kept out by the dark corners of the home, and the language in which a community performs its mental functions, as normally as one breathes, should be the language through which education is imparted. Only then can education purify the bloodstream of a community and enter its entire life process. Tagore says he did not mean to insinuate that the present universities were not serving any positive or negative purpose. He merely intends to say that our universities are unable to establish roots in the minds of our people;[14] they exist like architectural bubbles (*saudha budbud*). In his article, "The Centre of Indian Culture" Tagore writes,

> Our education should be in full touch with our complete life, economical, intellectual, aesthetic, social and spiritual; and our educational institutions should be in the heart of our society, connected with it by the living bonds of varied co-operations. For true education is to realize at every step how our training and knowledge have organic connection with our surroundings.[15]

---

13. "Siksha-r Herpher Prabandhe-er Anubritti".
14. Ibid., p. 503.
15. Rabindranath Tagore, "The Centre of Indian Culture", p. 469.

He commented that tomorrow if the British leave the country those enormous towers will have no place to stand. Well, after Tagore's death the British did leave India, and the institutions of learning founded by the British apparently did not collapse. Many more institutions have been established, since India's Independence, on similar structural patterns. This, however, does not falsify Tagore's prophecy that those whom you have left behind will pull you backward. Those whose darkness of ignorance is being masked by us will in turn mask our well-being and create a great divide.[16] To be educated meant for Tagore to be able to use and develop one's faculties creatively, to be able to unite with all the members of society, and to be able to gradually proceed towards uniting with the universe in a harmonious way. Neither have we achieved this goal, nor have we been able to set an alternative goal. In 1965 S.N. Ganguly remarked, "to say that there is no plan in our education today may sound a little harsh, but it is certainly not false. If plan means any programme without a purpose, then, of course, we do have a plan."[17] The situation remains very much the same in 2011.

We are still grappling with the problem of illiteracy; we are still crippled with the lack of a link language. Tagore, along with Gokhale and Gandhi, dreamt of integrating the country into a cultural whole not merely into a political unit. This remains an illusive goal even today. The wide schism between the "educated" elite and the backward masses is ever widening. Ironically our present government now plans to invite foreign capital into our education sector, and to welcome

---

16. *Agyāner andhakāre ārale dhakichho jare/ tomār maṅgal dhāki garichhe se ghor vyavadhān* in "Apamānita" written in 1910, included in the Bengali version of *Gītāñjalī.*

17. S.N. Ganguly, "A Plan for Education in India", *Sodha-Bharati,* A Journal of the Nehru Research Institute, vol. 1, July-December 1965, p. 67.

foreign universities to solve our education problem (referred to as "the problem of human resource development" in contemporary parlance). Where did we go wrong? The paradox is that scholars trained in India are successfully competing with their peers abroad, yet we need foreign help to solve our educational problem at home! The genesis of this problem can be traced far back into history.

Tagore began identifying the crux of our education problem in 1892; he continued writing on this subject till the end of his life. He found multiple defects in what was being imparted as education. One of the drawbacks pinpointed by him was the exclusionary approach adopted by our system of education. He observed many other problems in our system, yet he thought exclusion was one of the major problems. Education was encoded in a language that did not have roots in our culture, and therefore, could not easily be decoded by the learner. Due to this language problem, long years of an individual's exposure to education failed to trigger one's imagination or to fertilise one's creativity. Tagore comments, "when we are compelled to learn through the medium of English, the knocking at the gate and turning of the key take away the best part of our life."[18] The handful of learners who were capable of overcoming these obstacles formed a privileged isolated group. The excluded majority remained as the "other." Tagore felt this was an insult to the masses and a day will come when we shall all have to share their insult.[19]

The debate over the preferred medium of instruction for the educational institutions in India began long before Tagore wrote his article "Siksha-r Herpher." Charles Grant and

---

18. "The Centre of Indian Culture", p. 478.

19. *"Hey mor durbhāgā deśa, jāder korechho apamān/apamāne hote hobe tāhāder sabār samān"* in "Apamānita".

Wilberforce strongly urged the Company to introduce Christianity and English education in India. In 1813 the British Parliament renewed the Company's Charter. A clause was introduced in the Charter that authorised the Governor-General in India to set apart "a sum of not less than Rs. 1 lakh" a year to be "applied to the revival and improvement of literature" and for the introduction and promotion of knowledge of the sciences among the inhabitants of the British territories in India.[20] This was undoubtedly a handsome amount, and more so since it came from a colonising government. Obviously there was a hidden agenda. N.K. Sinha reports that Charles Grant between 1792 and 1797 propagated "his idea of imitating the Roman conquerors who had civilised and improved nations. He wrote: 'by planting our language, our knowledge, our opinions and our religion, in our Asiatic territories we shall put our great work beyond the reach of contingencies'."[21] Datta writes, "in 1823 a Committee of Public Instruction was formed. . . . A new difficulty soon arose, as to whether the medium of instruction was to be English or vernacular."[22] This became an issue of debate with the British as well as with the Indians. Thus the debate began much before Tagore's birth (1861).

Datta says, Macaulay was appointed Law Member of the Council of Governor-General of India. He reached India on 8 June 1834. He was subsequently appointed President of the Committee of Public Instruction. In his well-known Minute, dated 2 February 1835 Macaulay wrote "we have to educate a people who cannot at present be educated by means of their mother tongue. We must teach them some foreign language. The claims of our own language it is hardly necessary to recapitulate. It stands pre-eminent even among the languages

20. See, Kali Kinkar Datta, *A Social History of Modern India*, pp. 49-50.

21. N.K. Sinha, *The Historian as an Archivist*, p. 88.

22. Ibid., p. 50.

of the West."[23] Thus Macaulay through his authority and power succeeded in silencing the dissenting voices. The implementation of this thesis was made possible by the help of Raja Rammohun Roy and other Indian educationists.

Sir Edward Hyde East and Alexander Duff, however, give very different accounts of how English language was introduced in education in Bengal. Sir Edward Hyde East was the Chief Justice of the Supreme Court. In one of his letters he writes,

> the meeting was held at my house on 14 May 1816 at which 50 and upwards of the most respectable Hindoo inhabitants of rank and wealth attended, including also the principal Pundits, when a sum of nearly half a lac [*sic*] of rupees was subscribed and many more subscriptions were promised . . . all expressed themselves in favour of making the acquisition of the English language a principal object of education together with its moral and scientific productions.[24]

Evidently this episode took place much before Macaulay's well-known Minute. It was the native Indians who thought that the British have come to stay and that the only way to be empowered under the present regime is by gaining through the British system and in the English language.

Alexander Duff's account further corroborates Sir Edward Hyde East's account. In 1853 Alexander Duff said,

> English education was in a manner forced upon the British Government; it did not itself spontaneously originate it. The system of English education commenced in the following very simple way in Bengal. There were two persons who had to do with it. The one was Mr. David Hare [a watchmaker]. The other was a native Ram Mohan Roy.[25]

23. See Kali Kinkar Datta, *A Social History of Modern India*, p. 51.
24. See N.K. Sinha, *The Historian as an Archivist*, p. 93.
25. Ibid.

There were several members on the British side who did not agree with Macaulay's views. H.T. Prinsep supported the orientalist camp but his views were rejected by Macaulay. Another opponent was Ramsey MacDonald. Kali Kinkar Datta reports that Ramsey MacDonald significantly remarked:

> to read Lord Macaulay's confused thinking in visible and dashing English is enlivening, to study it is melancholy. It mixed up subjects to be taught in the language in which they ought to be taught, and it displayed no appreciation of the fact that the Indian mind was a product of history and not a blank sheet of paper upon which anything could be written by the teacher.[26]

Tagore was trying to make a similar point, though much more forcefully, in his "Siksha-r Herpher" article. The simple point was that the Indian mind was a product of history and not a blank slate. Tagore also pointed out that the medium of education and the content of education are not one and the same thing; the two must not be confused. He was never against receiving knowledge from the West, nor did he ever speak against learning English as a second language.

English could be introduced at a very early stage, in a graded manner, but not as a medium of instruction. He held that there is such a thing as the methodology of learning; this has to be grasped by every new learner. The best way to grasp the method of learning is through one's mother tongue. Once the method is acquired the learner can easily enter into foreign territories. Without a grasp on the learning method the learner tries to acquire a skill of cramming, of copying, and in general avoiding a holistic approach to any subject.

I shall now give a brief account of Tagore's essay "Siksha-r Herpher". There can, of course, be no substitute for his exquisite

26. *Rammohun Centenary Volume*, part II, section I, p. 44 quoted by Kali Kinkar Datta, in *A Social History of Modern India*, p. 51.

Bengali prose and command over his thoughts. Tagore was also a master of analogies. All will agree that an apt analogy is often more helpful than a tortuous logical argument. Moreover, as a poet Tagore was always concerned with communicating his grief, pain and anguish. While talking about education he was addressing the problem of the growth and flourishing of the human subject. Our present government's reference to education as "human resource development" would have appeared abominable to Tagore. For him human beings are resources unto themselves, not resources for the government to manipulate and nurture according to their preferred politico-economic goals. By referring to education as "human resource development" education is being brought under the wider rubric of development economics. Development in order to be sustainable needs the development of human resources. In this way education is looked at as a means and not as an end in itself. He neither shunned nor rejected politics and economics; they were simply given a secondary position. Tagore envisioned a society where freedom and creativity were respected.

He begins his article "Siksha-r Herpher" by telling us how the present system of education is not a joyful experience for the learner; on the contrary, it causes pointless pain and distress. Much of what he says in regard to British colonial education remains true of our present system as well. The system is excessively utilitarian. Tagore says man can never be satisfied by remaining strictly confined to the domain of needs. We expect education to open up new vistas and broader horizons. Man is partly governed by rules, and he is partly free. This freedom needs to be nurtured and developed through education, just as rules have to be familiarised. Until and unless we have command over our freedom, our power of self-expression, we remain infants. Unfortunately, our education system does not give us the power of self-expression, it fails to turn us into independent adult thinkers, we remain immature throughout our lives.

There is no provision for space and frivolity in our education. Our thoughts are not allowed to stray away; we do not have the liberty to read books of our own choice. The system is so all-consuming that there is no leisure for such activity. Tagore says it is true that our appetites cannot be filled with thin air, we need food for thought, but to digest the food air intake is needed.

Tagore comments on the English language which was being introduced as the medium of education. English medium education still occupies an elitist position in contemporary India. We have not been able to solve the language problem. Every language is a cultural product. It is difficult to appreciate a foreign culture at a young age. The English language appears exceptionally alien to an Indian beginner. The syntax has no similarity with the syntax of Indian languages. On top of that, the Indian perception (*bhāva vinyāsa*) is so different. The context of their perception is also different. For instance the popular nursery rhyme "Ba ba black sheep have you any wool . . ." barely has an analogue to any Indian experiential context. It is difficult to teach a language through translation. Tagore says if we translate the sentence "the horse is a noble animal" in Bengali as *ghoṛā ekti mahān jantu* then it hardly makes sense. From the beginning to the end if there are no familiar catch-points in a lesson then one has to take recourse to memorising it before comprehending it. As a result one gulps the lesson before one chews it.

As youngsters in school we learn so little English, and so much of it is mistaken, that it is not possible to derive any satisfaction *rasa* from it, nor does anyone expect to do so. Both the teacher and the student say that they are not in search of *rasa* (or satisfaction); if we can somehow squeeze a meaning out of the text then we are saved, we pass the examination, we get a job. If this be the case then what actually is being gained from this education? On reaching adulthood the student does not have the capacity to use his intelligence to invent something, he cannot use his strength to overcome opposition, and he cannot hold his head high with his inborn strength. All he learns is to memorise, to copy, and to act as a slave. In his "The Centre for Indian Culture" Tagore remarks, "this has created a most unnatural situation for us, making our own language an obstacle in our pathway of success."[27]

Tagore says, if the child only learnt Bangla, he or she could have at least read the *Rāmāyaṇa* and the *Mahābhārata.* If the child had no education, then he could at least have the leisure to play, to climb trees, to swim, to pluck flowers, and have a healthy body and happy mind. In the process of trying to learn English the child neither learns nor plays, nor does he enter the world of nature's wisdom; the imaginary world of literature also remains closed.

A child is imprisoned in a foreign prison, encircled by a foreign grammar, and a dictionary. Nourishment of the mind, widening of sensibilities, and strengthening of character, are thus not achievable. On gaining adulthood these children will not be able to use their intelligence for inventions, nor their strength for overcoming barriers. They will always lack confidence and remain submissive. All they will learn is to memorise, to copy and to remain a slave.

In order to become a full human being we need both the capacity to think, and the capacity to imagine. One must nurture one's intelligence and imagination from a young age, or else these faculties will be lost, they will be of no use when their services are requisitioned. This is a familiar piece of ancient wisdom that we all know. Tagore feels the present education system has almost foreclosed the possibility of imagination.

27. "The Centre of Indian Culture", pp. 481-2.

The question is how to nurture these faculties? There is the problem of finding well-versed teachers who can guide a child into a foreign language. A teacher needs to familiarise the child not only with the language, but also with the spirit (*bhāva*) of the text. Tagore felt most teachers are not well equipped to perform this task. As a result the student has to wait for a very long time to even get vaguely acquainted with the spirit of English. The student's faculty of thought is kept idle during this long period, and over time this faculty becomes dysfunctional. Up to the School Leaving level the student merely gains a working knowledge of English. At the B.A. level the student is suddenly confronted with books that need deep contemplation. By then the student has neither the time, nor the power for contemplation. He just mixes all the material and ingests it in big gulps. As a child we are introduced to a language without having access to thoughts and emotions (*bhāva*), and as an adult we have thoughts and emotions but we do not have access to an adequate language for expression.

Tagore says there must be some provision in the system to read, and to simultaneously think about what has been read, what its implications are, what kind of additional information can be gathered, is it in any way relevant to the problems we confront in our daily life? Tagore's point can be further instantiated by an episode that he relates in a letter to Krishnadayal Basu in 1925. He had unmindfully written in his poem *Sharat* (the name of the third of the six Indian seasons) that loads of ripe paddy are being ferried across. This was a factual mistake. In Bengal paddy ripens in *Hemanta* (the fourth season) not in *Sharat*. This lapse was overlooked by the teachers for years; students were encouraged to recite this poem on many occasions. It was only when a school student of former East Bengal questioned the poet on this point that he realised his error.[28] Had this been an English poem, written

28. Tagore's letter to Krishnadayal Basu, 1925.

by a foreigner, this kind of alert detection by a student could hardly be expected, since the student would not have been familiar with the English cultural context.

It is useless to merely collect information and create a mound. The information must be constructively processed (*nirmāṇa*). We mistakenly believe that amassing material implies being constructively able to use it. This is not how the process of learning works. One cannot sequentially first amass information, and subsequently put it to creative use. The gathering of information and the application of it must go on together bit by bit; then only can education gain a solid structure. From the very early stage of education the child must not only be taught to gather information, the child must also be given ample time for contemplation and imagination. There is a period in an individual's trajectory of development when he needs to be nourished by living ideas, he needs to be ignited by new imagination. This is essential for the maturity of an individual. Once the ideal moment is allowed to pass unattended, no amount of retrospective action will rectify the damage. There is a stage when the individual needs to be nourished by heaps of literature. The literature must be such that the student can dip into its *rasa*.

The problem with English literature, Tagore feels, is that the Indian student cannot relate to it in an intimate way, there is always that alien feeling, that feeling of unfamiliarity. We use these ideas in our speeches and in our writings, but we are unable to relate them to our life and to our work. In this way whatever we try to learn for twenty to twenty-two years of our student life fails to permeate our lives. As a consequence our minds receive an absurd identity. Some of the learned ideas remain pasted together and the rest simply fall off over the years.

The roots of our existence, and the roots of education, are so distanced that the latter fails to enrich the former. We are not able to get over our dogmas and superstitions. When our language and thoughts are not in tandem a split personality develops. Then we find someone mouthing enlightened philosophical or scientific ideas or both, and yet indulging in all sorts of dogmatic practices. An unbridgeable gap occurs between theory and practice. Thus life and education fall apart. The more we disrespect education the greater becomes education's disregard for life. From childhood if we gain a facility in using language, and if we are simultaneously capable of commanding ideas, and alongside if we continue with our regular routine life, then we can establish a balance or harmony in our lives and we can lead a normal human existence. In this way Tagore wants us to be *sahaja mānuṣa.* Then only can the appropriate measure of all things be appreciated. Tagore's reference to the "appreciation of measure" as the goal of education strongly resembles Plato's "doctrine of the mean." Plato also maintained that there is a "just right" in all the affairs of life, and to go beyond it is to spoil one's performance.[29]

Tagore felt that all we learn through the imported British education is how to be commercially successful. We are being trained to be employees; education is not positively impacting our lives. This has caused a schism between our education and our practice. In this way, both our life and our education remain incomplete. Tagore comments, in both contexts (in the context of life and in the context of education) the Bengali lives a life of a clown (*saṅger prahasan*). He says that today all our energy needs to be focused on harmonising our life with our education. The only way to achieve this goal is through the Bengali language (read vernacular). English can only be a language of expedience (*kājer bhāṣā*), it cannot be a language of thought and emotion (*bhāv-er bhāṣā*). In whichever way we look at the problem of education, we shall find that we have lost the link between our thoughts/emotions, our language

29. A.E. Taylor, *Plato: the Man and his Work,* New York: Meridian Books, 1957, p. 269.

and our life. However, such was not always the case. India had a non-alienated lifestyle and a language of communication which united the literate and the illiterate population. Preachers could communicate subtle philosophical ideas through this language. Tagore cites the examples of Buddha who succeeded in reaching out to the masses through their common dialect Pāli. Śrī Caitanya in Bengal was able to reach out to the masses and convey the message of Vaiṣṇavism through the Bengali language.

The poet laments that we have lost our language, she has been long neglected. He wonders whether she will surface, the moment she is called upon, to serve as a medium of expression. Tagore answers this question in the negative. Has not our language been subjected to further neglect after India's independence, not to mention the present effect of globalisation? The media and the advertisement world has crippled and maimed language even further. Now we come across hybrid languages that offer sentences like *dil maange more*. An entirely new utilitarian language is emerging with the internet and SMS culture. Tagore identified a kind of condescension among those who are educated in English and are accustomed to writing in English. When they decide to write in Bengali they appear to be doing a favour to the Bengali language. He says if they are not lauded for this they will go back to work in the merchant office or for some media house.

So far we have tried to give a gist of Tagore's observations as found in his "Siksha-r Herpher" article. In his rejoinder to this article Tagore reminds us that in this article he was primarily addressing the problems of the medium of instruction at the school level. There is no reason to think that he made a separate set of prescriptions for higher education.

Sisir Kumar Das writes, "During his stay in Bangalore, Tagore was interviewed by V. Subrahmanya Iyer on the eve of the publication of the report of the Calcutta University

Commission." Iyer's note was published in *The Mysore Economic Journal* under the caption, "Sir Rabindranath Tagore's Views on some Educational Questions." The interview was subsequently published in *The Modern Review* 1919.[30] The fourth question of Iyer's questionnaire was *The Medium of Instruction in the University* — Tagore's reply was:

> As a general rule the mother tongue, *if it be one of the leading* vernaculars of India, should be made the medium of instruction. But the adoption of this principle should be *gradual.* . . . In the course of ten or fifteen years, all the subjects may be given in the vernacular. . . . English should be universally taught as a second, but *compulsory* language.[31]

Tagore felt that

> along with this study of our living languages, we must include our folk literature, in order to truly know the psychology of our people and the direction towards which our underground current of life is moving.[32]

On many occasions Tagore argued for the introduction of vernacular education at every level. In the limited scope of this paper it will not be possible to give an exegesis of all his arguments and observations. We shall concentrate only on some of Tagore's writings. In his Bengali article "Siksha-r Bahan" (The Medium of Education) Tagore begins by saying that knowledge is the greatest unifier of humanity, and ignorance is the greatest divider.[33] Unification through knowledge gives immense pleasure, and on no account should an individual be denied this pleasure. Tagore feels that India

30. Sisir Kumar Das (ed.), *The English Writings of Rabindranath Tagore*, vol. 3, New Delhi: Sahitya Akademi, 1996, p. 981.
31. Ibid. p. 747.
32. "The Centre of Indian Culture", p. 487.
33. "Siksha-r Bahan" first published in 1915. The present references are to *Rabindra-Rachanabali*, Visva-Bharati edn., vol. 18.

has made some progress in the field of education, but has failed miserably in spreading education. The main constraint to the spreading of education is the medium of education. We are grudgingly willing to allow primary education in vernacular, but we are hesitant to allow vernacular education at the higher level. Tagore asks whether this hesitance is going to remain a permanent feature. Will we never have the confidence to say that higher education will be given in Bengali (vernacular), that it is possible, and that is the only way to reap the harvest of education throughout the country? Tagore asks, if the person who speaks only in Bengali (mother tongue) is the śūdra of the contemporary *Manu-Saṁhitā*, does he become the twice born brāhmaṇa by gaining rebirth in English?

Tagore goes on to say that we need to learn English, it is even better if we can also learn French and German. At the same time it goes without saying that most Bengalis (Indians) will not learn English. How can we let those lakhs and lakhs of people remain unfed or undernourished? He wonders whether such an unnatural heartlessness can be found anywhere outside India. Tagore was not in favour of replacing English-medium higher education by vernacular education. Those who are proficient in English, and prefer to receive instructions through English may continue. Those who have a problem in mastering the language, yet are equally intelligent, should not be debarred from higher education. Tagore proposes the provision for both streams of education. He refers to the streams as Gaṅgā and Yamunā. He is aware that the two streams are referred to respectively as being white and black, these colours carry value tags. His response to this comment is that at least the two streams are flowing, they are not stagnant. He dreamt of seeing a young Bengali university taking its seat beside the old universities. He pleads for someone to take the responsibility of bringing the Bengali language to the ocean of university education; thousands of minds remain mute due to lack of education.

At times Tagore spoke of a parallel vernacular university, at other times he spoke of something much more radical. In his article "The Centre of Indian Culture" he writes,

> We must therefore think of the seat of our Indian learning as in excess of, and quite apart from, the existing university-controlled schools and colleges . . . we must beware [*sic*] even of calling it a University. For the name itself is bound to rouse an irrepressible tendency to comparison and feeble imitation.[34]

Tagore urges us

> not to imagine that we are one of these disinherited peoples of the world. The time has come for us to break open the treasure trove of our ancestors and use it for our commerce of life. Let us, with its help, make our future our own — never continue our existence as the eternal rag-picker at other people's dustbins.[35]

Answer scripts written either in English or in Bengali are permitted at the universities in Bengal today. There is, however, a dearth of quality textbooks in Bengali. Tagore had envisaged this problem. He admitted that there was a scarcity of reading material in Bengali, meant for higher education. He asks a rhetorical question, "How can there be educational books if there is no education?" Educational texts are not horticultural plants that are propagated in a greenhouse, nor are they weeds that grow hither and thither. Tagore felt that the only way to produce good textbooks is to first introduce the language as a medium of instruction. He remarked, "We cannot very well expect a mint to go on working if the coins are refused circulation."[36] He goes on to name the intellectual stalwarts who were present in Bengal

34. "The Centre of Indian Culture", p. 482.
35. Ibid., p. 487.
36. Ibid., p. 479.

during his time: Jagadishchandra, Prafullachandra, Brojendranath, Mahamahopadhyay Shastri and many others. He laments that students from abroad will come and take lessons from them, but the students of Bengal, who do not know English, will remain deprived.

Tagore ends his article "Siksha-r Bahan" by asking when will these Indian intellectuals come together and disseminate their knowledge through their mother tongue to the masses. He uses an analogy to explain the desired process of education: the water of the sea goes up in vapour, forms rain clouds and comes back in the form of rain to feed and sustain the earth. He observes that his closing remarks ("someone must take the responsibility of bringing the Bengali language to the ocean of university education"; "thousands of minds remain mute due to lack of education") are not utilitarian in nature, they are imaginary. However, he says, till date, utilitarian utterances have merely led to patchwork solutions; constructive work has been done through imagination.

Rabindranath's "Siksha-r Sangikaran" (The Internalisation of Education) was first published in the *Visva-Bharati Bulletin* in 1936. Subsequently it was published posthumously in 1942 (1000 copies). Here Tagore reiterates his concern regarding the alienation from the masses caused by higher education through the medium of English. This essay was read at Calcutta University Senate Hall during the Education Week. He says, the most known yet most ignored fact is that education is something living, not something mechanical. Tagore begins this article with the comment that a poor country's poverty is a matter of sorrow, whereas the paucity of education is a matter of shame. Our failure to spread education is weakening our national history; it is stunting our country's mental growth. Among all forms of parasitical existence the worst is dependency in education. Tagore knows he is repeating these points, but he felt many will not be able to detect this repetition because they never paid heed when he first uttered these concerns.

While speaking of the inaccessibility of the masses to higher education through English in our country Tagore uses an anecdote. A rich man got a two-storeyed house built with exquisite material. The foundation was strongly built. Once the construction was completed people realised they had never thought of building a staircase. Thus the two floors of the building were kept permanently apart. A society where the occupants of the upper storey are well looked after and the people on the ground floor either do not have a square meal or they starve and the society is oblivious of the situation, is a society suffering from paralysis of half its body. Tagore feels that this disease of immobility is a disease of barbarism. The resulting lifelessness cannot be quantified by merely preparing a list of the dead. Had it been possible to directly measure the lack of enthusiasm, tiredness, lack of energy, and propensity to illness we would see how death is continuously deriding life, from one end of the country to the other. It is an extremely sad state of affairs. Tagore goes on to say no civilised country can continue to passively witness this drama of death: this unacceptability has been instantiated by many countries outside India.

Education is only irrigating a thin upper crust of society. Tagore observes that layers and layers below the crust remain arid due to lack of education. There could be nothing more foolish and self-defeating than an attempt to cover up this lack with a veneer. Tagore says any country that is unable to adjust the exchange of wealth and the exchange of thought and judgement with the modern age will be continuously marginalised. Every civilised country has tried to eradicate the causes of such an eventuality; lack of funds has never been used as an excuse.

Tagore commends the courage of Akbar Hyderi who founded the University of Hyderabad and introduced Urdu as the medium of instruction at every level. In this context he refers back to his prior anecdote and says, in this instance a building was built with a staircase and people are walking in a bottom-up direction. To make education inclusive, to be able to reach out to all the segments of society, vernacular education must be introduced. Tagore remarks that he has said this on many prior occasions; he is repeating the same point. If he again fails to reach his targeted audience then he hopes there will be others there to take up his cause. He acknowledged the difficulty of the task, and feared that it may be postponed to a vague distant future, which would be another way of treating it as impossible.

It will be instructive to note that during the Nationalist movement almost all the leaders were in favour of introducing vernacular education. Other than Tagore and Gokhale, there was Bankim Chandra Chattopadhyay, Gandhi, Swamī Vivekananda and others. Gandhi wrote a letter in Hindi to Prabodh Chandra Sen in support of imparting education in Bengali at Visva-Bharati. He was also interested in introducing Hindi as a link language. In his letter he says all the residents of Visva-Bharati should know both Bengali and Hindi; those who come from outside Bengal must learn Bengali; English should not be made compulsory. He further desired that all the administrative work should be carried out in Hindi, if that was not possible then it should be done in Bengali; under no circumstances should English be used as the administrative language.[37]

Tagore was never against using Hindi as an administrative language. He however felt that Hindi should not be imposed by force. An interesting correspondence took place between

37. Prabodhchandra Sen, *Rabindranather Siksha-Chinta* (Rabindranath Tagore's Thoughts on Education) Kolkata: Paschimbanga Rajya Pustak Parisad, 1961, 4th impression 2007, pp. 39-40.

Gandhi and Tagore on this point. While preparing his Presidential Address for the forthcoming Hindi Sammelan, to be held at Indore in 1918, Gandhi sent out a questionnaire to the National "leaders of thought." Gandhi felt that if the national servants are to come in contact with the masses all over India the questions need an immediate solution.[38] Gandhi's questions included the following two: "Is not Hindi (as *bhāṣa* or Urdu) the only possible national language for inter-provincial intercourse and for all other national proceedings?" He also asked "Is it not desirable and possible to give the highest teaching in our schools and colleges through the vernaculars?" Tagore's prompt reply was

> I can only answer in the affirmative the question you have sent to me from Motihari. Of course Hindi is the only possible national language for inter provincial intercourse in India. But, about its introduction at the Congress, I think we cannot enforce it for a long time to come. . . .[39]

In 1923 soon after Gandhi's Non-co-operation movement Hindi was being widely accepted as the national language for India. During this time Tagore was invited to Varanasi to address the north Indian *Banga Sahitya Sammelan.* In that speech he reacted to the demand of accepting Hindi as the national language. He said that he had even heard comments such as the Bengalis are creating a rift in national unity by concentrating on the growth and development of the Bengali language. He did not agree with this observation. Tagore maintained a difference between the role of Hindi as a national language, and the role of vernacular as a language of self-expression. Much later in 1938 he remarked that Hindi may be used as the national language, this would be an artificial

38. *The Mahatma and the Poet: The Debates between Gandhi and Tagore 1915-1941*, comp. and ed. Sabyasachi Bhattacharya, New Delhi: National Book Trust, 1997, 5th impression 2008, p. 45.

39. Ibid.

acceptance for some pragmatic purpose; the purpose of the State could thus be served. But, language has another important purpose and that is the need to nourish the mind, this can only be done in one's own language.[40] He says,

> Languages are jealous. They do not give up their best treasures to those who try to deal with them through an intermediary belonging to an alien rival. We have to court them in person and dance attendance on them. Poems are not like market commodities transferable. We cannot receive the smiles and glances of our sweetheart through an attorney, however diligent and dutiful he may be.[41]

Tagore says, "we must bravely accept the inconvenient fact of the diversity of our languages."[42] Every country has its specific set of problems. Our problem is how to maintain our rich cultural variety while unifying as a nation and there is no reason to be daunted by it. Tagore points out that there was a time when the whole of Europe had Latin for her language of learning. He observes, "the perfection of her mental unfolding was not represented by that oneness of her literary vehicle. When the great European countries found their individual languages, then only the true federation of culture became possible in the West and the very differences of the channels made the commerce of ideas in Europe so richly copious and so variedly active."[43] He goes on to say, "In fact, when natural differences find their harmony, then it is true unity; but

---

40. This point has been discussed in detail by Prabodhchandra Sen in his article "Visva-Bharatir Sikshaniti" in *Rabindranather Siksha-Chinta,* pp. 34-51.
41. Rabindranath Tagore, "The Religion of an Artist" in *The English Writings of Rabindranath Tagore,* (*EWRT*) vol. 3, ed. Sisir Kumar Das, New Delhi: Sahitya Akademi, 1996, p. 686.
42. Rabindranath Tagore, "The Centre of Indian Culture" in *EWRT,* vol. 2, p. 480.
43. Ibid., p. 480.

artificial uniformity leads to lifelessness."[44] The dictatorship of Hitler and the ensuing European calamity exemplifies this point. Tagore repeatedly asserted that unity cannot be achieved through external force, it must come from within. Individuals will have to reach out to each other and create bonds of togetherness. Language no doubt is a major bonding agent. This bond cannot, however, be used mechanically or artificially.

Sisir Kumar Das, the editor of *The English Writings of Rabindranath Tagore,* makes a slightly different comment on the comparison between linguistic pluralism as it is found in Europe and its parallel in India. In Europe the minor languages were part of the western cultural universe whereas in India during Tagore's time and even today they are not accommodated under any broader national rubric. Das clarifies the distinction between what is meant by a major language and what is a minor language. Das writes,

> by a "major" language I do not mean only a language spoken by a large number of people, spoken over a large territory, or a language rich in literature and philosophy. To achieve the status of a major language, it must be associated with power: political, economic and ideological. None of the Indian languages, despite their long and distinguished literary history and enormously large number of speakers, is a "major" language.[45]

He goes on to say that India had its multilingualism even before the introduction of the English language and there was a hierarchy among these languages.

> English being the language of the ruling power altered that hierarchy in such a manner that the relation between it and

44. Rabindranath Tagore, "The Centre of Indian Culture" in *EWRT*, vol. 2, p. 480.
45. Sisir Kumar Das, Introduction, *EWRT*, vol. 1, p. 17.

> other Indian languages was turned into a relation of opposition between a 'major' and a 'minor' language.[46]

The damage did not stop with the creation of this binary. The power hierarchy was further intensified by the leaders of independent India. Das writes, "This opposition was later redefined as that of 'international' and 'national,' 'national' and 'regional,' by the ruling elite of India after Independence."[47] From the perspective of a power matrix, naturally the national is weaker than the international and similarly the regional is weaker than the national. Since power in this context signifies political, economic and ideological power the regional language exponent is destined to be weaker on all three accounts.

We have already mentioned that Tagore gave the example of Europe to show how literature and philosophy began to flourish with the shift from Latin to the regional languages since it generated multiculturalism in place of mono-culturalism. Das agrees that the "minor" languages in Europe continue to flourish without any threat of disempowerment or extinction. This he thinks has been possible due to a favourable juxtaposition between the "major" European languages and the "minor" European languages. Nevertheless the minor language-using countries in Europe had to opt for bilingualism. Das says,

> being less powerful, politically and otherwise, these nations could not afford to be monolingual and were obliged to learn a "major" language. However, very few writers from Romania or Poland, Czechoslovakia or Bulgaria, Holland or Scandinavia, Greece or Iceland would have thought of abandoning their "mother tongue" in preference to a major language like English, or French or German.[48]

46. Sisir Kumar Das, Introduction, *EWRT*, vol. 1, p. 17.
47. Ibid.
48. Ibid., p. 17-18.

It is generally found that in a pond of mixed fish the big ones gobble up the little ones. It would be interesting to know what survival technique is followed by these European "minor" language communities. Das writes,

> Fortunately for them there always existed a group of intermediaries including translators, critics and publishers who tried to overcome the constraints of "minor" languages.[49]

From our experience in contemporary Bengal it could be said that having active intermediaries alone cannot solve the problem. The presence of publishers, translators and critics is only part of the solution, no doubt a necessary part. In addition there must be a patronage from the big powers and such patronage is abundantly available in Europe. As Das observes,

> The functions of such intermediaries have been patronised by the major languages, mainly because they are components of the western cultural universe.[50]

Unfortunately, in India there is no such Indian cultural universe prepared to patronise the minor languages at the national level. This is because we have neglected a study of history and tradition and have failed to create a cultural identity. All our energy has been spent in negotiating power with external forces. Tagore says, "there are some who are insularly modern, who believe that the past is the bankrupt time, leaving no assets for us, but only a legacy of debts."[51] But Tagore reminds us that "the unfortunate people, who have lost the harvest of their past, have lost their present age."[52] Tagore believed that the "inner spirit was calling to us to

---

49. Sisir Kumar Das, Introduction, *EWRT*, vol. 1, p. 18.
50. Ibid.
51. "The Centre of Indian Culture", *EWRT*, vol. 2, p. 487.
52. Ibid., p. 487.

establish in this land great centres, where all her intellectual forces will gather for the purpose of creation, and all her resources of knowledge and thought, Eastern and Western, will unite in perfect harmony."[53] Had all the intellectual forces gathered earlier this problem of accommodating the minor regional languages would not have occurred. Since this harmony is lacking and it is yet to be achieved, India's language problem cannot be compared with that of multilingual Europe.

The acceptance of any form of artificial bonding, or bonding by force, necessarily leads to servitude and loss of freedom. The vitality of any language is related to creativity; without freedom there can be no creativity. Language can either be used as a medium of emancipation, or as an instrument of bondage. During the British period, and immediately after, the great thinkers of India agreed that English language and the foreign mode of education could never be vehicles of emancipation. Tagore remarked, "English being our court language, it acts like an artificial tariff, gradually driving away our mother tongue from our life of culture into the insignificance of domestic use."[54] In an extended sense English remains the court language, the language of trade and commerce, even today. What Tagore was battling against was the primacy of trade and commerce in our life. Man has a basic need for literature, philosophy and art in life.

There is a primacy of trade and commerce in the present global culture too. Needless to say, trade and commerce generates its own model of art and philosophy. It is not as if there is a vacuum left by the pursuance of commerce. Tagore would argue that commerce is built on the philosophy of ruthless competition, and an aggressive market policy that in

53. *EWRT*, vol. 2, pp. 485-86.

54. Ibid., p. 481.

time is going to increase the divide among nations and their citizens. He felt certain that this philosophy will prove to be self-defeating. It will lead away from a power-sharing unifying process.

In all his writings on education Tagore has projected the concept of a "complete man" who is capable of cultivating various facets of human existence. He envisages an educated individual "who is intellectual as well as economic, bound by social bonds and aspiring towards spiritual freedom."[55] Among all these facets Tagore would consider spiritual freedom to be the most important. If we look at his article "The Religion of an Artist" closely we shall find by spiritual freedom Tagore refers to a secular type of freedom not bound by any theistic faith. He believes the path to spiritual freedom is not a final step in the sequential journey from trade and commerce through social bonding to spirituality. The "complete man" is expected to participate in all the dimensions of life simultaneously. The path to spiritual freedom is not a lonely path to be traversed by the isolated traveller through a monolithic insular culture wrapped in one's own mother tongue. For this we need a co-ordination of different elements, which we must primarily derive from our own lived experience and not in the form of dried and desiccated packaged food wrapped in some foreign language.[56] Tagore agrees that "intellectual co-operation is to be the keynote of the coming age."[57] But before we enter into a co-operative intellectual venture we must "be able to take our own views of Truth, from the standpoint of our own vantage ground."[58] It is only then that we shall be able to adjust our knowledge through a comparative study.[59]

55. *EWRT*, vol. 2, p. 490.
56. Ibid, pp. 489-90
57. Ibid., p. 485
58. Ibid.
59. Ibid.

The problem of being capable of incorporating lived-experience into one's own standpoint of knowledge is connected with the problem of establishing one's personal identity or what Tagore referred to as personality. He maintained that personality, freedom and creativity are interlinked in such a way that one cannot be achieved in the absence of the other. He saw a mutual relation of dependence between personality, freedom and creativity on the one hand and vernacular language on the other. These two sets nourished and sustained each other's growth. He also believed that there was no alternative to this relation of cross-fertilisation.

In Tagore's discussions on vernacular as a medium of instruction, at all levels of education, his main thrust is on two points. One is the appropriateness of the mother tongue as a medium of initiation into education — what he calls acquiring the methodology of learning. Obviously learning does not mean learning the three Rs (reading, writing and arithmetic) regarded as the fundamentals of learning. Learning means being able to relate information to one's lived experience creatively, and also to be capable of expressing one's thoughts and emotions in a creative manner. This process must begin through the familiar mother tongue. Tagore's second concern was to forge a social bonding through vernacular education. In this way the huge gap between the English educated elite and the uneducated common man could develop a two-way passage of exchange of ideas, of course, through a process of translation. This would lead to the strength of a country.

After India's Independence great educators like Meghnad Saha, Sarvepalli Radhakrishnan, and others agreed that at all levels education should be imparted in the mother tongue. The Radhakrishnan Commission Report, 1949, makes the following recommendation, that

(i) pupils at the Higher Secondary and University stages be made conversant with three languages, the regional language, the federal language [read Hindi] and English (the last one in order *to acquire the ability to read books in English*), and the

(ii) *Higher education be imparted through the instrumentality of the regional* language with the option to use the medium of instruction either for some subjects or for all subjects.[60]

This recommendation was made two years after India gained Independence. An opportunity was thus created at the government level to assuage Tagore's unmitigated pain. Evidently the government had other political priorities, and these recommendations were never implemented. India's Education Minister K.L. Srimali said (in his Tagore Centenary Address, delivered at Sriniketan on 6 February 1961)

> It is [a] great irony of fate that after independence when we have full freedom to develop our languages, . . . we are clamouring for the retention of English not only as an alternative official language but also as a medium of instruction in our universities.

Srimali reminds us

> Gandhi, Tagore and Radhakrishnan, and all our great thinkers who have thought seriously about the problems of Indian education have explained in unequivocal terms that *a foreign language cannot be the true medium of education*. . . .[61]

If the then Education Minister of India had his way, in all policy matters, Tagore's dreams may have been fulfilled.

---

60. Radhakrishnan Commisssion Report, 1949, p. 326. See Prabodhchandra Sen, *Rabindranather Siksha-Chinta,* p. 30.

61. See Prabodhchandra Sen, "Visva-Bharatir Sikshaniti", in *Rabindranather Siksha-Chinta,* p. 48.

Till date we have not adopted the prescription made by Tagore, and other great educationists of India, nor have we been able to come to any unanimous national policy of language. Our indecision and lack of focus has created a conducive vacuum ready for appropriation by forces now beyond our control. The language of commerce is invading our cultural space. A new hybrid language is developing known as Hinglish (Hindi-English cross-breed). There is also the language of abbreviations used by the internet and mobile SMS (short message system) device. The winds of change are blowing so rapidly in every sphere of human existence that one can hardly envisage the future and plan accordingly. A gradual normative approach to life is being disrupted by multiple counter-finalities. Tagore's notions of personality, creativity and freedom presuppose a belief in a unified world invested in universal values of love, whereas today's trend is to equate values with pragmatic decisions aimed at promoting economic and political goals. The goal of education is also geared towards the realisation of these pragmatic aims. In this age of globalisation, political and economic goals are not set at the local level. The related pragmatic decisions are also beyond local control. It is more so for a country like India which is lagging behind in the global context of competition. Had we heeded to Tagore's advice during his time, we would perhaps have been in a stronger bargaining position today.

The position we are in now is one of somehow keeping afloat in the global stream of change while exerting a minimum agency of intervention. All our resources and efforts are geared towards adjusting to global pressures. At times we display a great deal of efficiency in performing this role. Tagore felt efficiency was not enough; to avoid insult we must have a clear vision regarding our own contribution to a global culture. The comments he made in 1919 sound extremely relevant and contemporary today. He said,

> But before we are in a position to stand a comparison with the other cultures of the world, or truly co-operate with them, we must base our own structure on a synthesis of all the different cultures we have. When, taking our stand at such a centre [of comparison], we turn towards the West, our gaze shall no longer be timid and dazed; our heads shall remain erect, safe from insult.[62]

No doubt, today India is an important participant in global commerce, yet Tagore's anxiety remains. Is not her gaze still timid and dazed? Is she not still vulnerable to insult? But then we cannot expect someone to try and mitigate an unfelt injury. If some day we are conscious of the feeling of timidity and insult we may find some worth in Tagore's prescription for education through the mother tongue, provided that still remains an option. As long as we are sailing on the clouds of efficiency and gaining recognition for that, we are not likely to be sensitive to Tagore's concern for the development of our personality, our identity, our own language.

If the present trend continues around the world, the heterogeneity of human history will gradually be destroyed. A mixed hybrid culture will be the only available culture. The lesson that we have learnt from the life scientist is, bio-diversity is essential for the survival of the biosphere. By analogy the same seems to be true of the cultural sphere. Regional variations in culture are essential for the enrichment of human history. One may comment, after all Tagore did dream of a seamless world. Why do we then lament about the loss of regional languages and identitics? Did he not look forward to a future "where the world has not been broken up into fragments by narrow domestic walls."[63] What he implied was a world not fragmented by hate, suspicion and all the other

62. "The Centre of Indian Culture", *EWRT*, vol. 2, p. 485.

63. *EWRT*, vol. 1, p. 53.

degenerating emotions that go along with aggressive market competition. Tagore was never in favour of a monolithic global culture, nor did he endorse a polarised world. His aim was always one of unity in diversity, without compromising on freedom and creativity.

In his personal life Tagore tried to realise this goal by establishing a deep bond both with his mother tongue Bengali, and a bond with the world community through his English writings. Most other proponents of education through the mother tongue did not maintain an equal attachment to a "major" language and to a "minor" language. Bankim Chandra Chattopadhyay for instance began his literary career by writing in English, but once he switched over to Bengali, he wrote exclusively in Bengali. Same was the case with Michael Madhusudan Datta. He writes, "if there be anyone among us anxious to leave a name behind him, let him devote himself to his mother tongue, . . . but *when we speak to the world, let us speak in our own language*" and that is precisely what he continued to do.[64] Tagore agreed with Datta that the mother tongue was the natural channel of literature, but he did not think that one could reach the world through one's mother tongue. Sisir Das writes,

> Tagore's faith in the mother tongue being the natural channel of literature remained unshaken, but he had to come to terms finally with the major-minor linguistic opposition that conditioned India's colonial history.[65]

Unlike Bankim and Madhusudhan, Tagore remained bilingual till the very end. Das writes, "What is important is that Tagore did not surrender totally to a language of power but continued

---

64. This he wrote on 26 January 1865. Quoted in Prabodhchandra Sen, *Rabindranather Siksha-Chinta*, pp. 46-47.

65. *EWRT*, vol. 1, p. 18.

to remain a bilingual writer till the end of his life."[66] This was his way of solving the major-minor language tension. For him this was a healthy tension. It was a human problem that could not be wished away; it was a problem that needed to be acknowledged and solved. Das rightly points out,

> we do not know of any writer in the history of literature who wrote so much in an alien language and yet remained as prolific and as important in his mother tongue as he was before he became a bilingual writer.[67]

In spite of remaining bilingual Tagore continued to maintain that to understand his literary works fully one must be conversant in Bengali. W.B. Yeats acknowledges this in his Introduction to *Gitanjali*. Yeats writes, "these lyrics, which are in the original, my Indian [friends] tell me, full of subtlety of rhythm, of untranslatable delicacies of colour, of metrical invention . . .".[68] Tagore endorses this observation in his "Talks in China," where he writes, "this is as it should be. Man cannot reach the shrine, if he does not make the pilgrimage. . . . I hope that this may make you want to learn Bengali some day."[69] Tagore gained the recognition of being a world poet *viśvakavi*, by remaining rooted in his mother tongue. He never felt the predicament of education (*Sikshā-r Herpher*) in his own development. He, however, failed to convince his countrymen of the urgency of this educational ideal. Other national priorities stood in the way of adaptation.

66. *EWRT*, vol. 1, p. 18.

67. Ibid.

68. Ibid., p. 15.

69. *EWRT*, vol. 2, p. 588.

8

Gandhian Education
Aesthetic Perspectives

Mohit Chakrabarti

EDUCATION is always an endless enquiry into the inner self. To Mahatma Gandhi, it is more than that. It is to ceaselessly explore and manifest the harmony of the body, mind and spirit with the fusion of best thoughts, purest emotions, highest sense and noblest sensibilities. This is why his thoughts and experiments on education are always adorned with the aesthetics of Truth, Beauty and Goodness. As an aesthetic visionary in education, he wants a total and radical revolution whereby dull, drab, mechanical, artificial and life-destroying principles and practice in education will be fully replaced by living, spontaneous, value-savvy and aesthetic education that adorns serenity and poignancy, spiritual grandeur and excellence. Education for mere intellectual development is meaningless and hardly contributes to the development of the inner man, the man that always looks forward to assuring efflorescence of spirituality in course of the exercise of aesthetic serenity already in him. Gandhi significantly advocates:

> I hold that true education of the intellect can only come through a proper exercise and training of the bodily organs, e.g. hands, feet, eyes, ears, nose, etc. In other words, an intelligent use of the bodily organs in a child provides the best and quickest

> way of developing his intellect. But unless the development of the mind and body goes hand in hand with a corresponding awakening of the soul, the former alone would prove to be a poor lopsided affair.[1]

As an aesthetic visionary in education, Gandhi extends the horizon of the mind where hands and brain are continuously in search of aesthetic cohesion. Innovation and critical consciousness should always contribute to intellectual freshness and depth of vision. What, then, should be our ends-in-view of education? Here is Gandhi's categorical answer:

> Our education has to be revolutionised. The brain should be educated through the hand. If I were a poet, I could write poetry on the possibilities of the five fingers. And why should you think that the mind is everything and the hands and the feet are nothing? Those who do not train their hands, who go through the ordinary rut of education, lack "music" in their life. All their faculties are not trained. Mere book knowledge does not interest the child so as to hold his attention fully. The brain gets weary of mere words, and the child's mind begins to wander. The hand does the thing it ought not to do, the eye sees the things it ought not to see, and the ear hears the things it ought not to hear, and they do not do, see or hear, respectively, what they ought to. They are not taught to make the right choice and so their education often proves their ruin. An education which does not teach us to discriminate between good and bad, to assimilate the one and eschew the other, is a misnomer.[2]

Education for advancement of socio-aesthetics as Gandhi has always emphasised is primarily based on some of the fundamental components as follows:

(i) Education is essentially related to self-growth and self-development. For this, it honours and accelerates the

1. M.K. Gandhi, *Harijan*, 8 May 1937.
2. D.G. Tendulkar, *Mahatma*, New Delhi: Publications Division, Ministry of Information and Broadcasting, Government of India, vol. V, p. 43.

truth: I exist because I am Truth. I hold Truth and I am the serene disseminator of Truth to the last breath of my life and beyond it. This is education *par excellence*.

(ii) The fundamental philosophy of one's existence in terms of education is the philosophy of self-refinement. It is possible to succeed in learning and practising self-refinement only by means of truth. When truth remains absent from self-refinement in education, it is neither education nor refinement of the self.

(iii) For education as a passport to ascent and excellence, Truth is to be discovered, defined, analysed, applied, evaluated and rediscovered in order to be reassured of its fullness and perfection in theory and practice.

(iv) For continual and sustained advancement of personality, truth, as it were, serves as a backbone in education for enrichment of consciousness.

How would one realise truth through education? What guidelines in education should one follow in pursuit of truth? As an aesthetic visionary in education Gandhi prescribes self-discipline:

> He must be completely free from anger and lust, greed and attachment, pride and fear. He must reduce himself to zero and have perfect control over all his senses — beginning with the palate or tongue. Tongue is the organ of speech as well as of taste. It is with the tongue that we indulge in exaggeration, untruth and speech that hurts. The craving for taste makes us slaves to the palate so that like animals we live to eat. But with proper discipline, we can make ourselves into being only "a little below the angels." He who has mastered his senses is the first and foremost among men. All virtues reside in him. God manifests Himself through him. Such is the power of self-discipline.[3]

3. Pyarelal, *Mahatma Gandhi: The Last Phase*, Ahmedabad: Navajivan Publishing House, 1958, vol. II, p. 233.

The spirit of self-discipline for aesthetic development as Gandhi inspires in education should also be strengthened with the exercise of tolerance. Tolerance as an aesthetic component has no alternative. It acts as a solid foundation of education for self-refinement. One recalls how he clearly rejects coercion in the involvement of pupils in the non-co-operation movement:

> Some students have revived the ancient form of barbarity in the form of "sitting *dharnā*." I call it "barbarity" for it is a crude way of using coercion. It is also cowardly because one who "sits *dharnā*" knows that he is not going to be trampled over. It is difficult to call the practice violence, but it is certainly worse. If we fight our opponent, we at least enable him to return the blow. But when we challenge him to walk over us, we, knowing that he will not, place him in a most awkward and humiliating position. I know that the over-zealous students who "sat *dharnā*" never thought of the barbarity of the deed, but one, who is expected to follow the voice of conscience and stand even singlehanded in the face of odds cannot afford to be thoughtless. Non-co-operation, if it fails, will fail only through internal weakness. There is no such thing as defeat in non-co-operation. It never fails. Its so-called representatives may so badly represent their cause that it may appear to the spectators to have failed. Let non-co-operationists therefore beware of everything they do. There must be no impatience, no barbarity, no insolence, no undue pressure. If we want to cultivate the true spirit of democracy, we cannot afford to be intolerant. Intolerance betrays want of faith in one's cause.[4]

The education of self-analysis and self-evaluation as components of aesthetic upbringing contributes a lot to the refinement of man in softer sensibilities and greater visions of fullness and excellence. Gandhi further adorns it with spirituality. As he characteristically asserts:

---

4. M.K. Gandhi, *Young India*, 2 February 1921.

> It is not for us to find fault with anyone else and sit in judgement over him. We should be exhausted judging ourselves only, and so long as we notice a single fault in ourselves and wish our relations and friends not to forsake us in spite of such fault, we have no right to poke our nose into other people's conduct. If in spite of ourselves we notice another's fault, we would ask him if we have the power and think it proper to do so, but we have no right to ask anybody else.[5]

For self-satisfaction by means of exercise of austerity as an unparalleled aesthetic component of education, Gandhi advocates a synthesis between physical and intellectual wants. His experiments on socio-aesthetics in education harbour on this moderation that promotes social and humane relationship between man and man. As he characteristically observes:

> A certain degree of physical harmony and comfort is necessary, but above that level, it becomes a hindrance instead of help. Therefore, the idea of creating an unlimited number of wants and satisfying them seems to be a delusion and a snare. The satisfaction of one's physical needs, even the intellectual needs of one's narrow self, must meet at a point a dead stop before it degenerates into physical and intellectual voluptuousness. A man must arrange his physical and cultural circumstances so that they may not hinder him in his service of humanity, on which all his energies should be concentrated.[6]

How to be justified to the aesthetic education of self-consciousness? How to be self-assured of one's sincere endeavour in education? According to Gandhi, one must rise above all undesirable constraints like hatred, repulsion or attachment. For this one must be free from fear, and in order to be fearless one must exercise the education of self-

5. Mahadev Desai, *The Diary of Mahadev Desai*, Ahmedabad: Navajivan Publishing House, 1953, vol. I, p. 93.
6. M.K. Gandhi, *Harijan*, 29 August 1936.

purification. Then, how to attain perfect purity through the education of fearlessness — *abhaya*? Here is Gandhi's incomparable answer well crystallised in aesthetic education:

> To attain to perfect purity one has to become absolutely passion-free in thought, speech and action; to rise above the opposing currents of love and hatred, attachment and repulsion. I know that I have not in me as yet that triple purity, in spite of constant, ceaseless striving for it. That is why the world's praise fails to move me, indeed it very often stinks me. To conquer the subtle passions seems to me to be harder far than the physical conquest of the arms.[7]

The education of love as an essential component of aesthetics as Gandhi introduces is based on the philosophy of altruism. True education as he thinks and experiments promotes a sense of unity and co-operation, sincerity and devotion. Such education makes a union between man and man by dint of exercise of love and toleration, sympathy and co-operation. When Gandhi speaks of *sarvodaya*, this aesthetic vision of altruism in terms of thought for the others in and around us — *parārtha-bhāvanā* is manifested. In Gandhi's own words this can be further illustrated as follows:

> I should love all the men — not only in India but in the world . . . belonging to the different faiths, to become better people by contact with one another, and if that happens, the world will be a much better place to live in than it is today. I plead for the broadest toleration, and I am working to that end. I ask people to examine every religion from the point of the religionists themselves. I do not expect the India of my dream to develop one religion, i.e. to be wholly Hindu, or wholly Christian, or wholly Mussalman, but I want to be wholly tolerant, with its religions working side by side with one another.[8]

---

7. M.K. Gandhi, *The Story of My Experiments with Truth*, Ahmedabad: Navajivan Publishing House, 1929, vol. II, p. 592.
8. M.K. Gandhi, *Young India*, 22 December 1927.

To be really sincere in aesthetic education, one cannot but be self-controlled in thought and action, in promise and perfection. Gandhi advocates self-serenity and self-perfection in negotiating the ends-in-view of aesthetic education. He takes recourse to celibacy or *brahmacarya* not in terms of mere religion as it normally stands for but in terms of aesthetics which should be cultivated in the theory and practice of education. This is not only a physical practice but also a psychological one which brings forth balance of mind side by side with justice and dignity in one's activities. Gandhi introduces *brahmacarya* in education with the spirit of aesthetics. It is the aesthetics of transparency and transcendence of whatever stands best for the good of mankind. As he significantly advocates:

> *Brahmacarya* must be observed in thought, word and deed. It may be harmful to suppress the body, if the mind is at the same time allowed to go astray. Where the mind wanders, the body must follow sooner or later.
>
> It is necessary here to appreciate a distinction. It is one thing to allow the mind to harbour impure thoughts; it is a different thing altogether if it strays among them in spite of ourselves. Victory will be ours in the end, if we non-co-operate with the mind in its evil wanderings.
>
> We experience every moment of our lives, that often while the body is subject to our control, the mind is not. This physical control should never be relaxed, and in addition we must put forth a constant endeavour to bring the mind under control.[9]

Gandhi's concern for non-violence is entirely based on the aesthetic philosophy of education. Such education replaces hatred by love, untruth by truth and ignorance by enlightenment. His *satyāgraha* clarifies this point very explicitly:

---

9. M.K. Gandhi, *From Yeravda Mandir*, Ahmedabad: Navajivan Publishing House, 1935, p. 18.

> My mission is to teach by example and precept under severe restraint the use of the matchless weapon of *satyāgraha*, which is direct corollary of non-violence and truth. I am anxious, indeed I am impatient to demonstrate that there is no remedy for the many ills of life save that of non-violence.
>
> * * * *
>
> When I have become incapable of evil and when nothing harsh or haughty occupies, be it momentarily, my thought-world, then, and not till then, my non-violence will move all the hearts of the world. I have placed before me and the reader no impossible ideal or ordeal. It is man's prerogative and birthright. We have lost the paradise only to regain it.[10]

To regain the lost paradise is to introduce the aesthetic education of non-violence and to introduce as such is to take recourse to making a cordial relationship between man and man anywhere and everywhere. This requires the education of how to love mankind irrespective of caste, creed or community, colour, clime or character. It is really very difficult to understand, acknowledge and appreciate the aesthetics of non-violence which works wonders in education. The education of liberty, self-expression and self-analysis finds newer connotations in symphony with the education of non-violence where the role of aesthetics is to guarantee lasting peace and prosperity of humanity. Admittedly, Gandhi categorically asserts:

> Non-violence is not an easy thing to understand, still less to practise, weak as we are. We must all act prayerfully and humbly and continually asking God to open the eyes of our understandings, being ever ready to act according to the light as we daily receive it. My task as a lover and promoter of peace, therefore, today consists in unflinching devotion to non-violence in the prosecution of the campaign for

10. M.K. Gandhi, *Young India*, 2 July 1925.

> regaining our liberty. And if India succeeds in so regaining it, it will be the greatest contribution to the world peace.[11]

The practice of the nature and principles of non-violence in aesthetic education that Gandhi introduces in the Tolstoy Farm and the Phoenix School in South Africa is not only incomparable in the whole history of education throughout the world but also an unparalleled pointer to excellence in quality education. In fact, the lesson on non-violence that a child learns right from the beginning of school education goes a long way in learning the aesthetic components of love, truth and self-suffering. Moreover, as non-violence as he clearly asserts, stands for love-force, truth-force and soul-force, the education that a child receives out of its own direct involvement strengthens the foundation of education of fullness and perfection. Gandhi exquisitely spells out this point:

> It should be an essential of real education that a child should learn that, in the struggle of life, it can easily conquer hate by love, untruth by truth, violence by self-suffering. It was because, I felt the force of this truth that, during the latter part of the struggle, I endeavoured as much as I could to train the children of the Tolstoy Farm and then at Phoenix along these lines, and one of the reasons for my departure to India is still further to realise as I already do in part, my own imperfection as a passive resister and then to try to perfect myself; for I believe that it is in India that the nearest approach to perfection is most possible.[12]

The education of detachment as a very essential and invaluable component of aesthetics can be best learnt through non-violence. Gandhi introduces the study of non-violence as a lesson for learning the inherent and undying faith in truth and goodness of humankind. This goes far beyond reasoning

---

11. M.K. Gandhi, *Young India*, 7 February 1928.
12. M.K. Gandhi, *Speeches and Writings of Mahatma Gandhi*, Madras: G.A. Natesan & Co., 1934, p. 189.

and, in fact, refines and reschedules it for the benefit of one and all. This is why learning the lesson of patience as a very effective aesthetic component of non-violence in theory and practice becomes meaningful, purposeful and permanent. As Gandhi characteristically explains:

> Immediately we begin to think of things as our opponents think of them we shall be able to do them full justice. I know that this requires a detached state of mind, and it is a state very difficult to reach. Nevertheless, for a *satyāgrahī* it is absolutely essential. Three-fourths of the miseries and misunderstandings of the world will disappear, if we step into the shoes of our adversaries and understand their standpoint. We will then agree with our adversaries quickly or think of them charitably.
>
> * * * *
>
> I have found that mere appeal to reason does not answer where prejudices are age-long and based on supposed religious authority. Reason has to be strengthened by suffering and suffering opens the eyes of understanding. Therefore, there must be no trace of compulsion in our acts. We must not be impatient, and we must have an undying faith in the means we are adopting.[13]

The education of non-violence as an aesthetic advancement of man maimed and massacred in violence and farewell to conscience is actually an endless pursuit of education for elimination of hatred and fear, falsehood and absence of forbearance. It is learning the lesson of safeguarding self-respect and self-identity in terms of truth, beauty and goodness. Gandhi strongly advocates:

> Just as one must learn the art of killing in the training for violence, so one must learn the art of dying in the training

13. M.K. Gandhi, *Young India*, 19 March 1925.

> for non-violence. Violence does not mean emancipation from fear, but discovering the means of combating the cause of fear. Non-violence, on the other hand, has no cause for fear. The votary of non-violence has to cultivate the capacity for sacrifice of the highest type in order to be free from fear. He recks not if he should lose his land, his wealth, his life. He who has not overcome all fear cannot practise *ahiṁsā* to perfection. The votary of *ahiṁsā* has only one fear, that is of God. He who seeks refuge in God ought to have a glimpse of the *ātman* that transcends the body; and the moment one has a glimpse of the imperishable *ātman* one sheds the love of the perishable body. Training in non-violence is thus diametrically opposed to training in violence. Violence is needed for the protection of things external, non-violence is needed for the protection of *ātman,* for the protection of one's honour.[14]

The aesthetic lesson of *satyāgraha* that Gandhi has time and again introduced is self-suffering as a positive component of non-violence. He does not like violence because it destroys all good sense and sensibilities and makes one an inevitable prey to hatred and immoral activities. As he strongly observes:

> The doctrine of violence has reference only to the doing of injury by one to another. Suffering injury in one's own person is on the contrary the essence of non-violence and is the chosen substitute for violence to others. It is not because I value life low that I can countenance with joy thousands voluntarily losing their lives for *satyāgraha,* but because I know that it results in the long run in the least loss of life and what is more, it ennobles those who lose their lives and morally enriches the world for their sacrifices.[15]

The aesthetic value of non-violence in the serene and blessed manifestation of calmness and humility as Gandhi envisions

14. M.K. Gandhi, *Harijan,* 1 September 1940.
15. M.K. Gandhi, *Young India,* 8 October 1925.

and experiments proves the fact that the spirit of goodness never dies. How does he prepare himself for such aesthetic vision of non-violence? He recalls Shelley:

> Stand ye calm and resolute,
> Like a forest close and mute,
> With folded arms and looks which are
> Weapons of unvanquished war.
>
> And if then the tyrants dare,
> Let them ride among you there,
> Slash, and stab, and maim and hew, —
> What they like, that let them do.
>
> With folded arms and steady eyes,
> And little fear, and less surprise,
> Look upon them as they slay
> Till their rage has died away.
>
> Then they will return with shame
> To the place from which they came,
> And the blood thus shed will speak
> In hot blushes on their cheek.
>
> Rise like lions after slumber
> In unvanquishable number —
> Shake your chains to earth like dew
> Which in sleep had fallen on you —
> We are many — they are few.[16]

The beauty Gandhi introduces in and through *satyāgraha* is the power of tolerance. It is this aesthetic power which never knows defeat or disaster, decay or destruction. It is the power that is based on the inward aesthetic and spiritual vision of truth. The quest for truth, one of the most significant ends-in-view of aesthetic education, is the endless one for learning

16. P.B. Shelley, "The Mask of Anarchy".

the indomitable power of the soul-force. Gandhi encourages us to exercise soul-force in order to have a true vision of the All True:

> No search is possible without some workable assumptions. If we grant nothing, we find nothing, ever since its commencement, the world — the wise and the foolish included — has proceeded upon the assumption that, if we are, God is and that, if God is not, we are not. And since belief in God is coexistent with the human kind, existence of God is treated as a fact more definite than the fact that the sun is. This living faith has solved a large number of puzzles of life. It has alleviated our misery. It sustains us in life, it is our one solace in death. The very search for Truth becomes interesting and worthwhile, because of this belief. But search for Truth is search for God. Truth is God. God is, because Truth is. We embark upon the search, because we believe that there is Truth and that it can be found by diligent search and meticulous observance of the well-known and well-tried rules of search. There is no record in history of the failure of such search. Even the atheists who have pretended to disbelieve in God, have believed in Truth. The trick they have performed is that of giving God another, not a new, name. His names are legion. Truth is the crown of them all.[17]

Gandhi also exposes the true aesthetic nature of faith that serves as the true identity of man. The education of faith is one of spiritual consciousness crystallised in aesthetic purity of erudition and edification. It continually calls for an inner askance backed and revaluated by a series of counter askance in search of Truth.

Gandhi, the man who is the ever-living example of aesthetics with endless wonder and humane excellence:

---

17. D.G. Tendulkar, *Mahatma*, vol. III, pp. 293-94.

This was a Man
The essence of simplicity
With bifocals, sandals
And his hand-made "dhoti".
He wove intricately the
Cloth of human nobility
Into beautiful patterns
Of self-respect.[18]

When comes such an incomparable colossus?

18. Jitnarine Ganessing, Quoted by Pran Chopra in *The Sage in Revolt*, New Delhi: Gandhi Peace Foundation, 1972, p. 11.

9

Nationalists' Quest for Deeper Principles of Education

Anirban Ganguly

SRI Aurobindo's (1872-1950) political activism can be divided into two distinct phases. The first period that lasted from 1906 to 1908 was full of rhetoric and fire brimming with political polemics. The efforts that he made during this phase as a leading member of the nationalist front were political, public and mass-oriented. The second phase, though shorter and lasted from May 1909 to February 1910 when he left Calcutta, was richer in literary and creative output. The journalistic output during the first phase was generally political in nature and the writings during the second phase mostly dealt with topics and issues that Sri Aurobindo believed would eventually be central to the discourse of identity of post-colonial India. He communicated mainly through his then newly launched vehicle of thought, the English weekly, *Karmayogin*.

I propose to study some of the themes Sri Aurobindo discussed during this phase in the *Karmayogin*, about ancient Indian educational principles in their diverse aspects such as psychological, artistic and aesthetic. Sri Aurobindo unravelled and reassessed some of the deeper fundamentals of Indian education as practised through the ages and argued for their re-evaluation, re-examination and reinstatement in a new national system of education that he believed India would eventually have to evolve. He believed that the retention of certain indigenous educational principles in a new national system of education would prevent the Indian mind from being thoroughly refashioned and restructured by an unresponsive and unsuitable colonial education machinery. In order to make the exploration broad-based and provide an insight into the currents of thoughts and ideas that developed in a nationalist quest for the roots of Indian education, I have also made a comparative approach to the thoughts of some of the leading Indian minds of the period (1909-10) when Sri Aurobindo, on his part, initiated this discussion. The present study thus, while keeping Sri Aurobindo's ideas on the theme central, explores the ideas of his contemporaries too. This study may be seen as an exploration into the essential elements in the Indian educational thought as derived from various discussions, formulations and assessments of India's epoch-making thinkers and interpreters of culture. I have thus included the thoughts of Sister Nivedita (1867-1911) and that of the celebrated art historian and interpreter of Indian culture, Ananda K. Coomaraswamy (1877-1947). The debate that percolated through their discussion has not lost its contemporaneity and can perhaps still provide direction to a much neglected area in the national scheme of education, the training of the artistic, aesthetic emotions, which is evident as one proceeds to explore it.

The early Indian nationalists, as portrayed through these selected thinkers, do not appear to be blind revisionists, nor do they seem to adhere to an attitude of relegating and erasing all that belonged to the Indian past. They appear instead to have painstakingly searched for the principles, for the spirit, for the idea that, renewing itself through the ages, could still inspire a new direction and help develop a new system — a system which they believed, would largely reflect India's past civilisational achievements and yet respond to her modern needs and aspirations.

The Brain of India: Psychological Principles of Ancient Indian Education

The *Karmayogin* had, as mentioned above, a distinct trait; it not only commented on political issues of the day but began to gradually focus on topics such as philosophy, yoga, culture, art, literature and education. Sri Aurobindo, it will be seen, clearly toned down the political rhetoric during this phase perceiving that "the movement has drawn back to await a farther and truer impulse" and that it would be worthwhile in the meanwhile to focus on other issues of national importance that needed urgent attention and direction. Thus one sees him producing a series "The Brain of India" between 9 October and 13 November 1909, the objects of which were "to indicate the nature and psychological ideas of the old system and point out its essential relation of cause and effect to the splendid achievement of our ancestors."[1] In the series Sri Aurobindo analyses the Indian practice of *brahmacarya,* its integrality in the scheme of ancient Indian education and its relevance to the present. He also discusses the ancient educational discipline of Hinduism, its system of segregating the constitution of man according to the "three principles of nature." Taking humans to be constitutionally of three types, the ancient system of education practised by the Hindus, suggested three sorts of training. Sri Aurobindo was impressed by this idea, as he thought this practice to convey the idea that the psychological type of a person is a determiner for the kind of education to be imparted to him or her. It is part of our search to attempt to examine some of the classical concepts of Indian education as Sri Aurobindo saw them. "The Brain of India" series briefly offers us that opportunity.

Historically speaking, the time when Sri Aurobindo was writing "The Brain of India" was a period marked by

1. *Complete Works of Sri Aurobindo* (*CWSA*), vol. 1, 2003, p. 378.

perplexed reactions towards the new set of circumstances by the national mind, especially the Bengali mind. What the new circumstances are, is not clearly stated; it may be an allusion to the stalemate and confusion that prevailed at that point of time in terms of the direction the nationalist movement would adopt or alternately it may be a reference to the future, when the advent of self-determination would create entirely new requirements demanding new modes of thinking and functioning. For such an eventuality the national mind had to begin preparing itself through a new system of training. Therefore Sri Aurobindo suggests that for the "work of the present, and still more, for the work of the future, it is imperatively necessary to create a centre of thought and knowledge which will revolutionise the brain of the nation. . . ."[2] This revolutionising of the brain and the evolving of a new centre of thought required "a new centre of education." But under the present university system, Sri Aurobindo argues, such a hope is unrealisable. In a severe indictment of the university system he criticises it as one which "ignores the psychology of man, loads the mind laboriously with numerous little packets of information carefully tied with red-tape, and, by the methods used in this loading process, damages or atrophies the faculties and instruments by which man assimilates, creates and grows in intellect, manhood and energy."[3] The National Education experiment as inaugurated in Bengal did succeed to a certain reasonable extent to alter a number of these approaches and methods. Sri Aurobindo argues, "to enlarge the field of knowledge to which the student was introduced" the National Education Movement laid emphasis on "observation" and "experiment" and "employed the natural and easy instrument of the vernacular" and

2. *Complete Works of Sri Aurobindo* (CWSA), vol. 1, p. 367.

3. Ibid., p. 368.

encouraged the habit of thought "on the subject of study,"[4] these being certain essential features absent in the official system. But the new attempt too [National Education experiment] was not free from the taint of old habits, a number of "the vicious methods and ideas employed by the old system were faithfully cherished by the new" because the new too came to be dominated by men who were "wedded to the old lines" and this cast "a most unfavourable effect on the integrity of the system in its most progressive features,"[5] the new progressive features too thus did not have scope of adequate expression.

Sri Aurobindo had by now (1909) begun to openly analyse the systemic defects in the new educational attempt. His principal complaint against the attempt was that those leading it were still inspired by the officially constructed system and the one thing that was ignored was the "psychology of the race" — he perhaps qualifies this by saying that a surface approach to educational reform would never be sufficient to introduce into the system an Indianness, "the mere inclusion of the matter of Indian thought and culture in the field of knowledge does not make a system of education Indian."[6] It was this point that generated constant debate on what could make a system truly Indian and national — in fact, this remained a major area of challenge for the Swadeshi Movement itself. According to Sri Aurobindo's perception the Bengal National College version of the system was only "an improved European system."[7] Improved, perhaps because it at least did focus on Indian subjects and issues, attempted to impart certain moral-spiritual training and sought to perceive the learner as a questioning mind instead of a mere receiver of information

4. *Complete Works of Sri Aurobindo* (CWSA), vol. 1, p. 368.
5. Ibid.
6. Ibid.
7. Ibid.

nuggets. But here too Sri Aurobindo cautions against adopting extreme postures: the demand and seeking of an indigenous system of education, the aspiration for a Swadeshi education ought not to give rise to an irrational demand for retrogression. He clarifies that this retrogression must definitely not seek to revive the eighteenth-century system of indigenous education in Bengal, which in any case he felt could not reflect the modern aspirations of a race and nation in the throes of self-determination. He calls it an "error which has to be avoided" and which does attract "careless minds." Terming the argument that "in order to be National, education must reproduce the features of the old *tol* system of Bengal" as a "reactionary idea" he clearly states that "it is not eighteenth-century India, the India which by its moral and intellectual deficiencies gave itself into the keeping of foreigners" that is to be revived but rather "the spirit, ideals and methods of the ancient and mightier India in a yet more effective form and with a modern organisation."[8]

8. Ibid., pp. 368, 369. Sri Aurobindo, it appears from his stand, had little consideration for the revival of the old *tol* system of education. It is however difficult to say that Sri Aurobindo would have condemned the system even in its pristine manifestation. His criticism instead appears to be directed towards its later degenerative expression. His two contemporaries, whose views we have decided to induct into our discussions at various turns, seem to have some appreciation for the indigenous system especially evident in Bengal and do recall its utility. Sister Nivedita in her discussion on "The Mediaeval University of India" talks of the "formal and absorbing" organisation of "Tols or schools of Sanskrit" with which "India was netted from end to end, and men would come from the most distant parts to sit at the feet of some renowned teacher. . . ." In these centres of learning students were moved to work year after year "for pure love of knowledge" implying the link these centres had to the ancient Indian classical concept of education which talked of a learning inspired by the pure and selfless seeking of knowledge and wisdom. She saw the ancient university system of the fifteenth century "Nuddea" [Nāḍiā district of Bengal famous for its Sanskrit teaching schools] came down in an intact form to the present day →

Contemplating on ancient Indian society's capacity to create diversely, Sri Aurobindo wonders as to what could have pushed the race towards such massive and original creations

→ and extols its virtues as heard from an "older generation." Nivedita sees the routine of the old *tols* as revealing a "marvellously intense and earnest life." A system, she describes, where the "college" of a single teacher was made up of a household of "some 50 or 60 students, distributed over a number of mud cottages arranged round a central tank." Describing a *tol* in Bengal she says students from Maharashtra were admitted in it indicating the pan-Indian recognition that these educational institutions of Bengal had earned. The courses in these institutions were widely recognised and sought after, Nivedita points out, the "fame of Bengal logic went far and wide, and all India knew the names of its best teachers." She thus sees the *tols* as institutions where "was lived out the great ideal of *brahmacarya* — the celibate student dwelling as a son in his master's house." [Sister Nivedita, *Complete Works of Sister Nivedita (CWSN)* vol. 2, "The Mediaeval University of India" in *Studies from an Eastern Home*, 1999, pp. 341-43.] Sri Aurobindo, when referring to the working out of the *brahmacarya*, as we shall see, seems to refer to an earlier period and has therefore no high regard for the efficacy and utility of the *tol* system. Both appealed to the nationalist mind, one saw in the preservation of the indigenous system, as she witnessed it, the possibility of perpetuating certain fundamental Indian principles and the other saw the working out of an entirely new system inspired by principles of the classical Indian education principles as the way ahead for the national education discourse. The other contemporary mind, Ananda Coomaraswamy, in his study of education, culture and nationalism in India, written during the same period (1909), argues that unlike the indigenous system, the official school system functioned apart from the Indian life and environment. He identifies the disconnectedness of schools from the Indian life as the "great tragedy of the present situation." Schools, he argues, are not part of Indian life "as were the *tols* and *maktabs* of the past" and instead are antagonistic to it. [Ananda Coomaraswamy, *Essays in National Idealism*, 1909, p. 99.] Coomaraswamy implies that the *tols* of old, part of the indigenous education system were much more connected to, supportive of and in fact formed an inseparable part of the Indian life system while the colonial system adopted an adverse stance towards Indian life and its systems. He does not extol on the virtues of the *tol* system but simply indicates they were a part of the Indian life and thus easily adopted by the vast populace.

that demonstrated a huge intellectual, physical and moral energy — what could have been the secret of the "gigantic intellectuality, spirituality and superhuman moral force" that permeated the epics, the ancient philosophy, art, sculpture, architecture of ancient India. What driving energy and vision could be at the base of the "incomparable," feats of "public works and engineering achievements," the industries, scientific outputs, jurisprudence, logic, metaphysics and social structure?[9] What was it that generated a "national vitality and endurance," what was it that supported a civilisation that was unique in the "massiveness of its outlines" and the "perfection of its details?"[10] Sri Aurobindo's answer to the question is that there must have existed a wide and deep support system of "a unique

9. Sri Aurobindo was to deal extensively with this theme and question later during his early Pondicherry period in a series of essays on the Indian renaissance. He was to thoroughly refute the allegation of Indian civilisational incapacity in material creation and world understanding. Describing the European [read Western] narrative of Indian culture and civilisation as one that saw Indian civilisation as dominantly metaphysical with a distinct inclination towards the trait of "other worldliness" Sri Aurobindo then sums up the Western reading of Indian capacities. The perception of India that this reading came to present, was, Sri Aurobindo points out, that of a civilisation with a controlling mind that was mainly "abstract," "metaphysical" and "religious" "overpowered by the sense of the infinite, not apt for life, dreamy, unpractical, turning away from life and action as Maya." A phase of Indian quiescence to this view was followed by a realisation that though "spirituality [remained] the master key of the Indian mind" such a spiritual emphasis was not based in a void. The Indian civilisational view, Sri Aurobindo argues, was "alive to the greatness of material laws and forces" and for an uninterrupted period of "three thousand years at least" indeed much longer India created "abundantly, incessantly, lavishly, with an inexhaustible many-sidedness" creations that included republics, kingdoms, empires, temples, monuments, palaces, public works, etc." All of them signs that the much misjudged Indic civilisation did possess a balanced mastery of the metaphysical as well as the physical [*CWSA* vol. 20, 1997, pp. 6-8].

10. *CWSA* vol. 1, p. 369.

discipline involving a perfect education of the soul, mind,"[11] as the absence of such a system would have made impossible the achievements of such immense dimensions. The key then was to look for the "principle and basis on which the details" of such an education were founded. To look for the secret of the success of the ancient system in the details of the instructions in the old ashramas and universities as they have percolated to the present age would be an "error." He was clear that these ancient methods of instructions need not be replicated under modern conditions, rather what was far more important for him were the principles and guiding ideals that formed the base of this grand educational edifice that could generate such inexhaustible creativity.[12]

Sri Aurobindo then analyses the ancient Indian discipline of *brahmacarya* which, he argues, provided a strong foundation for "building up a great intellectual superstructure." He analyses its importance and centrality in the ancient Indian educational system as one that preserved the creative energy and prevented its dissipation and dilution. It is in course of this discussion that one is exposed to some of Sri Aurobindo's insights on education. He attacks the convoluted approach to education which believes that merely "supplying the student with a large or well-selected mass of information on the various subjects which comprised the best part of human culture at the time"[13] was sufficient to build a foundation. Such an approach did neither take into account the student's preparedness to absorb such a mass of information nor did it question whether the student had received an adequate training to be able to absorb the supplied mass of information. The general formula that appears to emerge from such an approach and one that seems to be broadly followed was that

11. *CWSA* vol. 1, p. 369.
12. Ibid.
13. Ibid.

the "school gives the materials, it is for the student to use them."[14] But such a formula did not seek to unveil before the student the path and method that could be taken to assimilate and put to effective use these materials. It did not perhaps also question the very utility or usability of the materials given as part of the exercise of educating. Such a formula was based, Sri Aurobindo observes, on a "fundamental error" — that of considering "information" to be the "foundation of intelligence." " Information," he argues, "cannot be the foundation of intelligence, it can only be part of the material out of which the knower builds the knowledge, the starting-point, the nucleus of fresh discovery and enlarged creation."[15] One may surmise that the habit of believing the imparting of information to be the sole aim of education, has developed with the growth of the centralised examination system, which created overdependence on prescribed textbooks to pass examinations — a system that was institutionalised by the colonial version of education adopted in the country. It invariably fails to develop the "various faculties of memory, judgement, imagination, perception, reasoning, which build the edifice of thought and knowledge for the knower. . . ."[16] Ancient Indian education had deeper layers to its educational vision — it focused on man as a part of the universe — it did not remain solely concerned with the development of his mind and his capacity to store information, it sought rather to develop him into a greater receptacle [*ādhāra*] of the Universal Energy. Sri Aurobindo terms Universal Energy here as an "infinite energy, *prakṛti*, *māyā* or *śakti* [that] pervades the world, pours itself into every name and form, and the clod, the plant, the insect, the animal, the man" in their phenomenal existence are "more or less efficient *ādhāra*s of this Energy." The ancient

14. *CWSA* vol. 1, p. 369.
15. Ibid., pp. 369-70.
16. Ibid., p. 370.

education system focused on increasing in man the capacity to store this energy because the continual improvement of the *ādhāra* and the increase in its capacity to hold the infinite Energy was believed to be the aim of evolution. And when the *ādhāra* was perfected and developed itself to the highest level to hold that Energy then was a man judged and recognised as a *siddha* (the perfected soul, the "fulfilled or perfect man"). The aim of education then, during the ancient epoch, was the creation of the perfected man and in order to achieve that perfection the storehouse of the infinite Energy had to be allowed greater uninterrupted flow in the individual himself and for this flow to remain perennial, obstructions in the channel of communication between the individual and the universal energy had to be cleared.

Extrapolating from this point Sri Aurobindo argues that if this theory of increasing capacity to hold the universal energy be correct then "the energy at the basis of the operation of intelligence must be" in the individual too, and must be "capable of greater expansion and richer use" and that the perception that "the more we can increase and enrich the energy, the greater will be the potential range, power and activity of the functions of our mind and the consequent vigour of our intellectuality and the greatness of our achievement" appears to be a sound principle. The ancient Indians thus based their education on this first principle and the "chief process which they used for increasing storage of energy, was the practice of *brahmacarya*."[17] The ancient system designated the practice of *brahmacarya* as the "first and most necessary condition of increasing the force within and turning it to such uses as may benefit the possessor or mankind." *Brahmacarya* thus was the cornerstone of the ancient educational discipline.[18]

17. *CWSA* vol. 1, pp. 370-71.

18. A detailed study of the concept of *brahmacarya* I shall not undertake here, a lack of proficiency being the simple reason. However, a few →

Sri Aurobindo then places his analysis of the ancient Indian concept of the individual's energy conservation and

→ collated thoughts on the term would put in perspective the centrality of the concept in the ancient Indian educational scheme. *Brahmacarya* was to be the life of abstinence and self-control. It was not limited to physical self-control only but possessed a wider connotation that included other areas of human action and reaction that needed restraint and sublimation. It meant a complete control over all the senses, thus a wave of impure thought became "a breach of *brahmacarya*" as was a reaction engendered by a spark of anger; such was Mahatma Gandhi's analysis of the term in the pages of his *Harijan* issue of 23 July 1938. According to Radha Kumud Mookerji [himself an outstanding product of the national education movement who formed among the "core of the teaching staff" and who had already begun making a name for himself through "research work in ancient Indian history and culture. . ." — (vide Sumit Sarkar, *The Swadeshi Movement in Bengal (1903-1908)*, 1973, p. 168). It is perhaps this connection that has prompted me to consult his seminal Ancient Indian Education when discussing or seeking light on education in the ancient period.] the system of education in ancient India was standardised and fixed based on a certain "universally accepted ideals and practices connoted by the term *brahmacarya* which form[ed] the foundation of the entire structure of Hindu thought and life." The system or framework of studentship in ancient Indian educational system, observes Mookerjee, retained "universal validity," it did not admit change according to "age" or "clime." [Radha Kumud Mookerji, *Ancient Indian Education*, 1969, p. 67.] The *Atharvaveda* "extols," "exalts" and "expounds" the fundamental principal system of the *brahmacarya*. [Mookerjee, op. cit., p. 67.] Discussing the Brahmanical system of education in ancient India, Mookerjee describes how a student had to find his teacher and formally apply for being inducted as a pupil: "I am come for the *brahmacarya*, I desire to be a *brahmacārin*." The teacher on his part as a sign of acceptance "ties the girdle around him [the pupil] gives him the staff into his hand, and explains to him the *brahmacarya* (the rules of conduct of a religious student") in the following words: "Thou art *brahmacārin*; drink water; perform service; sleep not by day; study the Veda obediently to thy teacher." [Ibid., p. 394.] Sri Aurobindo analyses the benefits of the discipline of *brahmacarya* and how an adherence to the system expands the energy base of the individual. A brief survey of the material demands of the system would be in order here. The ceremony of initiating the pupil (*upanayana*) by his selected teacher (*ācārya*) into the world of

→

enhancement. The ancient Hindus, he wrote, clearly perceived that the "source of life and energy is not material but spiritual,

---

→ knowledge and discipline of *brahmacarya* culminated in the pupil having a second birth — a spiritual birth (*dvija* or twice born). This birth was a psychological transmutation, an unfolding "of the mind and soul." The teacher, as it were, while accepting the pupil, initiates the exercise of recreating/remoulding the pupil's whole personality — *ācāryaḥ antaḥ vidyaśarīrasya madhye garbham kṛnute* (Sāyaṇa) "the teacher recreates the pupil in a new body of learning". The initiation of the pupil into *brahmacarya* required him to follow a twofold discipline — external and internal — the external enjoined the following of certain specific physical acts and discipline while the internal (inner) discipline required the pupil to practise and adhere to "*Śrama* (self-restraint), *Tapas* (practice of penance), *Dīkṣā* (consecration to a life of discipline through prescribed regulations) . . ." (Sāyaṇa). [Ibid., p. 67.] Thus in "The Scheme of Life and Education in Ancient India" the period of *brahmacarya* seems to possess a great centrality, it connoted the pupil's emergence into self-reliance and self-discovery through a rigorous pursuit of a knowledge and physical discipline. It was a period that generally lasted for 25 years and the pupil's "life spent in his professor's house [was designated as the] life of *brahmacarya*." The period was a great leveller too, any distinction of class, caste and position was equalised, the newly accepted "student would be treated equally with his compeers." The other positive social qualities and perceptions that it evolved was self-reliance — through the process of *bhikṣā*, respect for manual labour by tilling the master's fields, tending to his cattle, etc. The life of *brahmacarya* does not appear to be solely an academic one that segregated the pupil from his surrounding life and environment but one that was dedicated to developing an integral and holistic perception of life. [vide Swami Ramakrishnananda, *For Thinkers on Education*, 1949, pp. 3-5.] Arguing against the perception of the teacher-student relation as being monolithic and hierarchical in ancient India, especially arguing against that perception during the *brahmacarya* phase, Kireet Joshi observes that the pupil during the *brahmacarya* phase and in general was looked upon as a "seeker not to be silenced by any dogmatic answers, but to be lifted in higher processes of thought, meditation and direct experience or realisation." The pupil, the *brahmacārin* was devoted to "self-control and *askesis*," the discipline was not imposed and arbitrary, the *brahmacārin* obeyed "the command of the teacher, knowing very well that the teacher takes nothing arbitrary" and instead directed the path through which "self-perfection" was attainable. The pupil →

[and that] the basis, the foundation on which the life and energy stand and work, is physical." This distinction between the *kāraṇa* and *pratiṣṭhā* — "[e]arth or gross matter is the *pratiṣṭhā, Brahman* or spirit is the *kāraṇa*" — was well recognised by the ancient educators who thus propounded the raising up of the physical to the spiritual as *brahmacarya*. The interlacing of the two enables the energy "which starts from one and produces the other" to enhance and fulfil itself.[19]

The other fundamental view on which Hinduism based its educational discipline was the one which believed that "all knowledge is within and has to be evoked by education rather than instilled from outside."[20] The idea and practice of imposition was absent in ancient Hindu educational discourse. The teacher accepted his function as that of an "observer, helper [and] guide." The taskmaster's instructional approach was absent and he taught through the "example of his wisdom

→ and teacher's lives were intertwined, joint — it was a life of "joint prayer, joint endeavour, of joint conquest of knowledge." As the student sought for a teacher, so too the teacher sought pupils — the *Taittirīya Upaniṣad* thus portrays the teacher as saying — "May the *brahmacārins* come unto me. From here and there, may the *brahmacārins* come unto me." And in fact for the *brahmacārin* "the home of the teacher represented the fabric of life" which was subtly interlinked with " educational process" in such a way that life itself was education and educational activities were not segregated from "life-experience" [Kireet Joshi, *Education at Crossroads*, 2007, pp. 126-27] And so what emerges is the fact that the *brahmacārin*'s — the pupil following the discipline of *brahmacarya* — life was a multi-layered one, evolving and developing under a process of simultaneity and throughout the phase, the pupil is seen to be treated differently at two separate levels — at physical/material he is levelled, co-equalled with his peers of varying background and nature and at the psycho-spiritual level he is treated with a great finesse so as to assist in the sublimation of his nature and emotional being as in the evolution of his spiritual being which encourages simultaneously a growth of a unitary perception and vision.

19. *CWSA*, vol. 1, pp. 371-72.
20. Ibid., p. 373. This formed the seed expression of what was to be later much discussed as Sri Aurobindo's first principle of teaching (p. 384).

and character."[21] The other fundamental view of the Hindu system of education was that man's constitution "consists of three principles of nature [the three *guṇas*] *sattva*[22] (comprehensive), *rajas* (active), and *tamas* (passive) which manifest," Sri Aurobindo observes, as "knowledge, passion, ignorance."[23] Each of the *guṇas* influences, depending on their predominance, thoughts and actions of the individual and Sri Aurobindo does give here a succinct description of the three principles:

> *Tamas* is a constitutional dullness or passivity which obscures the knowledge within and creates ignorance, mental inertia, slowness, forgetfulness, disinclination to study, inability to grasp and distinguish.[24] *Rajas* is an undisciplined activity which obscures knowledge by passion, attachment, prejudgement, predilection and wrong ideas. *Sattva* is an illumination which reveals the hidden knowledge and brings it to the surface where the observation can grasp and the memory record it.

Adhering to this conception of the three composing principles of man the main task of the teacher thus was the "removal of *tamas*, the disciplining of *rajas* and the awakening of *sattva*."[25]

---

21. Joshi, op. cit., p. 126.
22. As per his [Sri Aurobindo's] various expressions of the three terms: *sattva* — clarity, principle of assimilation, equilibrium and harmony [which] translates in quality as good and harmony and happiness and light," *rajas* — "force of kinesis, translates in quality as struggle and effort, passion and action," *tamas* — "principle and power of inertia, translates in quality as obscurity and incapacity and inaction." [M.P. Pandit (ed.), *Glossary of Sanskrit Terms in Sri Aurobindo's Works*, 2002, pp. 53, 63-64, 70.]
23. *CWSA*, vol. 1, p. 373.
24. The principles if understood by the present-day tutor would further facilitate her/his understanding and appreciation of the learner and the difficulties — emotional, psychological, temperamental all nature-induced hurdles that the learner faces while undergoing the academic discipline.
25. *CWSA*, vol. 1, pp. 373-74.

The principle of *rajas* was disciplined through the adherence to "a strict moral discipline which induced a calm, clear, receptive state of mind free from intellectual self-will and pride" and the obscure shadings of passion — it was this discipline, celebrated as the one followed by the *brahmacārī*, which was the foundation of the morals and culture of ancient India.[26] The "wrong ideas"-induced disturbance was attempted to be arrested by a "strict mental submission to the teacher during the receptive period" which was the period when the "ascertained knowledge," "right ideas," already in collective racial and civilisational possession was "explained to him [pupil] and committed to memory."[27] *Tamas* was sought to be removed through the discipline of "moral purity" and through *tapasyā* (*askesis*, austerity of personal will, spiritual austerity), the system was thus trained to be a "reservoir of mental force and clarity."

The teacher had one fundamental task — the training of the learner to be "receptive of illumination from within" — which he had to perform and which was believed to be the essential training in education of that age. The guiding belief was that knowledge lay within the individual and the right approach to education would be to link that source with the learner.[28] The awakening or facilitating of this illumination

26. *CWSA*, vol. 1, p. 374.

27. Ibid.

28. The first principle of Sri Aurobindo's formulation of education thus comes in here again as a relevant corollary. The idea that all knowledge is within and should be evoked through education forms one of the core formulations of his educational theorem and according to it the role of the teacher undergoes a thorough repositioning, as one who is less of an imparter and imposer and more of a helper and guide. Thus I wish to argue that in the formulation of his first educational principle — we shall not go into all the three principles (or seven as enumerated by Jugal Kishore Mukherjee in his *Principles and Goals of Integral Education*, Pondicherry, 2008) at this juncture — Sri Aurobindo as evident →

was engineered through a well-defined method — a "triple method of repetition, meditation and discussion."[29] *Āvṛtti* (repetition) "was meant to fill the recording part of the mind with *śabda* (word) so that the *artha* (meaning) might of itself rise from within." This probably deconstructs assumed theories on a supposed tradition of rote-learning in ancient Indian educational systems. The emphasis on the necessity of giving rise to the *artha* (meaning) is quite clear, and repetition (*āvṛtti*)[30]

→ from his earlier writings and interpretations in the *Karmayogin* (1909-10) was inspired by classical Indian educational formulations. This emerges especially from the treatment of the ancient discipline in his opuscule under discussion.

29. *CWSA*, vol. 1, p. 374.

30. An aside here on the position of memory in the scheme of ancient Indian education would perhaps be relevant. In an analysis of the role of memory in the ancient Indian scheme of education Coomaraswamy argues that the role of repetition in the Indian system was not for mere memorising but served several purposes and played several training roles — e.g. Coomaraswamy argues that repetition trained the concentration. By way of illustration he draws upon the learning of concentration in the "atmosphere of Hindu culture." "A part of the *sandhyā* or daily prayer of the Hindus," he argues, "consists in the mental repetition of certain prayers (*mantras*) a certain number of times" (108 times in many cases he says). Though this could easily convert itself into a "mind-deadening mechanical process" a careful guard was taken against such a degeneration and the exercise was turned instead into a "good practice in concentration." The counting was insisted upon, for it was believed that "repetition without keeping count leads to mental vacuity" and the keeping of count while repeating was itself a mental gymnastic of no mean measure. "Let anyone," Coomaraswamy challenges his readers in support of the dexterity he says is needed to count and repeat, "try to repeat any two lines of poetry exactly 108 times, and see whether it does not require mental concentration to do it without failure." Counting along with repetition was not all that there was to the process, Coomaraswamy points out that certain "physical practices, especially that of breathing, retaining and expelling the breath, while prayers are repeated a certain number of times had to be simultaneously followed" and this could certainly not be done "without intense attention." The aim was to throw the whole mind →

was useful in only as much as it aided and promoted the rise and assimilation of that meaning — a concept quite different, it appears, from the present method of rote-learning and memorisation in order to pass through a standardised system of examination. Obvious similarities and inspirations are evident in Sri Aurobindo's highlighting the triple method of the ancient system and the classical evidences of the same in ancient Indian educational discourse. The ancient Indian system, it appears, insisted on the learner's understanding of the deeper underlying meaning of the text in order to complete the process of internalising them. The first step thus was undoubtedly the committing of texts to memory. "There was a method by which the teacher recited the texts. He recited them in the form of metres, pronouncing every letter, syllable, and word according to standardised rules regulating accent and stresses and giving scope to the vibrations of every sound so as to call up its inner sense." The learner, initially, had to follow the method with "mechanical precision and monotony, like a body of "croaking frogs." But the mastery of the texts was "only the first step of learning. The more important step was the mastery of meaning," mastery of text (*akṣara-prāpti*) had to be followed by *artha-bodha* (perception of meaning). For one who was a *kevalapāṭhaka* (mere crammer) the texts did indeed become a burden.[31] Sri Aurobindo too emphasises the

→ into the effort of worship and not approach the exercise in a "slovenly fashion," there had to evolve a *saṅkalpa* (resolve) to perform the *sandhyā* and on a "strong determination of the mental effort [depended] the efficacy of the worship." The repetition thus of the name during the prayer had to have the active mind behind it and if the "mind is not put into the act, it is done mechanically and loses half its value." [Coomaraswamy , op. cit., pp. 123-24.] Repetition thus was never an isolated process only to serve the purpose of retention, in fact, it may be argued that the concept of examination and testing itself was perhaps structurally and conceptually different in the ancient context and was nowhere similar to its modern colonially engineered counterpart.

31. Mookerjee, op. cit., pp. 35-36.

point that a "mechanical repetition was not likely to produce" the effect of the word gradually becoming self-evident.[32] The argument may, of course, be forwarded that the system faced eventual erosion and deteriorated into a mechanical habit. But the following argument too, that the habit of memorising without comprehensively internalising the meaning was a unique contribution made to Indian society by the colonial system of education, which inaugurated the system of examinations, has its merits. A centralised examination system required students to "rehearse endlessly the skills of reproduction from memory, summarising, and essay-type writing on any topic. Students were examined on their study of specific texts, not on their understanding of concepts or problems."[33] The pressure of examinations and the demands of meritoriously passing in them eventually sidelined the teacher, who merely became the executor of the textbook's will and vanquished her/his capacity to innovate, originate and enliven the process of learning.[34] Thus repetition in the classical Indian educational context had a much wider connotation and did not appear to be the dominant element useful only for information storing but was rather looked upon as an important aid towards evolving a genuine understanding of the topic or word discussed.

And how would the focus, the contemplation on the word — that would eventually help in revealing the meaning — be effectuated? Along with the *āvṛtti* of the *śabda*, *dhyāna* (meditation) "that clear still receptivity and that waiting upon the word or thing with the contemplative part of the mind"

32. *CWSA* vol. 1, p. 374.

33. Krishna Kumar, "Origins of the Textbook Culture" in *What is Worth Teaching*, 2004, p. 31.

34. For this argument see, e.g. Krishna Kumar, *Political Agenda of Education: A Study of Colonialist and Nationalist Ideas*, New Delhi: Sage, 2nd edn. 2005.

must also occur.[35] This was emphasised by the ancient system too. Sri Aurobindo places here a concrete example of the effect of *dhyāna* in the entire process of evoking the meaning, an observation that must have remained with him from the Baroda period (1893-1906) when he spent long hours of study. "All of us have felt," he writes, "when studying a language, difficulties which seemed insoluble while grappling with a text, suddenly melt away and a clear understanding arise without assistance from book or teacher after putting away the book from our mind for a brief period." He extends the experience to learning of languages,

> Many of us have experienced also, the strangeness of taking up a language or subject, after a brief discontinuance, to find that we understand it much better than when we took it up, know the meaning of words we had never met before and can explain sentences which, before we discontinued the study, would have baffled our understanding.

Such a manifestation of understanding is possible, he observes, "because the *jñātā* or knower within has had his attention called to the subject and has been busy in the interval drawing upon the source of knowledge within in connection with it." One whose sāttvic element has been greatly aroused and trained is capable of such an experience.[36] Thus adhering to his position that the ancient believed knowledge and illumination to be intrinsic, Sri Aurobindo argues that they had also drawn up certain methods and practices which could empirically demonstrate the validity of that belief.

35. Or as Ananda Coomaraswamy puts it while discussing memory in education ". . . all knowledge is founded on a knowledge of the self. How is this self to be controlled and focused? Only by the power of concentration, the capacity for fixing the attention of the whole mind for more than a brief moment upon a single aim or thought . . ." As an example he points to the *Mahābhārata* episode of Arjuna describing "a bird's head, and in that head only the eye." (op. cit., pp. 122-23.)

36. *CWSA*, vol. 1, pp. 374-75.

The ultimate expressions of an advanced sāttvic development, Sri Aurobindo concludes, are witnessed when the learner dispenses "often or habitually with outside aids, the teacher or the textbook, grammar and dictionary and learn a subject largely or wholly from within" but such a possibility visited only the *yogī* through a "successful prosecution of the discipline of Yoga." He was quite frank though that the majority was never expected to rise to this level of self-education.[37] The result of this placing of energies at the "service of the brain" Sri Aurobindo argues had far-reaching results, the training of *brahmacarya* "not only strengthened the *medhā* (grasping power), the *dhi* (subtlety) and swiftness of thought conception, the memory and the creative intellectual force" and made comprehensive and analytic the "triple force of memory, invention [and] judgement." The range of the mind was greatly enlarged as was strengthened its "absorbing, storing and generative mental activities" and this enabled it to accomplish those extraordinary "feats of memory, various comprehensions and versatility of creative work" such as was achieved by only a few "extraordinary intellects" in the West. In ancient India these achievements were common. In keeping with the spirit of the age when a process of self-examination and re-evaluation was in the process inspired and expedited by the nationalist movement, Sri Aurobindo draws a parallel with Gladstone (1809-1989)[38] who "was considered to be the possessor of an

37. Ibid., p. 375. Jugal Kishore Mukherjee cites this as one of the examples of evoking knowledge from within; he refers to this passage and indicates this to be the "beneficial result of the process" of evocation. (op. cit., p. 12.) What remains un-elucidated though is the actual process of evoking the knowledge within. Sri Aurobindo in the above passage indicates a certain outline of that process inspired from the classical Indian educational thought and method.

38. Homer seems to have been a constant companion of William Gladstone, four times British prime minister. In fact, his political biographers have dwelt on this aspect of his life — a near inseparable link and association with the Homerian world. Amidst his political →

astonishing memory because he could repeat the whole of Homer's *Iliad*, beginning from any passage suggested to him and flowing on as long as required" but such a capacity Sri Aurobindo argued was quite commonplace in ancient India and would be considered by the brāhmaṇa of old to be a capacity "neither unusual nor astonishing, but rather, petty and limited."

The ordinary, general curriculum of that age had a certain universality, "it was for every student and not for the exceptional few, and it implied, not a tasting of many subjects after the modern plan, but a thorough mastery of all."[39] Sri Aurobindo was to go back to this theme of his in the series on education where he denounces the modern practice of teaching by "snippets."[40] Further discussing the achievements of the

→ struggles gladstone found time to dwell and contemplate on Homer. "He was," writes Richard Shannon in his *Gladstone-II: 1865-1898* (University of North Carolina Press, 1999) "nursing a plan to produce a revised edition of his *Studies on Homer of 1858*." He started work on this plan in 1867 and would eventually complete it in 1869 as *Juventus Mundi: The Gods and Men of the Heroic Age* (p. 44). In fact, such an obsession or release was Homer for Gladstone that one sees Shannon quoting his relieved exclamation, "worked 6½ hours on Homeric primer. What a treat!" (p. 218.) During most of Sri Aurobindo's stay in England Gladstone dominated the political scene as prime minister, his feats of memory must have already become part of the lore by then!

39. *CWSA*, vol. 1, pp. 376-77.

40. "A remarkable feature of modern training which has," he castigates, "been subjected in India to a *reductio ad absurdum*. . . . A subject is taught a little at a time, in conjunction with a host of others, with the result that what might be well learnt in a single year is badly learnt in seven and the boy goes out ill-equipped, served with imperfect parcels of knowledge, master of none of the great departments of human knowledge." In the same piece he accuses the National Council of heightening this practice by following the method at start and the middle and then without sufficient preparation exposing the learner to a "grandiose specialism at the top." (*CWSA*, vol. 1, p. 393 (*A System of National Education: Some Preliminary Ideas*).

Indian mind and genius, which at that period was necessitated in order to reinstate the nation's faith in its intellectual prowess and performance — past and future — he talks of the "original achievements of a Kālidāsa accomplishing the highest in every line of poetic creation . . . paralleled in the arena of philosophy by Śaṅkara in a short lifespan of thirty-two years" and points to the "universal mastery of all possible spiritual knowledge and experience of Sri Ramakriṣhna" and says that these were instances of pure creative genius, examples of what the Indian mind, in its supreme capacity, was essentially capable of. Though these instances were not "so common as others" in Europe such parallels were "with a single modern exception, non-existent." In Europe the excelling has been in "one field of a single intellectual province or at most in two" whereas in India it is the "greatest who have been the most versatile and passed from one field of achievement to another" with easy and unfaltering mastery. The many-sided genius of the Indian mind was made possible because of the practice of *brahmacarya* which "developed *sattva* or inner illumination." This inner illumination made the "acquisition of knowledge" and all other intellectual operations and performances "easy, spontaneous, swift, decisive and comparatively unfatiguing to body or brain." Thus, Sri Aurobindo argues in conclusion, that it was finally *brahmacarya* and the sāttvic development that held the secret of ancient Indian "intellectual achievement"; it were these, he argued, that "created the brain of India."

Having thus discussed the psychological principles, Sri Aurobindo brings up current problems and questions of education and one sees that the issues remain contemporary even 100 years later. He accepts the common complaint that students "are too heavily burdened with many subjects and the studying of many books" but points to what he perceives to be the other truth that the "range of studies is pitifully narrow and the books read miserably few" and the reason for this paradox is that the creation of the base is neglected — the young mind being exposed to "snippet" education — and the foundation thus remains weak and unable to bear even the "paltry and meagre edifice of our imparted knowledge." And then follows a severe indictment of the effects of a colonial education on the Indian mind which is "still in potentiality what it was" but is being gradually "damaged, stunted and defaced." "The greatness of its innate possibilities is hidden by the greatness of its surface deterioration."[41] One of the chief causes of this deterioration and damage was — as nationalist educators constantly argued — "study in a foreign language which was not even imperfectly mastered at a time when the student was called upon to learn in that impossible medium a variety of alien and unfamiliar subjects."[42] The vernacular versus foreign tongue evoked much emotion and

41. *A System of National Education: Some Preliminary Ideas*, p. 377.

42. Sri Aurobindo had been highlighting this issue since his early days in India, his assessment of Bankim Chandra Chattopadhyay where he emphasises the imperativeness of an education that was rooted to the learner's surrounding and to his vernacular. [*CWSA* vol. 1, "Bankim Chandra Chatterjee." The pieces on Bankim appeared in seven instalments in the *Indu Prakash* a leading Marathi-English weekly of Bombay, between July and August 1894.] Sri Aurobindo also spoke for it in a scheme of national education, insisting that "one who has mastered his own language, has one very necessary facility for mastering another [and] with the linguistic faculty unsatisfactorily developed in one's own tongue, to master others is impossible" and therefore the mother tongue was the "proper medium of instruction" and the child's initial energies had to be directed towards its mastery. (*CWSA* vol. 1, p. 394.) He raised this issue as a vital component of the nationalist education discourse. The continuity of his tilt and support for the vernacular is evident in his "Preface on National Education" written decades later in 1920-21 where he supports the need for learning Sanskrit — he did not give up the language as impeding the growth of a scientific temper — through a method that was "most natural, efficient and stimulating to the mind," there was no necessity to cling "to any past or present manner of teaching." But the vital question was, as he saw it, how was Sanskrit and other indigenous languages to be →

debate, since the question was one of adequate self-expression and the medium of that self-expression was to be one that would facilitate and promote it. Sri Aurobindo was one among the principal Indian thought leaders to have dwelt on this aspect, his perception of this need and its importance in shaping the Indian mind had developed since his return to India. Sir Gurudas Banerjee had already presented the argument in his note on the vernacular language as the vehicle of education submitted to the Indian Universities Commission in 1902. "Teaching," he argued, "specially during the earlier stages of a student's progress, must be easier and more rapid if it can be conducted through the medium of his vernacular, because in that case, as a rule, the only unknown matters to be made known will be the things and thoughts connected

→ used to "get to the heart and intimate sense of our own culture and establish a vivid continuity between the still living power of our past and the yet uncreated power of our future." There was no segregation in the approach, it was not to be a total reverting to the past nor a complete rupture with it. Instead, the use of the indigenous tongues was to serve as a bridge. In a stance that indicated a greater global approach, an evolving internationalism in his thoughts that negated a narrow isolationist spirit, Sri Aurobindo also includes in the vital question the issue of the role that English or for that matter any other foreign language were to play in the new educational outlook. Training in these languages would enable one to "know helpfully the life, ideas and culture of other countries and establish our right relations with the world around us." He now saw national education as accepting the role of the foreign tongue, a tongue that would not dominate but would facilitate a cultural and ideational exchange. This was to be the principal aim of a "true national education" one that did not ignore, overlook or refuse "modern truth and knowledge" while taking along one's own "foundation," "being," "mind" [and] "spirit" [*CWSA*, vol. 1, p. 421]. The philosophical basis of the national education quest could perhaps be located in these lines, it came years after the storm of political activism had abated in Sri Aurobindo's life.

with the different subjects of study, and not also the words and sentences which express them. . . ."[43]

The two contemporary minds with whom we are concerned because of their links to Sri Aurobindo also saw this necessity and were vocal in its promotion realising its indispensability in re-creating the Indian mind. Coomaraswamy, for example, brings out a fundamental problem in education in India — though not referring directly in this instance to the medium of instruction through English — he however points towards a more deep-seated and connected or resultant problem, that of Indian students being instructed by Englishmen. Men who, he argued, could never really be "true educators of the Indian people" because of their inability to not only inherit Indian indigenous traditions but also to evolve a "spirit of perfect reverence for those traditions." He saw the necessity for the English professor to undertake a rigorous, assiduous and "sympathetic study of Indian religious philosophy, Sanskrit or Pāli, some vernacular language, Indian history, [including the period when the "ideals of Indian civilisation" saw expression] art, music, literature and etiquette" in order to enable himself to understand the problems of Indian education. Such a study, Coomaraswamy argued, would develop an understanding in him and would make him less inclined to interfere in the Indian ideals "for he would be either Indianised at heart, or would have long realised the hopeless divergence between his own and Indian ideals."[44] But the prevailing system did not encourage or allow the undertaking of such a study, and English teachers, he lamented, "have neither the time nor the

43. *Report of the Indian Universities Commission, 1902, Vol. 5, Miscellaneous Papers* cited in Sabyasachi Bhattacharya et al. (eds.), *Educating the Nation: Documents on the Discourse of National Education in India: 1880-1920, 2003*, pp. 187-88.

44. Coomaraswamy, op. cit., p. 100.

inclination to spend 10 years, or even two, in such a study of Indian culture." The stark manifestations of such an omission are apparent when rapidly elevated to positions of power and eminence in the education system in India they [English instructors] doggedly attempt to apply solutions best suited to an English environment to the Indian educational issues and problems.[45] Two contemporaries writing around the same time (1909) highlighted a crucial issue in the nationalist education debate and discussed it from two separate angles — one directly referring to the ineligibility of English as the predominant medium of educational instruction in a country where the vernacular continued to make sense to the vast majority and the other pointing to the disconnected Englishman as a teacher unsuccessfully trying to communicate in and impose a foreign medium and system to vastly different Indian conditions and situations.

Sister Nivedita considers the language of a people to be their "highest and most spiritual" creation. The deepest of a nation and race is expressed through it, "In this is expressed the soul of nations." The Indian thought world, the Indian vision world best expressed itself through the vernacular. She takes the debate to the ideational level and sees the vernacular medium as the best means to penetrate and assimilate Indian thought, philosophy and way of life. "As one studies an Indian vernacular," she observes, "the vastness and distinctiveness of the Indian dream-world continually grows on one. First there are the philosophical ideas which give its tone to dream.

45. Ibid., p. 101. Coomaraswamy thus saw quite early the imperativeness of taking control of the educational scheme if freedom in the actual sense of the term was to be achieved. "The control of Indian education," he foresaw, "is of so much importance that the necessity of gaining this would alone justify the present endeavours to attain political freedom." (p. 188.) The basic argument in favour of control of the education by the nationalist leaders was with this objective — its control would in a sense provide an intellectual shape and direction to the movement.

Then there is the great gallery of ideal characters of which every Indian child by birth is made a freeman. . . ."[46] It was this vast repository of Indian traditional knowledge that was missed out through a forced foreign medium. In her "Hints on National Education in India" discussing "the Place of Foreign Culture in a True Education" Nivedita appears to be quite categorical with the foreign instructional element. In her characteristically vigorous tone she observes that a mind at an initiation stage fed on "foreign knowledge and ideas" is not rooted upon and bound by a "sense of intimacy" with its own surroundings, tradition and psyche and becomes like the "waif brought up in the stranger's home. The waif may behave well and reward his benefactor" but this would be forced from a mental sense of duty rather than love. Then in words strikingly similar to those expressed by Sri Aurobindo in the pages of the *Karmayogin* insisting that the child be engaged first with his surroundings and with the land and soil of his birth and growth, she observes that

> In a true education the place of foreign culture is never at the beginning [and that] all true development must proceed from the known to the unknown, from the familiar to the unfamiliar, from the near to the far.[47]

---

46. Sister Nivedita, *The Mediaeval University of India,* p. 340.

47. *CWSN*, vol. 4, "The Place of Foreign Culture in a True Education" in *Hints on National Education in India*, 1996, pp. 354-55. The similarity of approach to the problem is also evident in Sri Aurobindo, who during the period of his educational writings had close interactions and co-ordination with Nivedita. Enunciating his third principle of education Sri Aurobindo felt the need to give the child a measured exposure, one that would be from the "near to the far, from that which is to that which shall be." The intrinsic relevance and inseparability in an individual's pattern of growth of his surroundings, nationality, country, sustaining soil, the "air which he breathes, the sights, sounds [and] habits to which he is accustomed" can never be brushed aside, they form a vital part of the child's growth and mental evolution. (*CWSA*, vol. 1. pp. 384-85) Interestingly Coomaraswamy in his essays during the period →

The learner thus was being disassociated from his life and moorings and therefore the nationalist demand for the vernacular as the best suited medium for the Indian student. In fact, all three, though trained in the Western educational pattern, felt the overdose of the foreign exposure on the Indian mind, especially, perhaps, the bewildering impact it had on the young Indian unfamiliar with the urbanised surroundings and ways.

The primary concern was that the Indian mind, as Nivedita saw it, was losing its native land and this was mainly because of the "unprecedented influx of foreign knowledge and foreign criticism, from the early decades of the nineteenth century onwards," an influx that Nivedita believed lost to the country "many a mind and many a character that should have been

---

→ [discussed above] also refers to the same issue using similar expressions, stressing the point that a people's intelligence could be developed "primarily only by means of education in the national culture." He argues that it was essential that one understands first that "with which [one is] already familiar before it is possible to understand the unfamiliar, and relate it to one's life." An imitation without understanding and without relating to one's surroundings results in vulgarity. (Coomaraswamy, op. cit., p. 193.) The foreign medium of instruction and the practice of describing foreign scenes and subjects and the forced imitation it generated stunted free thinking and imagination and dislocated the young mind from his surroundings. Young Abanindranath Tagore (1871-1951), later to become the leader of the nationalist art movement in Bengal, recalled how in his childhood while being educated at home he was surrounded "with pictures of all kinds mostly Victorian" and how his impression of "rustic cottages" were engendered by English picture books. It was not until his first visit to rural Bengal, where he saw peasant dwellings "did he realise how different they were from the ones known to him." (Partha Mitter, *Art and Nationalism in Colonial India: 1850-1922*, 1994, p. 272.) The colonial system through a foreign medium, expression and imagery sought to delink the Indian mind from his native life and living. This was the basic point that the three contemporaries under study, deeply concerned with the idea of a national education, were making.

amongst the noblest of her sons."[48] The idea was to stem that "brain drain" and to recreate, reignite and reformulate the cultural identity which was essential to redefining the nation — an education in a foreign medium right from its early stages they saw was impeding this process. The essence of the issue was either the unwillingness or inability — both effects of a foreign medium — to develop a deep and intimate understanding of the Indian ethos and because the struggle was to create and weld a nation it was indispensable to train the Indian mind to at least know what is one's own and for that the familiar, the known had to be first re-introduced in an education that called itself national. When she wrote that "In all directions we find that only when deeply rooted in the familiar, we may safely take up the unfamiliar [and] in proportion as we rightly analyse the known, rightly distinguishing, even in what is familiar, between the ideal expressed and the form assumed, in that proportion will it open for us the book of the whole world" she was making a plain case not only for the promotion of the vernacular but at a deeper level for retraining the Indian mind to be at ease with the Indian traditions. Such a knowledge and training was an essential prerequisite if the newly forming nation was to assume a certain position in the larger world community an event that they felt, freedom would eventually usher in. For such a co-equal status it was essential to love what is one's own and more importantly to actually know what is one's own and one who is incapable of doing this or has neglected its practice "will never be received by any people as anything more than half a man,"[49] true co-equality shall remain forever elusive.

The Indian brain thus to continue with Sri Aurobindo's argument, "in this unnatural process" [that of having to learn

48. *CWSN*, vol. 4, pp. 358-59.

49. Ibid., p. 357.

a wide variety of unfamiliar subjects in an "impossible medium"] was crippled by the disuse of judgment, observation, comprehension and creation" and the habit of an unthinking memorisation developed. Sri Aurobindo terms it an "exclusive reliance on the deteriorating relics of the ancient Indian memory." It is to be noted that he criticises whatever expressions remain of the ancient knowledge of using memory for education, a knowledge which by his time appeared to be losing all inner significance and focus. Finally, exposed to the colonial education methods, the Indian mind was "beggared and degraded" and had to contend with "snippets [a word that appears to describe the exact method followed by the colonial education system while imparting education and a word that Sri Aurobindo uses repeatedly] and insufficient packets of information instead of being richly stored and powerfully equipped."[50]

The national education experiment in Bengal, Sri Aurobindo continues, tried to undo the degenerative evil "by employing the mother tongue," and attempted to encourage and restore the intellectual functions and also tried to provide "a richer and more real equipment of information." But in this it achieved limited success because the teachers and directors themselves of this new educational experiment were "minds already vitiated by the old system and not often with the best even of these." One more negative point was that the teachers "had themselves seldom a perfect grasp of the requirements of the new system." And the educational system itself, Sri Aurobindo complains, while terming itself national "neglected the very foundation of the great achievement of our forefathers and especially the perfection of the instrument of knowledge."[51] But the observations come with the

50. *CWSA*, vol. 1, p. 378. For the expression of "snippets" vide *CWSA*, vol. 1, "Simultaneous and Successive Teaching," p. 393.

51. Ibid., p. 378.

clarification — perhaps to stall any effort or demand that talks of a fallback to past systems — that the contention is not "that the actual system of ancient instruction be restored in its outward features. . . . Many of them are not suited to modern requirements." But the argument is instead that the ancient system had certain fundamental principles that remain for all times and such a discipline could only be replaced by the "discovery of a still more effective discipline" which Western education was incapable of formulating. How the ideas or discipline of the ancient could be reapplied to the present, Sri Aurobindo does not discuss, perhaps he intended doing it sometime in the future and would have done so had the exigencies of politics and yoga not taken him along a different and unchartered route.

He explains thus certain principles of the ancient Indian education system, as he perceived it, and analyses some of the system's dominant psychological principles and practices which prepared the learner to excel and exceed assigning a wholly deeper meaning and significance, as compared to the then prevailing situation, to the term "education." Such an education had the development and evolution of the individual at the centre of its schemes. The write-up was also basically a case for developing the people's intelligence "through the medium of their own national culture."[52] And in that national culture the ancient principles of education — and not their now near defunct forms — formed an important and intrinsic part. In a sense, the contestation covered above was a call to recognise and reapply those principles to present conditions. Sri Aurobindo thus did discuss and engage himself with classical Indian educational concepts and principles and was concerned with the possibility of re-applying these to modern conditions and systems.

52. Coomaraswamy, op. cit., p. 106.

On Restoring the Artistic Emotion: The Value of Art in a Scheme of National Education

The other vital subject that Sri Aurobindo addresses in the arena of education and one that falls within his non-political writings and discussions of the issue is that of art, a necessity of training in aesthetics and its centrality in a scheme of national education. The researcher undertaking a study of Sri Aurobindo's thoughts and writings has to contend with the fact that Sri Aurobindo tackles a wide number of aspects even in the educational argument — one sees him discussing the political, technical, historical and philosophical as well as aesthetic aspects of the discourse. It is rather difficult to discuss all these facets of the arguments in detail within the constraints of the given space. Nevertheless Sri Aurobindo's observations on the necessity of an art-training, developing the aesthetical layer of the individual and placing this area of educational training in prominence in the national education scheme do deserve a reading however brief and cursory.

Sri Aurobindo's commentaries on what he termed "The National Value of Art" appeared in six instalments in his newly created thought-vehicle *Karmayogin* between November and December 1909. The Empire's Asian capital, Calcutta, had by this time emerged as the centre of the "Nationalist Art Movement" and become a remarkable arena for the growth and evolution of an "ideology of Swadeshi art."[53] It was but natural that Sri Aurobindo turned his attention to this important instrument of nationality formation and consolidation. He saw the inclusion of art-training in the national education curricula as essential for forging the

53. See, e.g. Elleke Boehmer, *Empire, the National and the Post-Colonial: 1890-1920-Resistance in Interaction*, New York: Oxford University Press, 2002; Partha Mitter, op. cit., and Sankariprasad Basu, *Nivedita Lokmata*, vol. 4, Kolkata: Ananda Publishers, Beng. 1401, for a detailed treatment of the nationalist art movement in India.

ideational unity between the individual's inner and outer personalities. The surface necessity was the regeneration of pride in the ever-living Indian forms of artistic expression, then clouded by a plethora of dominant Western artistic methods, techniques and manifestations. The inner, much deeper objective was to re-establish a link with the soul of the nation. The medium of art was felt to be one of the most credible and reliable instruments towards reviving that link.

Art as an Agent of National Unity and as a Restorer of the Racial Artistic Emotion

Sri Aurobindo participated in the movement encouraging its alternative forms of expressions and supporting the Indian nationalist effort to reclaim the field. The other two minds, whose ideas on the national education question we have begun examining, were themselves vigorous participants in this movement of nationalist art and were firm believers in the capacity of art to forge a new national mind and in the ineluctability of a training in art and aesthetics as part of the new national education. Sri Aurobindo had indicated earlier in the very pages of the *Karmayogin* that a "national awakening" which works itself out within a narrow or single confine can never be "vital and enduring." His contention was that the awakening of the national soul would express itself in manifold forms of expression themselves the manifestation of the "strength and the delight of the expansive spirit within."[54] In recognition of that manifold expression he threw his weight behind the Indian nationalist art movement and also argued in favour of trying to encourage the growth of a national aesthetics. His support for the new art movement was evident in the pages of the weekly where he highlighted not only its various facets and its place in the new awakening but also spoke in favour of those attempting to support and

54. *CWSA*, vol. 8, "The Awakening Soul of India, 26 June 1909", p. 63.

disseminate its ideas and expressions. Sri Aurobindo saw this awakening of the national soul in religion as a precursor to the awakening in a wider sphere of intellectual and cultural activities. He saw the religious awakening taking place, as he lyrically put it referring to Sri Ramakrishna, when "the flower of the educated youth of Calcutta bowed down at the feet of an illiterate Hindu ascetic, a self-illumined ecstatic and "mystic" without a single trace or touch of the alien thought or education upon him" — he saw this moment as announcing the triumph of the religious soul of India.[55] It was this churning of the religious mind in a new direction which not only revived certain robustness in the faith but also encouraged a wider quest in other areas of national activity and expressions.

Referring to these other activities Sri Aurobindo saw the needs of a religious and political life as eventually remoulding the national life in all its spheres. He saw the influence already at work in the sphere of art and literature and sought to strengthen its presence. In Bengal, *inter alia*, he saw the national spirit seeking to "satisfy itself in art and, for the first time since the decline of the Moguls, a new school of national art" with Abanindranath Tagore as "founder and master" developing itself. Though still influenced at times by foreign "though Asiatic" elements the new school was trying to express and work on the basic tenet of Indian art which was the effort to "express in form and limit something of that which is formless and illimitable."[56] The pages of the *Karmayogin* also began carrying his appreciations of recent paintings and current techniques of expressions.[57] At the same time appreciating the efforts of other nationalist journals in regularly doing the same he observes that by featuring prints of Indian paintings

55. *CWSA*, vol. 8, p. 62.

56. Ibid., pp. 63-64.

57. See, e.g. his write-ups on art and art appreciation in *CWSA*, vol. 1, pp. 455-64.

produced by the new school in Bengal and by others they were rendering a vital service to national regeneration. Talking of the efforts of the *Modern Review*, then just launched (1907) by the formidable Ramananda Chatterji (1865-1943)[58] and "quickly [to emerge] as a vital forum for the nationalist

58. Ramananda Chatterji was closely associated with the nationalists and was at times called upon to preside over their public meetings. He presided over at least one large public meeting held on 13 June 1909 at Beadon square in north Calcutta which had Sri Aurobindo as the main speaker. Keeping in mind that this was a phase when the revolutionary nationalists were facing severe administrative repression, Chatterji's presence at the meeting was significant. Referring to his ceaseless promotion of Indianness Sri Aurobindo called him an "indefatigable literary and patriotic worker" who was "well known to the Bengali public as a clear-minded, sober and fearless political speaker and writer." Among the many services Chatterji was rendering to his nation, his latest "introducing the masterpieces of the new school of Art to his readers" was, Sri Aurobindo felt, a "yet more valuable and lasting service to his country." [*CWSA*, vol. 1, p. 460.] In fact, Chatterji who had long been in search of an agent that would "bind the fissiparous languages and cultures of India" saw art as "a universal language" that offered him that opportunity. The binding through literature was hampered due to the inadequacy of translations, he saw instead the medium of visual arts as offering that scope. He saw in the revival of "artistic activity" a "factor silently making for national unity." [Partha Mitter, op.cit., p. 223.] The championing thus of the new school assumed urgency and reproduction in the pages of his journal facilitated and encouraged that silent unifying factor. It can be said that Sri Aurobindo too saw this unifying utility of the art movement and thus supported it. Nivedita had discussed in the pages of the *Modern Review* "The Function of Art in Shaping Nationality" indicating her collaboration with the editor in trying to discover and project art as a unifying agent of nationality. "Art . . . is charged," she declared in the piece, "with a spiritual message — in India today, the message of the Nationality." It had to be then pursued "like science, like education, like industry, like trade itself" with the sole objective of "remaking of the Motherland" and for no other aim". [*CWSN*, vol. 3, 2000, p. 14.] Coomaraswamy was as categorical on the issue, "nations are made by artists and by poets, not by traders and politicians" he declared and "it was by becoming artists and poets and by beginning again to understand "our own art and poetry" →

intelligentsia"[59] and its sister Bengali magazine *Prabasi,* Sri Aurobindo observes that the reviews by reproducing every month some work of art by contemporary Indian painter and by bringing them to thousands who had no opportunity to see the original were "restoring the sense of beauty and artistic emotion inborn in our race but almost blotted out by the long reign in our lives of the influence of Anglo-Saxon vulgarity and crude tasteless commercialism."[60] Implied in the statement was an attack on the official education system which seemed to encourage this tasteless commercialism. Most of the pictures he saw reproduced belonged to the "new school of Bengali art" which he saw as the only "living and original school now developing among us." Thus Sri Aurobindo's interest in art-training and his deliberations on its value in a national scheme of education does not seem to have suddenly cropped up nor was it isolated from his vision of national regeneration, it was part of the tradition that had by then (1906-09) made a space for itself in the national movement. In the regeneration, education was to play one of the most vital parts, not only would it lead to liberation, it would prepare the people to organise that liberation and an important component of this regeneration was the restoration of the "sense of beauty and artistic emotion inborn in [the] race." This is perhaps what led Sri Aurobindo to elaborate his thoughts on training in aesthetics for the nation.

The demand for including art-training in education had already been taken up by those who were directly involved

→ that one could attain the highest ideal of nationality . . ." [Coomaraswamy, op. cit., preface pp. i, ii.] Coomaraswamy was not advocating a soft approach to the issue of subjection but was rather pointing to the method that needed to be adopted to ward off the debilitating effects of a deeply entrenched cultural colonialism.

59. Ramachandra Guha, The Independent Journal of Opinion, *Seminar,* 481, 1999.

60. *CWSA,* vol. 1, p. 455.

in the revival of the Indian art movement. One Shyamacharan Srimani had set the pace early by producing a slim volume on *The Rise of the Fine Arts and the Artistic Skills of the Aryans* as far back as 1874. The work adjudged as an important "marker in the growth of cultural nationalism," was the "first history of art written in Bengali" and was looked upon as an early nationalist work.[61] E.B. Havell (1861-1934), one of the leading lights and voices calling for an Indian art and one who was instrumental in influencing the young Abanindranath — soon to lead the nationalist art movement — to turn towards and revive the Indian art forms had as early as 1901 urged the Congress leaders [in India] to "take a broader perspective and integrate art more fully into their national programme." Pursuing the same agenda he had published in 1903 an "Open Letter to Educated Indians" castigating them "for their indifference to their own art."[62] He argued in his essays on "Art and Education in India" (1901) that from a political standpoint it was not "a small thing that the artistic sentiment of the Indian peoples [was] being extinguished under our [British] rule," an argument that was to find echo nearly a decade later in Sri Aurobindo's writings on the issue. Havell saw the need of the people to be devoted to art, that devotion he saw as being erased by colonial rule. "A people devoted to art are a happy and contented people. A people without art are restless and unhappy"[63] was perhaps the reading that compelled him to take a hands-on approach to bring back the arts to the people. Similar to what Sri Aurobindo perceived Havell too saw India "as the only part of the British Empire where the aesthetic sense of the people, in spite of all that British philistinism has done to suppress it, [still] strongly

61. Partha Mitter, op. cit., p. 224.

62. Ibid., p. 251.

63. E.B. Havell, "Art and Education in India" in *Indian Art, Industry and Education*, 1901, p. 137.

influences their everyday life."[64] Therefore there had to be a national effort at restoring and preserving that sense. Sri Aurobindo stressed the necessity of this restoration too, for he lamented that the age was "bent on depriving life of its meaning by turning earth into a sort of glorified antheap" and that the value the ancients attached "to music, art and poetry has become almost unintelligible" to it.[65] The nationalist art movement attracted some of the most dynamic minds of the Swadeshi period and the triumvirate comprising Havell, Nivedita and Coomaraswamy were the ideologues of the nationalist art movement with Havell furnishing the

---

64. Ibid., p. 91. Sri Aurobindo beginning his series on "The National Value of Art" argues similarly that in modern times the tendency to "depreciate the value of the beautiful and overstress the value of the useful" is limited in India — a country and race subjected to a "mercenary and soulless education" that had cut it off from all its "ancient roots of culture and tradition" — only by the temperament of the people in which the "stress of imagination, emotion and spiritual delicacy" was "submerged but not yet destroyed." [*CWSA*, vol. 1, p. 433.] In his series on Indian art while defending Indian culture and discussing the Indian Renaissance, Sri Aurobindo refers to Havell and Coomaraswamy as the eminent two who had already done a considerable amount of work to clear away the "misconceptions about Indian sculpture and painting." While accepting during this period that a change in perception of Indian art had set in, Sri Aurobindo felt that the change had not yet gone far enough to develop a "thorough appreciation of the deepest and most characteristic spirit and inspiration of Indian work" [and that] "an eye or an effort like Havell's [was] still rare." [*CWSA*, vol. 20, pp. 254, 260.] Sri Aurobindo held the ideologues of the nationalist art movement in great esteem and valued their pioneering service towards the awakening of the national soul.
65. Ibid. According to Coomaraswamy, who discerned the "essential error in modern Indian education [by government/Anglicised Indians] [as the] refusal or inability to recognise any responsibility to the past". This break in the continuity of the historical tradition, [and the inability to understand it anymore would prove to be] fatal to Indian culture. [Coomaraswamy, op. cit., p. 186.]

"aesthetic," Nivedita providing the "moral" and Coomaraswamy supplying the "metaphysical content" to the Swadeshi doctrine of art.[66] Sri Aurobindo by lending his moral support and authority to the aspiration gave it a greater fillip and sanction.

Sri Aurobindo wished to work towards the restoration of the aesthetic and artistic emotion in the people. The age and education had nearly eradicated that emotion and sense. The education imparted — which was mainly looked upon as a "passport to jobs" — had by its neglect of the art or refusal to recognise the possibilities of an Indian art, rather encouraged this intelligibility of its value. But in the onward march of the evolution of collective existence Sri Aurobindo perceives that "whole of humanity" had reached a stage where it now demands "not merely the satisfaction of the body, the *anna,* but the satisfaction also of the *prāṇa* and the *citta,* the vital and emotional desires."[67] The new education had to recognise that urge and integrate the new schools of art so as to satisfy that larger demand. We shall not enter here into the detailed analysis that Sri Aurobindo undertakes in the series on the evolution of collectivities and their psychological and emotional yearnings and predilections; it would suffice, for our purpose to pick out the passages which highlight the need for an aesthetic training, though it is true that the issue cannot be subjected to a piecemeal treatment. Sri Aurobindo identifies the "thought" as "the highest that man has attained" and it was through the power of thought that man sought to create a new society and break the old formation. He sees thought as having two discernible aspects, "two separate sides" — "judgement or reason and imagination" both of which were necessary to "perfect ideation."[68] Each of these separate sides

66. Partha Mitter, op. cit., p. 246.

67. *CWSA,* vol. 1, p. 434.

68. Ibid., p. 436.

manifested a certain aspect of human sphere of activity — the former worked through the areas of science, philosophy and criticism; the other unveiled itself through art, poetry and idealism. Sri Aurobindo sees these as undermining the old state of humanity and laying the foundations for the new. While the contributions of science have been widely recognised by the mass of humanity the "more subtle and profound" value of the other has been less recognised by mass of men because of the "less visible and sensational character of its working." It was this value that had to be stressed and upheld.[69] An opening of these areas would enable the mass-mind to undergo a process of *cittaśuddhi* "or purification of the *citta*, the mindstuff, from the *prāṇa* full of animal, vital and emotional disturbances." That the national education system was to focus on man-making aspect was considered to be vital by Sri Aurobindo. One does not see him getting into much of a discussion on the technicalities of the education system and the areas of reforms required. He was, during this period as to a large extent during others, concerned with its deeper psychological and emotional aspects. This is what leads him to enunciate the position that a cultivated eye without a cultivated spirit — by this he broadly meant the refining, sublimation and training of the emotional and sensational aspects of the personality — cannot make "the highest type of man." The cultivation of the spirit could be brought about precisely through the subjects of language, literature, the arts, music, painting, sculpture or the study of philosophy, religion, history all converging on "the study and understanding of man through his works and of Nature and man through the interpretative as well as through the analytical faculties." This was the goal of a liberal education."[70]

The power of the arts to develop certain higher faculties,

69. *CWSA*, vol. 1, p. 437.

70. Ibid., pp. 437-38.

to cultivate the spirit was clearly recognised by the ideologues of the movement; they did discuss the issue and sought to give the subject a place of prominence in the new educational scheme. Havell, invoking the Greek philosophers and the civilisation they ideated, pointed out that one must realise "that it is no real education which does not help to develop all the higher imaginative faculties." They were in agreement that this developing of the higher faculties was being impeded by the governmental education then imparted. "It is not education," Havell quite boldly remarked, "but the most pernicious pedantry, which uses Western culture to blind the eyes and stop the ears of Indian youth to all that the nature, the art, and the culture of their own country have to teach them."[71] Coomaraswamy discussing "Music and Education in India" where he touches upon the necessity and utility of an education in art and culture, similarly invokes Plato and his views on the utility and effectivity of music in education which ensured the entry of a harmony "in the strongest manner into the inward part of the soul." Coomaraswamy too recognises, like his other illustrious contemporaries and co-ideologues, that "English education, as hitherto imparted and understood in India, has merely ignored the importance of music and art in education." Unfortunately there was no educational institution in the country under European guidance where "Indian music has any place whatever in the scheme of education." And there was no Indian university that recognised Indian music.[72] That was because, as Nivedita quoted Havell, "we, aliens in race, thought and religion, have never taken anything but a dilettante archaeological or commercial interest in [Indian art]." And its deeper meanings remain "hidden from us, and those spiritual longings and desires which come straight from the heart of a people, to

71. Havell, op. cit., pp. 105, 108.

72. Coomaraswamy, op. cit., pp. 187-88.

find expression in their poetry, music, and their art, strike no chord of sympathy in ours."[73] All three, Coomaraswamy, Havell and Sri Aurobindo were to continue to defend Indian art and argue that India, especially Hindu and Buddhist traditions, did support art, had a magnificent tradition of art and emphasised the necessity of an art-training.[74] The activism and ideas were not confined simply to the political heyday; this was an interest that saw continuous expression.

---

73. *CWSN*, vol. 3, p. 22. Nivedita, of course, cautions against the tendency to believe that "merely because there still existed a living, traditional and national art" in the Indian polity, "every chance thought and impulse that comes to us artistically are divinely inspired in this matter. . . ." Just as in the art of logic so in the field of art, Nivedita advocated a stern and rigorous training in order to develop the right judgement and sense of appreciation. She saw the nation as going through the "least hopeful and most chaotic transition" in the field of art. "European Commercialism" had completely shaken to the roots the race's "decorative faculty." If the Indian mind were to emerge from this confusion a preparation must be initiated by "building up a great art on a basis of sincere admiration of the truly beautiful for true reasons." The nationalist art movement and its works such as Havell's facilitated the growth of the mind's capacity of admiration and of relating "itself to Indian art." [Ibid.] Nivedita was to remain "a mentor of the Bengali artist [and one of the major moving forces behind their efforts and in the dissemination of their productions] until her early death" in 1911. [Partha Mitter, op. cit., p. 255.]
74. Sri Aurobindo, writing later, devoted four chapters on Indian art in his essays on the Indian renaissance and Havell, in a later work, highlighted the "ancient Universities of Northern India and their influence on Asiatic Art" and discussed the art-training given in these ancient institutions and argued that the "essential faculties of the artist, imagination and memory [given primacy in the Eastern universities] are those which are least considered in the curriculum of modern European academies, where the paraphernalia of the studio are used to make up for the deficiencies in the mental equipment of the student." [E.B. Havell, *The Ideals of Indian Art*, 1920, p. 41.] Naturally an art-training that ignored the basic tenets of the Indian approach could never really restore the aesthetic emotion of the nation, what was needed was a different training inspired by the Indian traditions.

There was thus an established effort and Sri Aurobindo being part of that age and one of the centres of the nationalist vortex naturally delved deep into the issue. A gleaning of some of his thoughts in the series gives one an interesting insight into his thinking on the issue. Continuing with his discussion on the national value of art and of art-training for the Indian mind one finds him aware of the tendency that ignores art and poetry as mere luxuries of the "rich and leisurely" with no relevance and necessity to the "mass of men or useful to life." Sri Aurobindo's opinion is that such a tendency developed largely because the "luxurious" few held these instruments and the world in their hands during a certain period of human progress.[75] In a sense Sri Aurobindo makes here a case for the subaltern voice. He realises their deprivation, recognises their toil and struggle for existence and yet demands that they too be made part of and ought to be included in and be capable of savouring the high tastes of subjects of art that may also in some measure mitigate their struggles, ennoble their existence and as a corollary elevate the national life in a general manner. It would be perhaps wrong to assume that Sri Aurobindo catered to a very exclusive circle, he was concerned and expressed in his own ways the plight of the masses and wished to include them in a national educational progress. In the same argument he recognises that the "aesthetic faculties entering into the enjoyment of the world" through the representations of the quotidian life such as "the beautiful in men and women, in food, in things, in articles of use and articles of pleasure" have done an immense service to elevate man, "to refine and purge his passions, to ennoble his emotions" and to lead him through the medium of the "heart and the imagination to the state of the intellectual man."[76] And that which has elevated man to

75. *CWSA*, vol. 1, pp. 438-39.

76. Ibid., p. 439.

the intellectual level must be preserved so that there is no backward slide. The danger of an undeveloped heart and spirit was that it would make man — "intellectually developed, mighty in scientific knowledge and the mastery of gross and subtle nature, using the elements as his servants and the world as his footstool" — an "inferior kind of *asura* using the powers of a demigod to satisfy the nature of an animal."[77] The continuous necessity therefore, of an aesthetic training remained. Sri Aurobindo did not limit the evolution and inclusion of an art education as necessary solely for the awakening of a binding national unity, he added to this his concern for the general "restoration" of artistic emotions. He saw the Bengal Art School as capable of creating and restoring this emotion to a great extent nationally.

Elaborating on this and discussing the role of music as part of an aesthetic training in a national system of education Coomaraswamy expresses much the same aim. His point is that a "proper education in music" has been generally accepted as "an invaluable aid in the training of character — [which is] the true aim of education." The arts therefore were to be invaluable aids to the training of character, the cultivation of the spirit. Coomaraswamy extrapolates the link further — and sets the perspective of a system of aesthetic training in a national education for self-reliance. He set the primary aim of education in India as the creation of "Indian citizens." The age demanded first a thorough training in Indian citizenship, only then could follow the true citizenship of the world. An immersion in one's roots had to precede any cosmopolitanism and in any case he felt it was "not the time for cosmopolitanism, it [was] the time when India herself needed Indian citizens" and he saw education in Indian music [for our purposes read Indian art as] an essential part of education in Indian

77. *CWSA*, vol. 1, p. 439.

citizenship."[78] And Havell on his part, staunchly believing in the strength of art to reshape the Indian mind and nationality and seeing a larger role for it in education demanded that Indian art, hitherto stifled under official direction and patronage, be set free "to follow its natural channel," and called for the removal of impediments that he saw being placed in its course. Once free, he argued, it [Indian art] can minister to the spiritual and intellectual needs of India and elevate the "moral and intellectual faculties" of the Indian students.[79] It was, of course, too much to expect that a colonial education system would undertake such liberating and revamping acts. The nationalists saw this as the task of the new education they were advocating and thus sought to enshrine art-training as an important charter of the new system.

Taking the reader through a gradual analysis of the place and role of aesthetics in human evolution Sri Aurobindo indicates that one of the highest roles of the artistic sense was the "direct purifying of the emotions"; he links the process to that of the Greek *katharsis*. In the series Sri Aurobindo argues that art and poetry had a "mighty utility" in mitigating the "pressing claims of the animal in man" and were fields where these claims could be excluded and the emotions, "working disinterestedly for the satisfaction of the heart and the imagination alone, [could] do the work of *katharsis*, emotional purification" which in the Indian context was *cittaśuddhi*, "the purification of the heart." It was through such a purification that man arrived at a greater fulfilment. Sri Aurobindo argued that if it could be shown, as he tried through his series on the subject, that art and poetry were "agents" and catalysts towards that end then their "supreme importance [could] be established." He concludes that these subjects did just that —

78. Coomaraswamy, op. cit., pp. 196-97.

79. Havell, *Art and Education in India*, op. cit., p. 108.

purification of emotions — and much more and the habit of looking upon these as mere ornamentations of life have reduced them to a secondary rank. Sri Aurobindo thus did not limit the utility of the subjects to the promotion of a national unity; he also perceived in them a deeper role affecting human conduct and the general psychological, emotional and spiritual state of being.[80] He perceived in them the capacity to generate a "sense of the beautiful" in the national life.

The Requirement of a "Universal Proficiency" in Art Training: A Call for the Democratisation of Aesthetics

A detailed reading of each of the ideas on the subject that Sri Aurobindo discusses in the series will, in my opinion, not be necessary for our explorations here. Those which we require for our understanding and reading are the ones that provide fairly accurately his ideas on the place, utility and role of these subjects in education and hence we have been selective in our approach while reading his art series.

Similar to Coomaraswamy's advocacy of the subject Sri Aurobindo discusses the role of music in the shaping of a national mentality. He invokes Plato and his *Republic* where the thinker "has dwelt with extraordinary emphasis on the importance of music in education" especially its role in shaping the national character of a people — "as is the music to which a people is accustomed, so, he [Plato] says in effect, is the character of that people."[81] In the same manner Sri Aurobindo

80. *CWSA*, vol. 1, pp. 444-45.

81. Ibid., p. 447. In the same vein Coomaraswamy, whose discussion on the role and place of music in Indian education we have already highlighted, says, the "importance of music in education could hardly be overestimated." Coomaraswamy too takes recourse to Plato in order to buttress his argument in favour of a steady tradition of music education. He quotes Plato as saying that education in music is of greatest importance because through it enters harmony "in the strongest manner into the inward part of the soul." The one →

sees the importance of painting and sculpture in education as hardly less. He does not enter into polemics of colonial versus nationalist but simply provides the subject's importance in the training of the mind to be open to the law of beauty and harmony. The points he makes here are relevant for that matter to educational systems anywhere. The mind he says is "profoundly influenced by what it sees" and a training of the eyes from childhood "to the contemplation and understanding of beauty, harmony and just arrangement in line and colour, the tastes, habits and character" will capacitate the individual to follow even later in life as an adult a "similar law of beauty, harmony and just arrangement." Sri Aurobindo points at this insistence on developing a "universal proficiency" in arts in societies such as ancient Greece, "in certain European ages, in Japan" and in India of a better time. It was a call for a re-look at this ancient tradition and for its revival in the present context. Sri Aurobindo argues that since "Art galleries could not be brought into every home" it would serve the purpose of trying to restore the aesthetic emotion of the race if the "appointments of our life and furniture of our homes are things of taste and beauty" and such a situation would perhaps inevitably raise, ennoble, harmonise the habits, thoughts and

---

→ who receives such an education develops faculties and capacities that "perceives in the quickest manner whatever workmanship is defective, and whatever execution is unhandsome . . . he will praise what is beautiful, rejoicing in it and receiving it into his soul, be nourished by it, and become a worthy and good man." [Coomaraswamy, op. cit., p. 187.] The same point was being made and supported, education in music developed the individual's capacity to seek after perfection, understand its manifestation, reject its distortion or misrepresentation and in general encourage goodness and expressions of harmony. As I have argued earlier, the national education activism was not merely political in nature, or reformatory in approach, it had deeper spiritual and intellectual undercurrents too. The effort to rejuvenate the people spiritually was made and in that the instruments of art, poetry and music were found to be valuable instruments and allies.

feelings of the people.[82] This ennobling and harmonisation of emotions also happens through a regular study "of beautiful and noble art." Like poetry, which works towards purifying the heart, spoken of earlier as *cittaśuddhi,* painting and sculpture too do much the same thing in their own manner. It is interesting to read here Sri Aurobindo's analysis of how the arts — painting, sculpture — train and elevate the emotion.[83] Paintings and sculptures, though they do not possess the movement of poetry and are still, fixed and the expressions of only a given moment these very attributes give them a separate value altogether. While poetry "raises the emotions and gives each its separate delight, [art] stills the emotions and teaches them the delight of a restrained and limited satisfaction. . . . Music deepens the emotions and harmonises them with each other."[84] Each component of an art and aesthetic education — music, art, poetry — contributed something distinctive to the development of individual — they are, Sri Aurobindo observes, "a perfect education for the soul," they keep the individual's emotional tendencies "purified, self-controlled, deep and harmonious." Sri Aurobindo saw these

82. *CWSA*, vol. 1, p. 447.

83. An interesting reference which reveals how Sri Aurobindo himself developed the artistic perspective may be given here. Assuaging the lamentations of a disciple much later he wrote with touching humility, "Don't be desperate about your incapacity as a connoisseur of painting. I was far worse in this respect: knew something about sculpture, but blind to painting. Suddenly one day in the Alipore Jail while meditating I saw some pictures on the walls of the cell and lo and behold! the artistic eye in me opened and I knew all about painting except of course the more material side of technique. I don't always know how to express though, because I lack the knowledge of the proper expressions, but that does not stand in the way of a keen and understanding appreciation." [Sri Aurobindo, *On Himself*, 1995, pp. 226-27.] The series on art was written a few months after release from prison.

84. *CWSA*, vol. 1, pp. 447-48.

as powerful agents, great civilising, educating and "edifying forces" if properly used and applied.[85]

Further analysing the effects of an art-training Sri Aurobindo talks of the "double character of intellectual activity" divided between the "imaginative, creative and sympathetic" on one side and the "critical, analytic and penetrative on the other." The latter he saw as "best trained" through science, criticism and observation and the former "by art, poetry, music, literature and the sympathetic study of man and his creations."[86] He sees art as a "powerful stimulator of sympathetic insight" because it raises images that have to be understood not by analysis but through "a self-identification with other minds." Art being "subtle and delicate" makes the mind in its movement subtle and delicate too, it is "suggestive" and thus a mind trained in the appreciation of art "is quick to catch suggestions." It is an instrument that opens individual to ways of deeper self-knowledge. It is this supreme value of art that was never sufficiently recognised by those who made language, poetry, history, philosophy instruments for training the imaginative, sympathetic and the creative side of intellectuality. They made these, Sri Aurobindo says, obligatory parts of a liberal education while the "immense educative force of music, painting and sculpture has not been duly recognised." They were treated, as he interestingly puts, as "by-paths" that have been treated as interesting and beautiful but not essential for the vast majority and thus to be confined to a limited few. Yet there persists an almost "universal impulse to enjoy the beauty and attractiveness of sound, to look at and live among pictures, colours [and] forms."[87] But this impulse Sri Aurobindo sees as not being given adequate recognition and no proper scope for a greater

85. *CWSA*, vol. 1., p. 448.

86. Ibid., p. 449.

87. Ibid., pp. 449, 450.

working. A national art-training or education would base itself first on the recognition of the existence of that impulse.

Arguing that if art were to reach its highest expression the "Indian tendency" must dominate, Sri Aurobindo briefly describes the Indian concept and practice of art as manifested in the race's civilisational expressions. We see him expounding here, like his contemporaries, Coomaraswamy and Havell, the metaphysical bases of Indian art as evident through the ages. He traces the noblest and higher uses of art as its "service to the growth of spirituality in the race." In Europe it was well recognised that there was this close connection of art with religion. The productions of art in Greece, [Renaissance] Italy and India have mostly given expressions to religious thoughts and have adorned temples and other such instruments of national religion. In the following passage he succinctly states the aims and ideals of the Indian art and also says what he means by a spiritual aspiration and growth and of art as an aid in that growth and quest. This perhaps requires quoting *in extenso*:

> This [art giving expression to religious thoughts] was not because Art is necessarily associated with the outward forms of religion, but because it was in the religion that men's spiritual aspirations centred themselves. Spirituality is a wider thing than formal religion and it is in the service of spirituality that Art reaches its highest self-expression. Spirituality is a single word expressive of three lines of human aspiration towards divine knowledge, divine love and joy, divine strength, and that will be the highest and most perfect Art which, while satisfying the physical requirements of the aesthetic sense, the laws of formal beauty, the emotional demand of humanity, the portrayal of life and the outward reality [requirements satisfied by the best of European art productions] reaches beyond them and expresses inner spiritual truth, the deeper not obvious

> reality of things, the joy of God in the world and its beauty and desirableness and the manifestation of divine force and energy in phenomenal creation. This is what Indian Art alone attempted thoroughly. . . .[88]

While doing this, Indian Art, Sri Aurobindo points out, often dispensed with the more material but not necessarily unimportant expressions that European Art focused upon. And it were these approaches to techniques and expressions of Art that have created the two divergent streams of European [read Western] and Asian art. This Asian tendency in art was for a long while imperfectly appreciated by the West and Sri Aurobindo, in keeping with his synthesising tendencies of course hopes that these two diverging streams would unite in future completing and developing in one "grandiose flood of artistic self-expression perfecting the aesthetic evolution of humanity."[89] But why look at all at the Indian tendency in

88. *CWSA*, vol. 1, p. 450.

89. Ibid., p. 451. For an insightful discussion of Sri Aurobindo's perception of the Indian tendency in art see, e.g. Nolini Kanta Gupta's "The Standpoint of Indian Art" in *Collected Works of Nolini Kanta Gupta (CWNKG)*, vol. 1, 1989, pp. 175-80. There was this distinction made, Indian art did not go so much for naturalism, it attempted to portray something deeper apparently hidden to the common sight. As Gupta, close political, literary and spiritual associate of Sri Aurobindo, analyses, the art of the East rejected the "scheme of sense-perceptions." The artist within this fold first sought "to get a focus within the mind, to discover a psychological standpoint, and from there in accordance with . . . conventions of inner vision create a world. . . . The aim was always to build from within, at the most, from within outwards, but not from without, not even from without inwards. . . ." [*CWNKG* vol. 1, p. 175.] The Indian point of view in art was a much discussed and debated issue of the period. What was it, how was it explained? Coomaraswamy delving on the same issue is rich and illustrative in his examples while trying to explain the inner vision and the practice of contemplation on it by the artist. The analogy he draws is between the "methods of the Indian worshipper and the Indian artist." The true artist, for him, is one who "does not "compose" (put together) his picture but "sees" it." And his desire is "to represent his vision in the material terms of →

Art? It is because, as Sri Aurobindo argues, this tendency was expected to dominate in the new training that the nationalist

→ light and colour." To great painters, says Coomaraswamy, these visions come crowding and in a continuous stream and the painter has to possess the ability to still these, dwell on them and give them expression and it is here that his approach is like the worshipper. As the worshipper daily adoring his *iṣṭa devatā* — "the special aspect of divinity that is to him all" — first through the "recitation of the brief mnemonic *mantram* detailing His [*iṣṭa devatā*'s] attributes, and then in silent concentration of thought upon the corresponding mental image." [Coomaraswamy, op. cit., pp. 20-21.] Similar is the mental images that the artist sees and the process of visualisation is the same. Invoking the sage Śukrācārya's *Śukranītisāra* — which contains almost the "whole philosophy of Indian art" — Coomaraswamy argues that the "method of visualisation upon the imager" was enjoined by this particular text which asked the creating artist/sculptor to "establish images in temples by meditation on the deities who are the objects of his devotion." It calls upon the artist to enter into a "*dhyāna yoga* (yoga of contemplation)" and goes on to describe the method of doing it, the elements and the characteristics of the image. The objective of Indian art has never been "mere representation of nature." And no truly Indian sculpture can be said to have been created direct from living models. The inability of the West to appreciate and comprehend Indian art and the consequent criticism of its expressions, points out Coomaraswamy, stem from the habit of trying to look for "something to recognise" in a work of art. And if there is a failure to identify that something recognisable, and if the "representation is of something they [the viewer] have not seen, or symbolises some unfamiliar abstract idea" it is seen as "untrue to nature" and therefore self-condemned. [Ibid., p. 23.] The Indian tendency in art never had as its object the "reproduction of the external forms of nature." In fact, it [Indian art] is "essentially religious [and its] conscious aim . . . is the intimation of Divinity". It is an attempt at expressing these deeper truths through symbolism. Śukrācārya's doctrine in this matter is quite explicit — "the aim of the highest art must always be the intimation of the Divinity behind all form, rather than the imitation of the form itself." Kṛṣṇa's play with the *gopīs* is a favourite depiction of Indian art panels but it is always done in "a spirit of religious idealism, [and] not for the mere sake of the sensuous imagery itself." [Ibid., pp. 23, 27, 31.] These are the basic issues that were highlighted in order to explain the uniqueness of the Indian approach to art, an approach that was, as the ideologues felt, being systematically erased by the dominance of the Western perspective and understanding of art.

advocated. Without the dominance of this tendency in an Indian art-training the whole exercise would never reflect the Indian ethos and psyche. It would be merely the developing of another technique devoid of the Indianness and incapable of expressing the Indian mind and emotions. Thus, Sri Aurobindo saw an enormous potential in Art as a medium of opening the national life to higher thoughts and expressions. Perhaps the following observation best illustrates the reason for his deep concern with the subject, for if man is destined to a higher life in his individuality as well as collectivity then art could be a powerful aid to that quest for perfection:

> Art can express eternal truth, it is not limited to the expression of form and appearance. So wonderfully has God made the world that a man using a simple combination of lines, an unpretentious harmony of colours, can raise this apparently insignificant medium to suggest absolute and profound truths with a perfection which language labours with difficulty to reach. What Nature is, what God is, what man is, can be triumphantly revealed in stone or on canvas. . . .[90]

This perhaps best explains the Indian approach to art.

In the series Sri Aurobindo principally discusses the enormous value that Art has to human evolution. What then of its value "as a factor in education"? Sri Aurobindo's stand is that no nation can afford to neglect "an element of such high importance" an element that has great importance to the cultural life of the people and to the training of the "higher intellectual, moral and aesthetic faculties of the young." A system of education that recognising this importance refuses to keep artistic training reserved for the specialist but introduces it "as a part of culture" equally in importance as science or literature will have taken a major step forward in the "perfection of national education and the general diffusion

90. *CWSA*, vol. 1, p. 451.

of a broad-based human culture."[91] The approach that art and training in its appreciation must be diffused and not limited to the privileged few is evident whenever he speaks of art in education. The view that there can be a general art-training was to be first accepted. The demand was not that art education be imparted in order to make every man an artist, the demand was for a general diffusion of the artistic impulse, it was rather that:

> [every man should have] his artistic faculty developed, his taste trained, his sense of beauty and insight into form and colour and that which is expressed in form and colour, made habitually active, correct and sensitive. It is necessary that those who create, whether in great things or small, whether in the unusual masterpieces of art and genius or in the small common things of use that surround a man's daily life, should be habituated to produce and the nation habituated to expect the beautiful in preference to the ugly, the noble in preference to the vulgar, the fine in preference to the crude, the harmonious in preference to the gaudy. A nation surrounded daily by the beautiful, noble, fine and harmonious becomes that which it is habituated to contemplate. . . .[92]

The point is self-evident; the reason for the demand and the demand's goal is clearly stated. Sri Aurobindo sees Art as having a fundamental service to render in a national scheme of education and every man, and not the elite few, would be covered by its sweep. It was a clear demand for the democratisation of a very important aspect of human development in education and it was made when the subaltern was as yet unable to speak! It is interesting to note that the issue retains a great degree of contemporaneity, whether or not a general effort has been made today towards achieving it requires a separate area of treatment altogether.

91. *CWSA*, vol. 1, p. 453.

92. Ibid.

Talking of the effort in this direction made by the national education system in Bengal, Sri Aurobindo says that though a beginning was made in this direction by the importance attached to "drawing and clay-modelling as elements of manual training" the "artistic ideal" was missing. The misconception of the true aim of manual training, lack of resources, the eventual dominancy of the commercial aim in education, of "English ideas, English methods and English predilections" rendered the whole effort ineffective. The formal and mechanical English method was useless to evoke and train an "inward vision of the relation and truth of things, an eye quick to note and distinguish, sensitive to design and to harmony in colour"[93] essential manifestations of a sustained artistic training. Writing in 1909 Sri Aurobindo saw the revival of a "truly national Art" as an already accomplished fact producing masterpieces that were comparable to the best work of other countries. He criticised, as unpardonable, the continued subsistence of the "crude formal teaching of English schools and the vulgar commercial aims and methods of the West." This subsistence was an indication that the country was "yet to evolve a system of education which shall be really national." For that tasks — as Sri Aurobindo saw them — yet remained to be accomplished: alien and unsuitable methods and the "taint of Occidental ideals" had to be purged from the national mind and nowhere was it more urgent than in the field of education which must ultimately become the "foundation of intellectual and aesthetic renovation." It is in this task that the resuscitation of the spirit of old Indian Art must be accomplished, the "dexterity of the Indian hand and the intuitive gaze of the Indian eye must be recovered" and the whole nation would see an elevation to the "high level of the ancient culture" and perhaps even surpass that some day.[94]

---

93. *CWSA*, vol. 1, p. 454.

94. Ibid.

The above exploration thus of some of the thoughts, reflections and exposition of the leading Indian nationalist thinkers (during 1900-10) provides an interesting insight into their approach to India's educational quest. A quest that kept opening up to advanced educational ideas and at the same time attempted to rediscover, reinterpret and refit what these thinkers perceived to be some of ancient India's core conception of education, to the developing educational discourse of their times. Among some of these fundamental elements of ancient education that they reinterpreted and re-explored was the unique Indian tradition of *brahmacarya*, the renewal of a universal artistic and aesthetic training for the nation and through them the method of restoring the artistic emotions of the people. The ideas that were generated from this quest did provide a firm intellectual base to the early nationalist educational movement apart from giving new directions in certain fields such as the new art movement. The other aspect that emerges from the exploration of the above thoughts is that the points made and discussed by these thinkers continue to remain relevant to the educational debate today. The question that perhaps emerges is how does the education system today assimilate and synthesise, if at all, some of the perennial educational principles that India's ancient civilisational past evolved? Can a national method or system for creating a universal proficiency in the arts be developed; can a system of training and nurturing the latent artistic and aesthetic emotion of the race be made part of the education system?

The other point that can be seen as emerging from the exploration may be linked to the ongoing cultural debate. In an age when there is an emerging discourse on issues of cultural hegemony, cultural co-option and a dominant-culture paradigm, the demand for a universal artistic proficiency, the perception that the collective artistic emotion needs nurturing assumes a renewed relevance. It is perhaps through such a training, through such a democratisation that each culture, each civilisation may still preserve its identity, its uniqueness and be capable of staving off an enforced cultural uniformity that remains one of the stark manifestations of the process of globalisation in our age.

Bibliography

Aurobindo, Sri, *Complete Works of Sri Aurobindo* (*CWSA*), vol. 20, Pondicherry: Sri Aurobindo Ashram Publication Department, 1997.

Aurobindo, Sri, *Complete Works of Sri Aurobindo* (*CWSA*), vol. 1, Pondicherry: Sri Aurobindo Ashram Publication Department, 2003.

Aurobindo, Sri, *Complete Works of Sri Aurobindo (CWSA)*, vol. 8, Pondicherry: Sri Aurobindo Ashram Publication Department, 1997.

Aurobindo, Sri, *On Himself*, Pondicherry: Sri Aurobindo Ashram, 6th impression, 1995.

Bhattacharya, Sabyasachi, et al., eds., *Educating the Nation: Documents on the Discourse of National Education in India: 1880-1920*, New Delhi: Kanishka Publishers-Educational Records Research Unit, Jawaharlal Nehru University, 2003.

Collected Works of Nolini Kanta Gupta (CWNKG), vol. 1, Kolkata: Nolini Kanta Gupta Birth Centenary edition, 1989.

Complete Works of Sister Nivedita (CWSN), vol. 2, "The Mediaeval University of India" in *Studies from an Eastern Home*, Kolkata: Advaita Ashrama, 4th impression, 1999.

Complete Works of Sister Nivedita (CWSN), vol. 3, Kolkata: Advaita Ashrama, 4th impression, 2000.

Complete Works of Sister Nivedita (CWSN), vol. 4, "The Place of Foreign Culture in a True Education" in *Hints on National Education in India*, Kolkata: Advaita Ashrama, 3rd impression, 1996.

Coomaraswamy, Ananda, *Essays in National Idealism,(1909)*, New Delhi: Munshiram Manoharlal, 1st Indian edn., 1981.

Guha, Ramachandra, "The Independent Journal of Opinion," *Seminar*, no. 481, New Delhi, 1999.

Havell, E.B., "Art and Education in India" in *Indian Art, Industry and Education*, Madras: G.A. Natesan & Co., 1901.

———, *The Ideals of Indian Art*, London: John Murray, 1911.

Joshi, Kireet, *Education at Crossroads*, New Delhi: The Mother's Institute of Research, 2nd edn., 2007.

Krishna Kumar, "Origins of the Textbook Culture" in *What is Worth Teaching*, New Delhi: Orient Longman, 2004.

——, *Political Agenda of Education: A Study of Colonialist and Nationalist Ideas*, New Delhi: Sage Publications, 2nd edn., 2005.

Mitter, Partha, *Art and Nationalism in Colonial India: 1850-1922*, Cambridge: Cambridge University Press, 1994.

Mookerjee, Radha Kumud, *Ancient Indian Education (Brahmanical and Buddhist)* (1947), Delhi: Motilal Banarsidass, 4th edn., 1969.

Pandit, M.P. (ed.), *Glossary of Sanskrit Terms in Sri Aurobindo's Works*, Pondicherry: Sri Aurobindo Ashram (1966), rpt., 2002.

Ramakrishnananda, Swami, *For Thinkers on Education*, Chennai: Sri Ramakrishna Math (1949), reprint date not stated.

Sarkar, Sumit, *The Swadeshi Movement in Bengal (1903-1908)*, New Delhi: People's Publishing House, 1973.

10

J. Krishnamurti's New Philosophy of Education

Atashee Chatterjee Sinha

> *In the fullness of co-operation, goodness, which is not sentimentality, can flower. It is authority that destroys co-operation, for love cannot possibly exist where there is authority. We have lived so long in the accepted patterns of life that it has become traditional, and freedom, love and co-operation have lost their fundamental meanings. Education is to break down these patterns. In the very breaking down of them is seeing of the truth of the new.*
>
> — Jiddu Krishnamurti

THE word "education" comes from the Latin *e-ducere* meaning "to lead out." Education encompasses teaching and learning specific skills, imparting of knowledge, positive ideals and culture from generation to generation. In this paper we shall discuss the nature and purpose of education, as conceived and practised by Jiddu Krishnamurti (1895-1986). Krishnamurti's work is large, subtle, and complex; he did not explicitly define his position; instead, his understanding is interwoven throughout his work. His insights on education do not tally with the traditional form of education; rather he introduced a radically different philosophy of education. Like Sri Aurobindo (1872-1950), his insight into education is unique and can be of immense significance in the present world. Krishnamurti stated,

> We may be highly educated, but if we are without deep integration of thought and feeling, our lives are incomplete, contradictory and torn with many fears; and as long as education does not cultivate an integrated outlook on life, it has very little significance. In our present civilisation we have divided life into so many departments that education has very little meaning, except in learning a particular technique or profession. Instead of awakening the integrated intelligence of the individual, education is encouraging him to conform to a pattern and so is hindering his comprehension of himself as a total process.[1]

Once we clarify Krishnamurti's vision about "the right kind of education", we can attempt to identify some important aspects shared among the educational centres founded by Aurobindo and Krishnamurti.

Krishnamurti states

> To bring about right education, we must obviously understand the meaning of life as a whole, and for that we have to be able to think, not consistently, but directly and truly. A consistent thinker is a thoughtless person, because he conforms to a pattern; he repeats phrases and thinks in a groove. We cannot understand existence abstractly or theoretically. To understand life is to understand ourselves and that is both the beginning and the end of education.[2]

He regards education as one of the most significant ways of communication, which is central to the transformation of the human mind and the creation of a new culture. Such a fundamental transformation takes place when the child, while being trained in various skills and disciplines, possesses the capacity to be awake to the processes of her own thinking, feeling and action. This alertness makes her self-critical and

---

1. *J. Krishnamurti, Education and the Significance of Life*, 1992, Krishnamurti Foundation, India, p. 11.
2. Ibid., p. 14.

observant and thus establishes integrity of perception, discrimination and action, crucial to gain maturity of a right relationship to other human beings, animals, nature and to the tools created by humans. He points out that the ignorant person is not the unlearned, but one who does not know herself. Understanding, in Krishnamurti's view, comes only through self-knowledge, which is awareness of one's total psychological process. Thus education, in the true sense, is the understanding of oneself; for it is within each one of us that the whole of existence is gathered. He points out that the present education is based on the cultivation of the intellect, of thought and knowledge which are all necessary in our day-to-day life, but they bear no significance in our psychological relationships with others, living with and around us. To impart knowledge of human discoveries is merely a part of education and not the whole of it. A more important part of education is helping the individual to understand herself, her mind and the inner movement of her thoughts. Krishnamurti, while addressing the students, said,

> This is the function of all education. We need to bring about a good society in which all human beings can live happily in peace, without violence, with security. You as a student are responsible for this. A good society doesn't come into existence through some ideal, a hero or a leader, or some carefully planned system. You have to be good because you are the future. You will make the world, either as it is, modified, or as a world in which you and others can live without wars, without brutalities, with generosity and affection.[3]

Education means learning. To inquire and to learn is the function of the mind. Krishnamurti says that learning is not

---

3. Ray Mcloy (ed.), *The Whole Movement of life is Learning: J. Krishnamurti's letters to his schools*, 2006, England: Krishnamurti Foundation Trust Ltd., Brockwood Park, p. 123.

mere cultivation of memory or accumulation of knowledge, rather it is the capacity to think clearly and sanely without illusion, without any prefixed standard, ideal or dogma. Learning, taken in this sense, implies the love of understanding and love of doing things for themselves. Such learning by children is possible only when there is no coercion or imposition of any kind from parents and teachers. Parents and teachers are both educators but the educators do not understand themselves, or their relationship with the child. Simply through stuffing them with information and making them pass examinations, we cannot possibly bring about a new kind of education. If the guide, the helper is herself confused and narrow-minded, biased and theory-ridden, then naturally the imparted education becomes a source of further confusion and strife. Krishnamurti realised that to educate the educators — that is, to have them understand themselves — is one of the most difficult undertakings, because most of us are already crystallised within a system of thought, ideology, religion, or a pattern of action. He often found that parents and teachers are occupied with their own personal conflicts and sorrows. Although they desire that children shall be equipped to get on in the world, that they must be educated to hold secure positions, yet they knowingly or unknowingly encourage the child into a general process of isolation and competition. In Krishnamurti's view, it is only when there is love and understanding that the walls of isolation are broken down, and then the family is no longer a closed circle, then the parents are in communion with their children and with others in the society.

Hence it is important that the educator helps in the education of the parents as well. The teacher must talk to them, explaining that the confused state of the world mirrors their own individual confusion. The teacher has to awaken the parents' confidence, by talking over with them the child's temperament, difficulties, aptitudes and so on. If the teacher takes a real interest in the child as an individual, the parents need to have confidence in her. In this process, the teacher is educating the parents as well as herself, while learning from them in return. Krishnamurti never supported a top-down structure among the educator and the learner. Right education is a mutual task demanding patience, consideration and affection. If parents truly love their children, they will do away with envy and strife, and will set about altering fundamentally the structure of present-day society. Both parents and teachers have to contribute so that children receive the kind of education that helps them to be sensitive, intelligent and integrated human beings.

The aim of education, according to Krishnamurti, is to create a new society and a new culture based on new values. He advocated as an aim of education, the enjoyment of beauty of nature and thus focused on developing an aesthetic sense, the art of observation and sensitivity among everyone. To him, learning is to think sanely and clearly without illusion, imagination or myth. Instead of using reward, punishment, competition, etc. as motivational factors, he advocated natural curiosity, interest, attention, fearlessness, and freedom. He has been a strong supporter of observation and meditation for understanding one's own self and others as well as for enjoying the beauty of nature and the whole world around us. He opposed the present-day examination system and proposed to keep a record of pupils' progress only for the use of teachers and parents. According to his writings, the qualities necessary for a good teacher were an unending desire to learn. A teacher must have patience, sensitivity, intelligence, and an attitude of equality with pupils. Krishnamurti strongly maintained that the pupils, teachers and parents must be closely interrelated for human progress.

The centres of learning founded by Krishnamurti are places where the children are open to a way of life which is not based on mere pleasure, or self-centred activities, but on the understanding of the mind, correct action, the depth and beauty of relationship, and the sacredness of a religious life. Here "religious life" has a very special meaning. He often stated that the purpose of education is to bring about freedom, love, "the flowering of goodness" and the complete transformation of society. He specifically contrasts this to what he feels are the intentions of most schools which emphasise preparing young people to succeed materially in the society that exists. A constant theme in Krishnamurti's declarations of the intentions of education is freedom. Undoubtedly, there is a connection between psychological freedom and outward compulsion — it is difficult to help a student find the former in a situation dominated by the latter — but it is not political freedom that interests Krishnamurti. Rather he is interested in the deeper freedom of the psyche and the spirit, the inner liberation that he felt was both the means and the ends of education. The intentions of education must be the inner transformation and liberation of the human being and, from that, society would be transformed.

He maintained that we are affected or informed by nature and the surroundings where we learn, and this is especially true of young impressionable minds. For instance, beauty is important, not just because it is pleasing, but because sensitivity to beauty is related to being religious and indispensable to the healthy growth of a child. Krishnamurti felt that some very important things could not be taught by prescription; rather they need to be lived in, by the learner. He felt that beauty was related to truth. For him, nature is both beautiful and a demonstration of order. Therefore, if one establishes a relationship with nature then one can truly communicate with other humans and have meaningful relationship with humanity. He further insisted that the schools should have special places for silence. He often spoke to the students of the importance of a quiet mind or silence so that they could observe their thoughts and practise meditation. Meditation means to have a very quiet, still mind, not a chattering mind; to have a really quiet body, quiet mind so that our mind becomes religious. All his educational centres reflect a religious atmosphere, often generated by aesthetics, the setting, and the effect of special location of the centres.

In Krishnamurti's view, a school or an educational centre is a place where one learns about the totality, the wholeness of life. Academic excellence is absolutely necessary, but a school includes much more than that. It is a place where both the teacher and the taught explore not only the outer world, the world of knowledge, but also their own thinking, their own behaviour. From this they begin to discover their own conditioning and how it distorts their thinking. Freedom from conditioning and its misery begins with this awareness. It is only in such freedom that true learning can take place. In this school it is the responsibility of the teacher to sustain with the student a careful exploration into the implications of conditioning and thus end it. A school is a place where one learns the importance of knowledge and its limitations. It is a place where one learns to observe the world not from any particular point of view or conclusion; one learns to look at the whole of man's endeavour, his search for beauty, his search for truth and for a way of living without conflict. There are, generally speaking, two kinds of participants in his educational centres: staff and students. Krishnamurti felt that any adult who is present regularly in one of the centres is a staff member (regardless of function) and because of their regular contact with the educational environment (if not the students), they are in the position of educators. There can be no real hierarchy between the students and staff. Although their responsibilities and experiences are different, in the central concerns of education, which is to do with inner liberation, both the students and the teachers are learners and therefore equal, and this is untouched by functional authority.

Since the educator is religious she is concerned first with "being", and then right "doing" or right actions would follow from it. Krishnamurti describes this relationship between "being" and "doing" frequently, in his talks. In his view, "doing" is derived from "being" rather than "being" deriving from "doing" — this is the reverse of convention. He always stressed the importance of the learner's "being" — their deepest sensitivities, their goodness and intelligence (this has nothing to do with conventional morality or IQ), the depth of their questions about themselves and the world. Although he wanted both staff and students to be intellectually sound, he never stressed academic prowess, cultural abilities, or capacities as being more important than the willingness and ability to lead what he called a religious life.

Krishnamurti's philosophy of education is closely related to some concepts, each one bearing special significance, backed by his understanding. These are the concepts of Truth, Intelligence, Understanding, Freedom, Goodness and Relationship. Let us very briefly consider each of these concepts:

Truth is something about one's own self which everyone has to find for herself. Krishnamurti says, "Truth is not something far away. It is the truth about the mind, truth about its activities from moment to moment."[4] Truth of things and individuals can be discovered when one possesses the capacity to think very simply, without any fixed ideals or desires. It is only the simple and direct mind that can find the real, the true. Truth arises through intelligence.

Intelligence is the spontaneous perception which makes a person strong and free. In order to help the child to be

4. Jiddu Krishnamurti, 2001, *The First and Last Freedom*, Krishnamurti Foundation, India, p. 113.

intelligent, both educators and/or parents have to break down within themselves the hindrances which make them dull and thoughtless. In Krishnamurti's view, our struggle for security is causing conflict and chaos in the world. So we must begin to awaken our own intelligence by being aware of our psychological processes; we must begin to question all the values which enclose us. We should not continue to fit thoughtlessly into the pattern in which we happen to have been brought up. Unless the educator understands herself, unless she sees her own conditioned responses and is beginning to free herself from existing values, she cannot possibly awaken intelligence in the child.

It is only by **understanding** the ways of our own thoughts and feelings that we can truly help the child to be a free human being; and if then we are vitally interested, we shall ask ourselves why and to what purpose we are educating the children and ourselves; we shall inquire into the meaning of existence, into the relationship of the individual to society, and so on. Educators must be aware of these problems and should try to help the child to discover the truth concerning them, without projecting upon the young mind their own idiosyncrasies and habits of thought.

To give **freedom** to the child, the educator must be aware of the implications and the full significance of freedom. Right values are not discovered through the authority of society or tradition; only individual thoughtfulness can reveal them. The teacher must understand this deeply and encourage the student from the very beginning to awaken insight into present-day individual and social values. The educator will help the child to be fearless, which means to be free from all domination, authority and bias whether by the teacher, the family or society, so that as an individual she can flower in love and goodness. In thus helping the student towards freedom, the educator changes her own values and begins flowering in love and goodness. This process of mutual education creates an altogether different relationship between the teacher and the student. A total development of the child can be brought about only where there is the right relationship between the teacher, the student and the parents.

All authority and domination is a hindrance, and it is essential that the educator should not become an authority for the student. The strength and certainty of the teacher gives assurance to the student, but such assurance is neither lasting nor true. A teacher who consciously or unconsciously encourages dependence can never be of great help to her students. Krishnamurti emphasises that freedom is necessary for intelligence. He points out, "freedom means not merely freedom from fear, anxiety, and sorrow, but freedom to inquire, to go deeply, profoundly into yourself, because that is all you have. You are the result of the society, the culture in which you have been brought up. That is the only thing you have, and therefore you have to investigate it, explore it, and see whether you can be completely free of all that."[5] To be the right kind of educator, a teacher must constantly be watchful to see that the students do not make of her an example, an ideal, and an authority. When the teacher desires to fulfil herself in her students, when their success is hers, then her teaching is detrimental to self-knowledge and freedom. The right kind of educator must be aware of all the material and psychological hindrances in order to help her students to be free, not only from her authority, but from their own self-enclosing pursuit. Further, educators must consider all children equally, irrespective of their economical status, social position, religious background, and individual temperament. Dedication to the right kind of education must be wholly voluntary. It should not be the result of any kind of persuasion, or of any

5. Jiddu Krishnamurti, 2002, *Why are you being educated? Talks at Indian Universities*, Krishnamurti Foundation, India, p. 70.

hope of personal gain; and it must be devoid of the fears that arise from the craving for success and achievement. If teaching is one's vocation, and if one perceives the grave importance of the right kind of education, one cannot help but be the right kind of educator. There is no need to follow any method. The very fact of understanding that the right kind of education is indispensable if we are to achieve the freedom and integration of the individual brings about a fundamental change in oneself. If one becomes aware that there can be peace and happiness for us only through right education, then one will naturally give one's whole life and interest to it.

He contends that goodness can flower only in freedom. Goodness shows itself in behaviour and relationship when the latter are based on sensitivity. The whole movement of thought is goodness. In his words, "Good behaviour is in essence the absence of the self, the "me", it shows itself in politeness, in consideration for others, in yielding without losing integrity."[6]

Krishnamurti's insights on education though remarkable and radical are none the less frequently misunderstood or dismissed as impractical prescriptions. This is probably due to the fact that Krishnamurti presents education as a religious activity in an age when most people still see it as preparation for succeeding in a secular world. Krishnamurti's view that a human has both a brain and a mind puts him at odds with most modern perspectives and most learning theories, which identify the two as one. In simple terms, Krishnamurti explained that the brain is the material centre of the nervous system and the organ of cognition. It is therefore responsible for co-ordination of the senses, memory, rationality, intellectual knowledge, etc. The mind, which is not material, is related to

6. Ray Mcloy (ed.), *The Whole Movement of life is Learning: J. Krishnamurti's Letters to his Schools,* 2006, Krishnamurti Foundation Trust Ltd., Brockwood Park, England, p. 4.

insight (non-visual perception), compassion, and the profound intelligence that he held as the real goal of life and therefore of education. One needs a brain that functions well like one needs a heart or a liver that functions well; but the real source of acting rightly, of goodness, and of a religious life is the mind. In this unequal relationship between the two, a good brain cannot ameliorate a mind, but a good mind does ameliorate the brain. The brain has an important role to play with the mind, and that role is freeing itself from its conditioning and from activities that inhibit the mind's healthy functioning (i.e. hate, fear, pride, etc.); and helping the brain do this is one of the main functions of education (not accumulating knowledge). The real issue for Krishnamurti is the quality of our mind: not its knowledge but the depth of the mind that meets knowledge. Mind is infinite, is the nature of the universe which has its own order, has its own immense energy. It is everlastingly free. The brain, as it is now, is the slave of knowledge and so is limited, finite, and fragmentary. When the brain frees itself from its conditioning, then the brain is infinite, then only there is no division between the mind and the brain. Education then is freedom from conditioning, from its vast accumulated knowledge as tradition. This does not deny the academic disciplines which have their own proper place in life. Krishnamurti felt that each person needs to explore themselves and reveal themselves to themselves rather than be shaped into something by others. The function of education, then, is to help one from childhood not to imitate anybody, but to be herself all the time.

Krishnamurti felt that not only was a person's nature and deepest aspects to be uncovered, but each person also has a unique vocation that needs to be discovered; what she really loves to do has to be found and pursued, and to do anything else is a deprivation of the worst kind, especially if such deprivation is in order to pursue success or other such cultural aspirations. The discovery of the natural vocation for an individual student and the student's understanding what she really loves to do may not fit into the plans of the parents or society, but it is an important part of understanding oneself and, consequently, of education. It does not matter what it is, whether it is to cook, or to be a gardener, but is something in which one puts her mind and heart.

Modern education fails to solve the world's problems, and is clearly unable to prepare people for the fundamental challenges of living. Krishnamurti's insights into education actually combined our most profound learning with everyday life. His concern for education started since 1912, when he made suggestions on the basis of his own memories of early school life where he experienced both the right way of teaching and the wrong way. And for the rest of his life he attempted to help others towards a better form of education.

We may now try to understand some converging visions shared by Aurobindo and Krishnamurti in proposing their own distinct philosophies of education. Both the thinkers have proposed to develop some kind of non-hierarchical relationship between teachers and students. Teachers facilitate the learning process for children, but simultaneously, they too learn about life and their own selves. Thus students and teachers consciously engage in a process of mutual learning and teaching. Teachers of the educational centres founded by Aurobindo as well as Krishnamurti are selected on the basis of their sensitivity and an adequate grasp on the subject, rather than merely on the basis of their formal qualification. Secondly, both philosophers lay great emphasis on a kind of non-competitive ethos. They were opposed to promoting values of aggressive individualism and cut-throat competition which are the main features of the present-day educational institutes. Thirdly, in their centres, Aurobindo and Krishnamurti had similar pursued goals. Academic excellence is encouraged but not seen as the sole aim of these centres. The real issue in education, as Krishnamurti suggested, is to see that when the child leaves the school, she/he is well established in goodness — both inwardly and outwardly. In Aurobindo's view, the aim of education is to help the child develop her/his intellectual, aesthetic, emotional, moral, spiritual being and her/his communal life and impulses out of her/his own temperament. The aim is "integral education," that is, education that develops each faculty — physical, vital, mental, psychic and spiritual. Both thinkers emphasised that education must address the whole person, so that by developing harmoniously the children can create new ways of life — for themselves as well as for others. Their centres provide hope that the children are brought up to co-operate rather than compete, would try to establish non-violence, peace, compassion and happiness. Both Aurobindo and Krishnamurti hoped that the world would change to the extent each person in the world truly changes inwardly and outwardly.

Bibliography

Anderson, Allan W., *A Wholly Different Way of Living: Krishnamurti in Dialogue with Professor Allan W. Anderson*, Victor Gollancz, 1991.

A Flame of Learning: Krishnamurti with Teachers, 2006, Krishnamurti Foundation India. *A Flame of Learning: Krishnamurti with Teachers*, 2006, Krishnamurti Foundation, India.

Krishnamurti, Jiddu, *The Urgency of Change*, ed. M. Lutyens, Harper and Row 1970.

———, *Education and the Significance of Life*, Gollancz: London, 1954.

———, *Education as Service*, Adyar, Madras: Theosophical Publishing Society, 1912.

———, (1948) *5th Public Talk*, 26 September, at Poona.

———, 1953, *6th Public Talk*, 5 July, at Ojai, CA.

———, 1953, *Education and the Significance of Life*, London: Victor Gollancz Ltd.

———, 1974, *On Education*, Pondicherry, India: All India Press.

———, 1975, *Dialogue on Education*, at Ojai.

———, 1979, *2nd Public Talk,* 26 August, at Brockwood Park.

———, 1998, *Krishnamurti on Education,* Krishnamurti Foundation, India.

———, 2000, *Life Ahead,* Krishnamurti Foundation India.

———, 2001, *The First and Last Freedom,* Krishnamurti Foundation, India.

———, 2002, Why are you being Educated? Talks at Indian Universities, Krishnamurti Foundation, India.

Mcloy, Ray (ed.), *The Whole Movement of life is Learning: J. Krishnamurti's Letters to his Schools,* 2006, Krishnamurti Foundation Trust Ltd., Brockwood Park, England.

Rajagopal, D. (ed.), *Think of these Things,* 2007, Krishnamurti Foundation India.

11

Sri Aurobindo and Dilip Kumar Roy

Sachidananda Mohanty

> I believe that what I have written is worthwhile not because of the part I have played in what I cannot help but call a drama, but because through my conflicts and aspirations an aspect of his incredible self comes to the fore, a self whose flowering neither our age nor circumstances could explain.
>
> — Dilip Kumar Roy on Sri Aurobindo

LIVES of great men and women never cease to interest and inspire us. And yet, in the literary domain, biographies and autobiographies have, in the past, not received the canonical status they deserve. The situation seems to have changed drastically of late. Biographies and autobiographies, along with diaries, memoirs and letters, are receiving a great deal of attention by literary critics especially in the domain of cultural studies in the post-colonial context.

In choosing to write this essay on Sri Aurobindo and Dilip Kumar Roy, I hope to underline the rich tradition of spiritual biographies and autobiographies of our country. I should like to explore here the theme of initiation central to the domain of the sacred. In the spiritual narratives of the world, the theme of initiation occupies a central, albeit, a somewhat enigmatic place. Its purpose and role are generally seen and acknowledged, but less understood even by the devout. Initiation and discipleship — of a formal and informal kind —

go hand in hand in all movements of the sacred. Indeed, they are true of the secular as well. The *guru-śiṣya paramparā* of India has acquired over millennia an axiomatic cult status. It parallels myriad other traditions that speak of the "circle" of the Master with His disciples. Thus, we speak of Jesus Christ, the Son of God, and his apostles. Similarly, Socrates, Plato and Aristotle, constitute the secular trinity that affirms the importance of mentors and disciples, common to both pedagogy and spirituality.

Secular education of the liberal kind informs us that the student ideally chooses his teacher. Esoteric traditions or mysticism, on the other hand, holds that like the Divine Grace, discipleship often comes in an unforeseen gratuitous manner, as a blessing or a boon from heaven. The working of the Divine Grace defies human reasoning or causal action of the existential kārmic kind.

For many years, I have been fascinated by the Dilip Kumar Roy story.[1] I have tried to trace his footsteps through his writings and those of Sri Aurobindo. Through the publications of the Hari Krishna Mandir, Pune, I began to have a clearer idea of D.K. Roy, especially in his later life after he left Pondicherry for the outside world following the passing away of Sri Aurobindo. I must thank Shankar Bandyopadhyaya of the Pune Ashram for the assistance I received.

The opportunity for writing this monograph on Dilip Kumar Roy came when I was invited by Indrani Sanyal of the Centre for Sri Aurobindo Studies of Jadavpur University, Kolkata, to deliver two lectures on Sri Aurobindo and Dilip Kumar Roy. I am grateful to Professor Sanyal for the opportunity to reflect upon this important topic.

---

1. *Dilip Kumar Roy and Indira Devi, Pilgrims of the Stars: Autobiography of Two Yogis*, USA: Timeless Books, 1985 (first published in 1973 by Macmillan Publishing Co.).

Part I
Dilip Kumar Roy: Life and Times

Initiation and discipleship are profound truths of spiritual life. The *guru* may be benign and benevolent towards each of his many disciples. And yet, in human terms, he may appear close to some and closer to others at different times. I shall take up the spiritual relationship between Sri Aurobindo and Dilip Kumar Roy for my purpose.

I do not mean to suggest that there are no other relationships of this kind in the Aurobindonean context. Indeed, one can right away think of several: Sri Aurobindo and Nolini Kanta Gupta, Sri Aurobindo and Nirodbaran, and so on. And yet, to the human mind, at least, there appears to be something special, and indeed, unique about the Dilip Kumar Roy story. The process of initiation and the outcome of the spiritual encounter leave little doubt in our mind about the depth and many-sided nature of the unique relationship between Sri Aurobindo and Dilip Kumar Roy.

I shall offer, in the first part of this essay, an outline of the life and career of Dilip Kumar Roy. I shall highlight aspects that intersect with the life and works of Sri Aurobindo. The method here will be that of a narrative history of the conventional kind.

In the second part, I shall look at some of the related dimensions of the encounter. It is not my claim that I will be able to cover all aspects of this fascinating relationship. Indeed, due to lack of space, I will not be able to deal, for instance, with the voluminous correspondence Dilip had with Sri Aurobindo over poetry and literature. And finally, I shall try and sum up what in my opinion is the larger significance of the master-disciple relationship in the Indic context.

Born as the only son of Dwijendra Lal Roy (or D.L. Roy as he is better known) in Calcutta to an aristocratic brāhmaṇa family, on 22 January 1897, Dilip Kumar Roy came from the legendary Nāḍiā district of Bengal, the birthplace of Śrī Caitanya. Dilip's forefathers followed the Vaiṣṇava Dharma of Śrī Caitanya. His father's mother traced a lineage of verifiable descent from the saintly Advaita Goswami.

Dilip lost his mother at the age of six and was taught by tutors till the age of eleven. Passing his matriculation in 1913, he joined the Presidency College on a scholarship. His grandfather Dr P.C. Mazumdar, a wealthy man, took charge of his education. Dilip passed his IA in 1915 and in 1918, he secured the BA degree with Honours in Mathematics.

Dilip had a pronounced spiritual interest from the beginning. But he was not drawn to traditional religiosity. "I did not want to be a monk," he recalled later, "cloistered in a monastery. I yearned to bow to the will of God the Lord but not to the will of a human being."[2]

Meeting Saradamani of Dakshineswar had a profound effect upon him. He was taken to her in order to be blessed. Dilip wrote:

> Mother Saradamani smiled and said: "My son, one who has loved Sri Ramakrishna need not worry about this and that. He has only to remember him in his heart and cherish him as the final inspirer who sought birth on earth only to give us all his lead of light." With these few words she blessed me, touching my head, as I bowed down to the ground at her feet. I was moved to my depths, and a lump in my throat prevented me from speaking. Besides, what was there to say to her, an incarnation of holy Motherhood? Had I not read about her greatness in Śrī Mā's *Kathāmṛta* and Swami Saradananda's *The Great Master*? Had I not been startled by Sri Ramakrishna's tribute to her when he said he saw the Divine Mother in her at the very start? Had I not

2. Dilip Kumar Roy and Indira Devi, op. cit., pp. 55-56.

> read about her power of love which had drawn all who came to her to be mothered and sustained by her light?[3]

As higher education in England beckoned Dilip, his grandfather was keen that the former married before undertaking his journey abroad. However, Dilip was against marriage and was firm in dedicating his life to God.

The grandfather remained sceptical and took him to meet Swāmī Brahmānanda, considered by Sri Ramakrishna as his *mānasa-putra* or "Spiritual Son". Dilip was asked by Swāmījī to sing a song about the Mother. He chose a song from the famous *Kālī Kīrtan* of the great devotee Kamalakanta. This is how Dilip records the experience, following his singing:

> We waited in silence till he (Swāmī Brahmānanda) came back to normal consciousness. Then he looked intently at me in silence. I lowered my eyes, soothed and, withal, a trifle embarrassed under his steadfast scrutiny. Suddenly he turned towards my grandfather and said with a beautiful smile: "Pratap Babu, have no misgivings: he will come to no harm abroad."
>
> My grandfather stared at him uncomprehendingly. Swāmījiī smiled again. "Do you know what I saw while he was singing? I saw an aura of protection around him. . . . Thakur's (Sri Ramakrishna's) aura, which is an armour, I tell you, and I know what I am speaking about. So let him go where he will — he will come back unscathed. He may indeed, stumble sometime — but I can assure you that he will not fail." Then turning his face towards me: "Come my boy — come nearer."
>
> I could hold myself no more and rested my brow on his feet as tears of joy and gratitude found an outlet at last.[4]

Dilip was sent to England in 1919. He studied Law beside Mathematics. He also learnt music. In 1920, he passed the Part

3. Dilip Kumar Roy and Indira Devi, op. cit., pp. 41-42.
4. Ibid., pp. 55-56

one of Maths Tripos. In Cambridge, he pursued Music and learnt German and Italian Music. In England, he met Bertrand Russell, Romain Rolland and Herman Hesse. He gave lectures in many institutions and toured cities like Vienna, Prague, Budapest, Rome, Florence and Naples. He had illustrious classmates like Subhas Chandra Bose and returned to India in 1922. Back home, Dilip studied the music of the different regions of India. He learnt under Abdul Karim, Fayyaz Khan and Chandar Dubey.

A crucial event took place in the spiritual life of Dilip in 1923, when he met, in Lucknow, the English Professor Ronald Nixon. From Nixon Dilip heard for the first time about Sri Aurobindo and his works. Inspired by his mentor, he read several books of Sri Aurobindo like *The Ideal of Human Unity*, *The Synthesis of Yoga*, *The Psychology of Social Development*, *Essays on the Gita* and *The Life Divine* that initially appeared in the journal *Arya*. In due course, Ronald Nixon took up *saṁnyāsa* in the Himalayas and came to be known as Sri Krishnaprem. Thanks to Dilip's help, he had the *darśana* of Sri Aurobindo in 1948. (After a life of spiritual attainments, Krishnaprem passed away at Nainital on 14 November 1965.) In the example of the Englishman who became a devout Hindu, Dilip learned that God did not belong to any community or nation, but to entire mankind.

Meeting Sri Aurobindo in 1924

Dilip's quest now centred on Sri Aurobindo. Obtaining the latter's permission, he met his future *guru*, for the first time, at Pondicherry in the forenoon of 24 January 1924. Dilip writes:

> It was about eight in the morning. Sri Aurobindo lived then in the house which stands at the main entrance to the ashram. He was seated in a chair on the front veranda. I bowed before him and took another chair in front. An oblong table stood before us.

> "A radiant personality" sang the very air about him. A deep aura of peace encircled him, an ineffable yet concrete peace that drew you almost at once into its magic orbit. But it was his eyes that fascinated me most — shine like beacons. His torso was bare except for a scarf thrown across.The greatest living *yogī* of India![5]

At the end of his meeting with Sri Aurobindo, Dilip asked Sri Aurobindo with a degree of eagerness: "But what about my *yoga*?"

> His glance cut into me like a knife. "Yours is still a mental seeking," he said. "For my *yoga* something more is needed. Why not wait till the time comes?"
>
> "When it does, may I count on your help?" I asked anxiously.
>
> He gave an affirmative and smiled.[6]

Depressed and downcast, Dilip returned to Calcutta in 1924. Here he engrossed himself in the arts, literature and music. He wrote a book entitled *Indian Music* in 1924, published *Diary of a Wanderer*, a novel, *Mana Parash* in 1925, *Dudhara* (*The Currents*) in 1927, *Dhola Dhalan* (*Vacillating Human Spirit in Quest of Certitude*). In addition, he wrote a number of stories, plays and essays. In 1924, he lent his voice to more than 100 compositions for the HMV Gramophone Company. In this effort, he was ably assisted by Uma Bose, Subbulakshmi, Indira Devi and Manju Gupta.

Despite all this, Dilip's spiritual vacillation continued. About to take *dīkṣā* from the monk Swāmī Abhedānanda following the latter's lecture, Dilip happened to meet a friend who was a disciple of Sri Aurobindo, "Sit down and close your eyes!"[7] he was told. Dilip did so and had a profound

---

5. Dilip Kumar Roy and Indira Devi, op. cit. , p. 118.
6. Ibid., p. 131.
7. *Parama Bhakta: Dilip Kumar Roy* (Oriya), by Panchanan Mohanty, Cuttack: Matru Bhavan, 2000, p. 6.

spiritual experience. His friend said: "You have been accepted by Sri Aurobindo, and therefore there is no need for you to seek a *guru*! All that remains is for you to be ready!" Meanwhile, worldly attractions beckoned him. Invited by Edison's Gramophone Company, for recording purposes, Dilip sailed for France on his way to the United States in March 1927. He was bid farewell by Rabindranath Tagore, Sarat Chandra Chatterjee, and Subhas Chandra Bose.

After reaching France, Dilip realised that some invisible Power wanted him to turn back to India. Following his inner voice, he decided against going to America and instead went to Nice in France. Here, he met many musicians and delivered lectures on Indian music at the residence of local hosts. One of the notable events that happened here was his meeting Paul Richard. Richard who had returned from India after a stay in the Himalayas and meeting Gandhi at the Ahmedabad Session of the Congress had parted from Mirra and Sri Aurobindo. He visited Dilip in the hotel suite that belonged to the ambassador of Czechoslovakia. Contents of their conversation appeared in *Among the Great* and *Pilgrims of the Stars*. More complete versions were published in the Bengali travel book, *E deshe O deshe*. Richard's admission of his failings and his reverence for Sri Aurobindo as a veritable Śiva incarnate will be taken up in the second part of my essay. Meanwhile, suffice it to state that after a series of lectures, Dilip returned to India in November 1927. Now, stronger than ever in his convictions, he was keen to travel to Pondicherry and become Sri Aurobindo's disciple.

It must be added at this point that aside from his considerable talent as a musician, Dilip began to achieve distinction as a biographer of great personalities. His conversation and recorded talks were invariably of a high order. They reveal not only the minds of the eminent figures, but his own insights, erudition and literary skill. This was the result of training and an earlier resolution dating back to his childhood days worth recalling.

At the age of 13, Dilip happened to read *Sri Ramakrishna Kathāmṛta*, later translated by Swāmī Nikhilānanda and published as *Gospel of Sri Ramakrishna*. The narrative that acquired an iconic status in course of time owes its origin to the notes taken by the biographer Mahendranath Gupta. Overwhelmed by emotions at the reading of the *Kathāmṛta*, Dilip visited Gupta who lived close by. Gupta advised Dilip to keep a record of his meetings with the great men and women he met.

Dilip would not forget this advice for the rest of his life. His book, *Among the Great*,[8] remains a classic in this sense. It contains interviews and correspondence with five eminent figures: Sri Aurobindo, Mahatma Gandhi, Rabindranath Tagore, Romain Rolland and Bertrand Russell. The foreword to this book was written by S. Radhakrishnan.

Pondicherry: Second Visit and Ashram Life

Meanwhile, arriving in Pondicherry for the second time in August 1928, Dilip learnt that Sri Aurobindo had withdrawn and Mirra, the Mother had taken charge of the Ashram in 1926. He made a request to meet her. From her, he learnt that Sri Aurobindo had said that time had come for him (Dilip) to begin the practice of Integral Yoga as his disciple.

Dilip remained an inmate of the Sri Aurobindo Ashram from 1928 to 1952. He recalls his days in the Ashram with a sense of deep gratitude:

> I was on the whole happy in the Pondicherry *Yogāśrama* but the norm of which is hailed as happiness is not bliss, which

8. *Among the Great* by Dilip Kumar Roy, Pune: Hari Krishna Mandir, 2006 (first published by Nalanda Publications, Bombay, 1945). Also see *Sri Aurobindo Came to Me* by Dilip Kumar Roy, Pondicherry: All India Books, 1984 (first published in August 1952).

> can come only when the soul opens to the Divine Grace. In Sri Aurobindo Ashram I experienced this "outpetalling of the soul flower" many a time, but most often through his letters showering love. It did, indeed, seem to me, time and time again that his letters held magic which soothed the scorch of my heart with their rain of love. I had received loving letters from friends galore as well as world celebrities, but Sri Aurobindo's letters were written in a very different vein. One of my greatest joys — culminating in thrills — was to receive his letters day after incredible days. I stayed in his ashram a little over two decades, assiduously writing letters till the very end.[9]

About his Ashram life, we get some idea from Nirodbaran's Bengali book *Rachana Bichitra*,[10] published from Calcutta on 15 August 1997. Readers will benefit by reading, in particular, the essay "Dilip Kumar Royer 'Basantakal Ashram Jiban'".

Nirodbaran asks: "What was the real personality of Dilip? His radiant, smiling face? His poetic figure or his heavenly voice?" And he answers: "It must indeed be his melodious voice! [11] For, Dilip and music always went hand in hand. Every Saturday, with the Mother's permission, there was organised a musical soirée in Dilip's house. The function often extended up to 10 p.m. It must be added that this building, later known as the "Trésor House", remained empty for many years. The Mother would not allow anyone to use it. She said the house belonged to Dilip and must be kept ready for a possible return of the singer. Meanwhile, at Dilip's initiative, poet Nishikanto joined the Ashram two to three years after Dilip arrived. This led to an artistic collaboration between the two. Nishikanto's Bengali poems that were approved by Sri Aurobindo were rendered into music by Dilip. Some of these songs include the

---

9. *Pilgrims of the Stars*, op. cit., p. 155.
10. See Panchanan Mohanty, op. cit., p. 10.
11. Ibid.

following: "Ei Prithwibir Pather Pare", "Jwalbar Mantradile More", and "Kanakojwal Sabita Barani". At times, the sessions were organised during daytime for the Mother. Once when she was unwell, for her benefit, Dilip sang in an adjacent room. The Mother exclaimed to people around that Dilip's songs are so magnificent, they could magically invoke the presence of the Lord.

Similarly, when Sri Aurobindo was confined to bed after his accident, Dilip and Sahana sang for him. At times, when Dilip was away from Pondicherry and his songs were broadcast, he would request Sri Aurobindo to listen to his songs on radio. Many of these moving accounts are found in the writings of Sahana.

Dilip's correspondence with Sri Aurobindo would easily occupy a special place in the annals of spiritual literature. Begun in 1930, when Sri Aurobindo was in seclusion, the correspondence between the two comprise around 4000 to 5000 letters, many of which appeared in the book *Anami*, currently unavailable, and in *Among the Great*, aside from many others. More recently, much of the correspondence has been included in two handy volumes under the title *Sri Aurobindo to Dilip* (vol. 1, 1929-33 and vol. 2, 1934-35), both published by Hari Krishna Mandir Trust, Pune and Mira Aditi, Mysore, 2003 and 2005 respectively.

According to Nirodbaran, Dilip's pleasing personality, radiant and smiling face, and gentle behaviour endeared him to several inmates of the Ashram. Nirodbaran felt inspired by Dilip to take up the composition of poetry. With Dilip, there was seldom the need for gossip or small talk. There was of course good food when the situation demanded. His only flaw, as Nirodbaran recalls, was that he was given to "Abhimāna". As Sri Aurobindo describes it in a light-hearted manner: "He (Dilip) was a spoilt child!" Once Dilip imagined that due to some reason the Mother was unhappy with him.

He therefore decided to leave the Ashram and join the Salt Satyagraha Movement of Gandhiji.[12] Luckily he was dissuaded from taking this path by a letter from Sri Aurobindo. In due course, Dilip visited the Ashram of Ramaṇa Maharṣi and Swāmī Rāmdās. He travelled to Calcutta for raising funds for the Ashram, and upon return to Pondicherry, devoted himself to music and the arts.

We also get glimpse of Dilip's personality from the writings on his niece Esha. Published in 1995, in the form of a book entitled *An Extraordinary Girl*, Esha's account, as rendered by Nirodbaran, offers many memorable vignettes regarding her famous uncle. Esha first came to the Ashram with Dilip in 1938 when she was 18. Her mother Maya Devi, however, was not happy with the decision, and after an unpleasant altercation at Pondicherry, succeeded in having Esha back in Calcutta.

Another chapter of Dilip's life comprises his companionship with Indira Devi. Born in 1920, Indira, a married woman from a respectable background, first met Dilip in Jabalpur. She expressed a desire to become his disciple. While Dilip hesitated to ask Sri Aurobindo, the Master, when asked, to everyone's surprise, gave a ready consent.

Towards the end of November 1950, Sri Aurobindo's physical condition worsened. He passed away on 5 December 1950. Dilip received the tragic news from Arindam Basu in Benares. He had the last *darśana* of his *guru* and confided sadly to Nirodbaran: "You can't imagine what I have lost!" He was plunged into grief for a while. Later he left for America on a lecture tour in the company of Indira Devi.

As a *sādhaka* at Pondicherry, he donated regularly his earnings to the Ashram. He declined to accept the Music Chair at the Benares Hindu University in 1925. Similarly, he declined the post of a Director in the Faculty of Arts at Annamalai

12. See Panchanan Mohanty, op. cit., p. 15.

University when the coveted position was offered to him.

Last Days: Hari Krishna Mandir, Pune

After Sri Aurobindo's passing, Dilip left Pondicherry. The place for him was not the same in the physical absence of the Master despite his reverence for the Mother. After his world tour in 1953, Dilip and Indira Devi visited Calcutta, Bombay, Madras, Delhi and Hardwar. A friend, C.V. Mehta, invited them to stay in the latter's guest house, "Dunlavin Cottage" in Poona. In 1959, thanks to generous donations by his followers, a temple dedicated to Kṛṣṇa was built at Poona in the same premises. Every Sunday, in the forenoon at "Hari Krishna Mandir", Dilip addressed the gatherings on topics like the *Bhagavad-Gītā* and *Sāvitrī*. As Nirodbaran recounts, Dilip continued to express his love for the Mother, in all his correspondence with Nolini Kanta Gupta.

Towards the end of his life, Dilip began to lose his sight, and more tragically, his hearing. One day in 1980, he heard of the imminent arrival of Sri Aurobindo's relics in Bombay. Although seriously ailing, Dilip, along with followers, travelled to Bombay. Eyes laden with tears, overwhelmed with emotions, he stretched his hands and received the relics. He remained in this condition and after two to three days, he left the earth in a state of *samādhi*.[13]

In life as in death, Dilip Kumar Roy remained steadfastly loyal to his *guru*. In his unflinching devotion and *guru bhakti*, he would be second to none. He travelled widely and met many legendary personalities of his times. However, he never courted anyone for favour or patronage. He was convinced about the spiritual approach to life and engaged in conversation with distinguished men and women. Some he met, like Bertrand Russell, were agnostics, others like Subhas were puzzled by Sri Aurobindo's spiritual stance and thought him

13. See Panchanan Mohanty, op. cit., p. 24.

(unfairly) an escapist. To each of them, Dilip spoke lovingly and patiently, explaining the significance of the evolution in his Master's thinking and consciousness. As a true *Vaiṣṇava*, from the land of Nāḍiā, he was a real *Kṛṣṇa-bhakta*. He combined a heightened intellect with devotional ardour. He was intoxicated by the love of God. Why would the others not be equally made steeped in divine joy, he mused.

Part II

What His Life Meant

Dilip Kumar Roy was one of the best known disciples of Sri Aurobindo. A multi-talented personality, Dilip travelled far and wide, across India and the world. He rubbed shoulders with the high and mighty, and was attracted especially to outstanding intellectuals and men of letters. He excelled in music and the arts and consequently could touch the chord of a wide cross-section in society. Unlike the anglicised men and women, Dilip was firmly rooted to the Indian soil and was exposed to wide cross-currents of contemporary thought. He was a critical modernist who was drawn to the philosophy of creative evolution and integral *yoga* envisioned by Sri Aurobindo. It seemed as though the sole mission of Dilip's life was to promote the Aurobindonean vision. His entire life and career appear to be a preparatory ground for meeting Sri Aurobindo.

As disciple, so also the Master! Sri Aurobindo and the Mother deeply loved Dilip, and later, his companion Indira Devi. They broke all Ashram rules for Dilip. If life in the early days of the Sri Aurobindo Ashram was austere and somewhat puritanical, musical soirées in individual houses were unheard of and frowned upon, Sri Aurobindo and the Mother made exception in the case of Dilip. Ashramites and visitors attended such sessions. Many of the present-day teachers and inmates of the Sri Aurobindo Ashram[14] recall with fondness their memories associated with Dilip Roy. A number of them joined his music classes and gave group performances.

In the early days of the Ashram, Ashramites and inmates seldom travelled outside. Again, an exception was made for Dilip. Travel to America? Well, the Mother was concerned: Indira Devi ought to accompany him, she said. Sri Aurobindo's views regarding *sādhaka*s becoming *guru*s were clear. He uniformly disfavoured the idea. This would have a negative fallout, he reasoned, and would lead to unhealthy desire and ambition among disciples. After all, the sole and one-pointed aim of Integral Yoga was to transcend the human ego. Again, an exception was made and Sri Aurobindo allowed Indira Devi to become the disciple of Dilip.

While many such exceptions, difficult to fathom by the human mind and reason, were made, there were a number of instances when the *guru* said a firm "No" to the star disciple. To begin with, for quite some time, Sri Aurobindo did not grant Dilip his wishes. He kept Dilip waiting and after a considerable period, accepted him as his disciple. But once the decision was made, there was no holding back. While the Master did not have time for writing a few messages to the famous and influential men in the outside world, he gave enough time and attention to Dilip and other disciples as may be seen in the countless letters Sri Aurobindo wrote to Dilip regarding life, literature and *yoga*.

A good instance of the case cited above is seen in the book *Sri Aurobindo Came to Me*. Pramatha Choudhury, a correspondent from Calcutta, entreated Sri Aurobindo to write a few lines as a tribute to Tagore for the proposed *Golden Book of Tagore*. This is what Sri Aurobindo wrote to Dilip in 1931:

---

14. Conversation with Amita Sen at the Sri Aurobindo Ashram, Pondicherry, 7 July 2010.

> I am afraid Pramatha Choudhury is asking from me a thing psychologically impossible. You know that I have forbidden myself to write anything for publication for some time past and some time to come. I am self-debarred from the press, platform and public. Even if it were otherwise, it would be impossible under present circumstances, to write at a week's notice. You will present him my excuses in your best and most tactful manner.[15]

When Choudhury persisted, the Master wrote again to Dilip:

> I take Pramatha Choudhury's remark — that Tagore's *Golden Book* will be incomplete without my contribution as a complimentary hyperbole. The *Golden Book* will be as golden and Tagore's work and fame as solid without any lucubration from me to gold the one or buttress the other.[16]

Dilip cannot help seeing that while Sri Aurobindo found no time to write tributes, he was supremely compassionate towards disciples like him. As he says:

> He not only went on encouraging the poems of such as we but went on actually correcting our English verse — and with what meticulous pains! I myself have written more than six hundred pages of English verse and produced at least two thousand pages in Bengali, and he not only found time to read all these carefully but to comment on most of them as well as throw out suggestions for improvement.[17]

And yet, when Dilip regretted the fact that Tagore "recanted his faith in the Divine, having been overwhelmed by the modern craze for humanity, with a big H, he asked me almost with a motherly solicitude not to criticise Tagore adversely for his volte face."[18]

15. *Sri Aurobindo Came to Me*, p. 240.
16. Ibid., p. 19.
17. Ibid., p. 241.
18. Ibid., p. 242.

The long note that Sri Aurobindo wrote to Dilip regarding this, explains in very clear terms Tagore's mastery contributions and concludes:

> We should (not) hastily conclude that Tagore's passing to the opposite camp is a certitude. He is sensitive and is perhaps a little affected by the positive, robustious slogan-fed practicality of the day — he has passed through Italy and Persia and was feted there. But I don't see how he can turn his back on all the ideas of a lifetime.[19]

Most of the correspondence that Dilip had with Sri Aurobindo was characterised by the former's remarks in the opening lines of his "Preface" to *Sri Aurobindo Came to Me*, 1952; 1984.

> I believe that what I have written is worthwhile not because of the part I have played in what I cannot help but call a drama, but because through my conflicts and aspirations an aspect of his incredible self comes to the fore, a self whose flowering neither our age nor circumstances could explain.[20]

An issue came up when Dr S. Radhakrishnan wanted Sri Aurobindo to write a philosophical article for the Westerners. Sri Aurobindo asked:

> Do these people expect me to turn myself again into a machine for producing articles? The time of *Bande Mataram* and *Arya* is over! I have now only the Ashram correspondence and that is overwhelming enough in all conscience without starting philosophy for standard books and the rest of it.[21]

When Dilip persisted and declared that Sri Aurobindo was not known in the West and Radhakrishnan would give the former wide publicity, the Master was firm that it was "impossible" for him to write philosophy to order (p. 50).

---

19. *Sri Aurobindo Came to Me*, p. 242.
20. Ibid., p. XIII.
21. Ibid., p. 49.

More importantly, he declared his approach to life in the following words:

> I do not care a button about having my name in any blessed place. I was never ardent about fame even in my political days; I preferred to remain behind the curtain, push people without their knowing it and get things done. It was the confounded British government that spoiled my game by prosecuting me and forcing me to be publicly known as a leader. Then again I don't believe in advertisement except for books, and in propaganda except politics and patent medicines. But for serious work it is poison. It means either a stunt or a boom, and stunts and booms exhaust the thing they carry on their crests and leave it lifeless and broken. . . .[22]

Several instances, absolutely hilarious, have been recorded by Dilip in *Sri Aurobindo Came to Me*. One such happened when a fellow *sādhaka* called Bindu was crestfallen that Sri Aurobindo had not relished the food prepared by him. As Bindu wrote:

> Gurudev, Nolini brought me back the dishes. I was stunned to find that you had hardly touched them. I am deeply pained, sorely disappointed, utterly dejected and mortally wounded, and cannot imagine why you are so unsympathetic to me.[23]

Sri Aurobindo's reply was marvellous:

> Bindu, Don't be absurd! Our sympathies towards you are perfect, but it cannot be measured by our sympathy towards the eatables.[24]

Similarly, there are instances of fun which "bordered upon irreverence". Here is Dilip in his inimitable best:

> O Guru, I send you a Bengali poem of mine called *Akirti* which I translated last night into English. Can you revise

22. *Sri Aurobindo Came to Me*, p. 51.
23. Ibid., p. 275.
24. Ibid.

> it? Is it good? Mediocre? Worthless? Frame opinion please! But what about Raihana's letter please? Won't return? You keep mum. What's up? Bridge building? Supramental? Wool gathering?[25]

Sri Aurobindo's repartee was equally hilarious. He wrote:

> I shall see if I can get a few minutes for revising your English translation. But you seem to have progressed greatly in your English verse — (How so quickly? Yogic force? Internal combustion? The Subliminal self?) Raihana's letter and drawing which have unaccountably turned up against me. (Poltergeist? Your inadvertence? Mine?)[26]

Dilip's misunderstanding of the Mother is narrated in the chapter entitled "The Mother". At one stage, he wrote to the Mother defiantly:

> If you choose to frown on me because I love Sri Aurobindo more than yourself then I must stay impenitent since I did come here primarily for him and accepted you because he had wanted me to turn to you. I never made a secret of this, as I saw no reason why I should stifle the voice of truth. . . .[27]

The answer of the Mother surprises Dilip totally! "The Mother has no intention of frowning on you," said Sri Aurobindo. The whole imbroglio ended on a note of shame for Dilip when the Mother observes compassionately:

> "But can I possibly be angry with anyone who loves Sri Aurobindo as you do," she said, very simply. Her eyes radiated a strange light, a marvellous blend of strength, tenderness and humility. "My own feelings apart, do I not know how Sri Aurobindo cherishes you? So, how could you think it possible for me to frown upon one whom he greets with a smile? Am I not here to serve him with all I have and am — even as you, his near and dear disciples are?"

25. *Sri Aurobindo Came to Me*, p. 278.
26. Ibid., p. 279.
27. Ibid.

She would have said more had I not burst into tears.[28]

Another correspondence engaged the attention of Dilip when sports or physical activities were introduced as integral to *yoga-sādhanā* in the Ashram. Dilip considered this development as "ultramodern", rather unnecessary and exchanged a series of letters with Sri Aurobindo. Sri Aurobindo wrote an article on this topic that appeared in the Bulletin of the Department of Physical Education of the Ashram. Here again, Sri Aurobindo was his characteristic self explaining to Dilip with patience, kindness and consideration — about the evolving nature of his supramental yoga.

Dilip's book, *Yogi Sri Krishnaprem* (Bharatiya Vidya Bhavan, Bombay, 1968; 1992), is another example of his commitment to Sri Aurobindo. The friendship that he shared with Ronald Nixon, an English Professor-turned-Yogi has already been referred to by me. The book shows Dilip as a letter writer *par excellence*. Through a primarily epistolary method, we see an evolving relationship between two God-ward individuals. Here again, the inextricable link is that of Sri Aurobindo. The letters, date marked, Lucknow, Brindavan, Almora, among other places explore the significance of the advent of Kr̥ṣṇa and the meaning of Kr̥ṣṇa Consciousness *vis-à-vis* Integral Yoga. Related issues both sacred and secular, are taken up. Often, Dilip would share Krishnaprem's letter with Sri Aurobindo and seek his comments. For instance, Krishnaprem's letter on "Hitler and the War" elicits a very significant reply from Sri Aurobindo. While not condoning the Allies for many of their serious flaws, Sri Aurobindo concluded:

> The Divine takes men as they are and uses man as His instruments even if they are not flawless in virtue, angelic, holy and pure. If they are of good will, if to use the Biblical phrase, they are on the Lord's side that is enough for the

---

28. *Sri Aurobindo Came to Me*, p. 432.

> work to be done. Even if I knew that the Allies would misuse their victory or bungle peace or partially at least spoil the opportunities open to the human world by that victory, I would still put my force behind them.[29]

Aside from the triangular exchange between Dilip, Krishnaprem and Sri Aurobindo, the book contains letters Krishnaprem wrote to others such as Govinda Gopal Mukhopadhyaya, Hem Chandra Majumdar, Abani Nath Roy and Salil Kumar Mukhopadhyaya. Also, these letters by Yasoda Ma and Madhava Ashish. All in all, a very fruitful exchange between like-minded seekers after the spiritual truth.

The first two parts of the book are written in a narrative style. Part One deals with "Sri Krishnaprem *vis-à-vis* Sri Aurobindo", Part Two, with reminiscences and Part Three with letters. In all these, the underlying refrain seems to be Dilip's search for the meaning of greatness in life. He quotes Aldous Huxley's memorable lines in his *Along the Road*:

> That it is difficult to tell the genuine from the sham is proved by the fact that enormous number of people have made mistakes and continue to make them. Genuineness always triumphs in the long run, but at any given moment, the majority of people, if they do not actually prefer the sham to the real, at least like it as much, paying homage to both.[30]

As the Mother aptly told Dilip one day in passing:

> Most people who called Sri Aurobindo great based their estimate on data which could not reveal the moral core of his greatness. That is why a true vision of what is the essence of greatness is indispensable, especially to the pilgrims of the spirit.[31]

If the earlier books of Dilip spoke eloquently of his homage to

---

29. *Sri Aurobindo Came to Me*, p. 434.
30. Letter dated 3 September 1943. See *Yogi Sri Krishnaprem*, op. cit., p. 229.
31. *Yogi Sri Krishnaprem*, p. 11.

Sri Aurobindo, the later ones like *Pilgrims of the Stars: Autobiography of Two Yogis, Dilip Kumar Roy and Indira Devi*, (Timeless Books, 1973; 1985) continue the same refrain, after the founding of the Hari Krishna Mandir. Divided into Part 1 and Part 2, the book covers familiar ground in a refreshing manner, and recapitulates his experience in life for a new readership. Many of the figures such as Swāmī Brahmānanda, Mahatma Gandhi, Ramaṇa Maharṣi and Rabindranath Tagore earlier encountered, are brought in again with fresh perspectives and additional information. The chapter on Madame Calve and Paul Richard offers a detailed account not seen in the earlier books. On the other hand, Part 2, by Indira Devi will appear completely new to readers. Earlier, she was in the background. She now acquires an equal status as a *yogī* in her own rights. Her narrative occupies exactly seventeen chapters, practically the same number as the one devoted to Dilip.

Readers will note that Sri Aurobindo is equally present in the story of Indira. In the Foreword to the volume, Frederick Spiegelberg an eminent Western scholar of spirituality who had the *darśana* of Sri Aurobindo for five seconds, says of Dilip:

> It remains for me to wonder. When five seconds could mean so much to your *Gurubhāī*, how huge must have been the transforming power of that spirit to a man, who like you, was privileged to be in close contact for almost a lifetime! Are you still yourself or have you become of something towering over all human possibilities?[32]

Two extracts are worth narration here. Both of these offer an extremely significant commentary on Sri Aurobindo's life. One comes from India's leading poet Rabindranath Tagore and the other from the French savant Paul Richard, husband of Mirra, the Mother. Richard, we know, collaborated with Sri

32. *Sri Aurobindo Came to Me*, p. 11.

Aurobindo in the philosophical journal *Arya*.

To Rabindranath, Dilip reads out a passage from *Synthesis of Yoga* to disprove the charge that his *guru* stood for individual salvation. As Sri Aurobindo wrote:

> An individual salvation in heavens beyond, careless of earth is not our highest objective: the liberation and self-fulfilment of others is as much our own concern — we might almost say, our divine self-interest — as our own liberation.[33]

Dilip persuades Rabindranath to meet Sri Aurobindo. The poet promises to do so, if an opportunity arises.[34] In 1928 on his way to Colombo the poet meets Sri Aurobindo and wrote an account of his conversation in *Modern Review:*

> At the very sight I could realise that he had been seeking for the soul and had gained it, and through this long process of realisation, had accumulated within him a silent power of inspiration. His face was radiant with an inner light and his serene presence made it evident to me that his soul was not crippled or cramped to the measure of some tyrannical doctrine which takes delight in inflicting wounds upon life.
>
> I felt the utterance of the ancient Hindu *ṛṣi* spoke from him of that equanimity which gives the human soul its freedom of entrance into the All. I said to him: "You have the Word and we are waiting to accept it from you. India will speak through your voice to the world. Hearken to me."
>
> Years ago, I saw Aurobindo in the atmosphere of his earlier heroic youth and I sang to him: "Aurobindo, accept the salutation of Rabindranath." Today I saw him in a deeper atmosphere of reticent richness of wisdom and again sang to him in silence: "Aurobindo, accept the salutation of Rabindranath."[35]

---

33. *Pilgrims of the Stars*, p. XII.
34. Ibid., p. 80.
35. Ibid., p. 81.

And as for Paul Richard on Sri Aurobindo let Dilip do the telling again. The conversation takes place in a hotel in Nice:

> Dilip (smiling) . . . . "I want you to tell me frankly, your opinion of Sri Aurobindo."
>
> Richard (after a pause): "I have not met his peer in the whole world. To me he is the Lord Śiva incarnate."
>
> Marthe: "Please go on monsieur."
>
> Richard: "I can assure you *Madame* that if Aurobindo came out of his seclusion today, he would overtop all others as a king of kings. But he has chosen to decline his country's invitation to resume his leadership — a renunciation I look upon as the most convincing proof of his spiritual royalty."[36]

And finally, we have the correspondence between Dilip and Subhas Chandra Bose regarding Sri Aurobindo. Bose was then in Mandalay Central Jail in Burma. Unlike his earlier admiration of the Master, now he could not appreciate Sri Aurobindo's decision to leave "politics for philosophy". In a letter dated 9 October 1925, to Dilip, this is what Subhas wrote:

> I subscribe to most of what you write about Sri Aurobindo, if not to all. He is a *dhyānī* (a contemplative) and I feel, goes even deeper than Vivekananda, though I have a profound reverence for the latter. So I agree with you when you say that one may from time to time — and on occasion for a long spell — remain withdrawn in silent contemplation in perfect seclusion. But here there is a danger: the active side of man might get atrophied if he remained cut-off for too long from the tides of life and society. . . . For a variety of reasons, our nation has been sliding pauselessly down to the zero line in the sphere of action. So what we badly need today is a double dose of the activist serum, *rajas*.[37]

But elsewhere, such as in his speech at the Hooghly District

36. *Pilgrims of the Stars*, p. 143.

37. *Netaji: Collected Works*, ed. Sisir Bose, vol. III, Calcutta, 1980, p. 2.

Students' Conference on 22 July 1929, Subhas spoke highly of Sri Aurobindo. Again, on 17 July 1931 at Narail, he said that Sri Aurobindo gave a "new form and shape," to the "nascent idea of freedom." However, in his speech at the Third Session of the All India Youth Congress held in Calcutta on 25 December 1928, Subhas spoke against the passivism taught by "two schools of thought which have their centres at Sabarmati and Pondicherry."[38]

Dilip's correspondence with Subhas continued. On 10 September 1932, from a jail in Madras, he said that he "appreciated Sri Aurobindo's action," ibid. vol. IV, p. 292. Later when he reached Vienna in March 1933, Dilip helped Subhas get in touch with his friends like Madame Müller, named as Nilima by Sri Aurobindo. However, as successive exchange between Dilip and Subhas showed misunderstanding between the two persisted. Subhas could not see a reconciliation between life- affirming altitude of Integral Yoga with the life of seclusion that many like Dilip and Anil Baran embraced.

However, a fruitful meeting eventually took place between Dilip and Subhas on 17 March 1937 in the old Elgin Road House. Subhas declared that it was an impulsive remark he had made and that "we don't always mean the things we say when we are rubbed the wrong way."[39]

According to historian Amalendu Dey, as the later events showed, Subhas did not heed the advice of Dilip. Sri Aurobindo had earlier said of Dilip's "despairing friend" Subhas: "all this insistence upon action is absurd if one has not the right by which to act."[40] As Dey concludes:

38. *Netaji: Collected Works*, ed. Sisir Bose, vol. V, pp. 272-74.

39. Ibid., p. 139.

40. *Sri Aurobindo, Max Müller, Subhas Chandra*, ed. Amalendu Dey, Kolkata: Sri Aurobindo Bhavan, 2005, p. 46.

The perception of Sri Aurobindo on contemporary political events was quite different from the perception of Subhas Chandra Bose as a politician during a crucial period of Indian history.[41]

Conclusion

It would thus be seen that Dilip Kumar Roy was a true disciple in the best sense of the term. He was sincere, loyal and dedicated to the Master and the ideals he stood for. He did not efface himself or silence his mind before a towering personality. Rather, he learnt to constantly open his rational and intuitive self to higher influences. He sought inspiration from Sri Aurobindo and in accordance to his teaching carved out a path for himself and his companion Indira Devi.

It is relatively easy for an ordinary mind to surrender to a *guru*. It is far more difficult for a talented, multifaceted personality intellectually gifted like Dilip Kumar Roy to give up the ego, to become a fitting instrument and spread the message of the *guru* in the world. One would recall here, the views of Huxley and the Mother regarding the meaning of greatness. It was Dilip Kumar Roy's singular good fortune that he discovered for himself, one of the greatest figures of the twentieth century and shaped his life under his abiding influence.

Note

I am indebted to my late father Panchanan Mohanty for his booklet *Parama Bhakta: Dilip Kumar Roy* (in Oriya), Cuttack: Matru Bhavan, 2000, for a brief but cogent narrative about D.K. Roy. It turned out to be a major source of inspiration for me.

---

41. *Sri Aurobindo, Max Müller, Subhas Chandra*, ed. Amalendu Dey, Kolkata: Sri Aurobindo Bhavan, 2005, p. 47.

12

Harindranath Chattopadhyay's "Spiritual Education" and Sri Aurobindo

Dilip Kumar Chatterjee

> That poets are born, no sensible person will deny; but it all depends on where they are born and when — in what period of history; into what family, what class, what society. And to say that they are not made is far from truth of the evolution of a poet who has at all mattered in literary history.[1]

HARINDRANATH Chattopadhyay, one of the most versatile and vigorous literary personalities of modern India, was born on 2 April 1898 in Hyderabad. He was the youngest son of an eminent Indian, Aghornath Chattopadhyay, a D.Sc. from Edinburg, and brother of Sarojini Naidu. His contribution in diverse fields, such as poetry, drama, films, music, painting and even politics made him one of India's fascinating literary and cultural personalities. He is often far more prolific than

---

1. This quote is from an incomplete autobiography of Harindranath, *Life and Myself,* first published by Nalanda Publications, Bombay, 1948. This is written in a fictional style with a consciousness of history. The quoted lines are from the chapter, "Poets are made not born." Here Harindranath admits the fact that he is made a poet out of his association and interactions with outstanding personalities; Sri Aurobindo is certainly one of them (see p. 57).

his sister Sarojini and his writings in diverse fields using different genres spread over more than half a century. He died in June 1990. His eventful creative life and multifaceted works, his direct involvement in all the significant social, political, cultural movements in pre-independent and post-independent India made him a unique figure in contemporary Indian English literature.

Harindranath is one of those few poets who had the privilege of interacting with Sri Aurobindo in the Pondicherry Ashram. It was his great fortune that the seer reviewed Harindranath's first poetical work. His aesthetic and spiritual interaction with Sri Aurobindo is an interesting field of research. Harindranath needs a reappraisal in two ways: first by replacing speculation and sensationalism about his bohemian life with scholarly research, and second by establishing his works as deserving of critical attention. Critics often dismiss Harindranath's short stay in the Ashram but these were the most formative years of Harindranath to grow as a unique Indian English poet. This paper attempts to explore the evolution of the poet under the direct spiritual guidance of Sri Aurobindo in Pondicherry Ashram where a good many Indian as well as non-Indian creative personalities flocked around the great seer only to be enlightened by his yoga.

Since the setting up of the Ashram at Pondicherry, there had been apprehension and misapprehension in the minds of people as to what Sri Aurobindo was doing there. A clear-cut characterisation about the kind of yoga Sri Aurobindo was pursuing is available in the well-known work of Nolini Kanta, *The Yoga of Sri Aurobindo.* Nolini Kanta writes:

> When they speak of Sri Aurobindo, they really have in their mind some of the old schools of spiritual discipline. But one of the marked aspects of Sri Aurobindo's teaching and practice has been precisely his insistence on putting aside

inert and life-shunning quietism, illusionism, asceticism and monasticism of a latter day and decadent India.[2]

Nolini Kanta's insightful remark in the above excerpt speaks volumes about the very essence of Sri Aurobindo's teachings and practices of spiritual education in the ashram. Sri Aurobindo's spiritual education provides man and his social existence with a progressive purpose to be fulfilled here and now. His is a metaphysic of hope and he envisions the essential and eventual Godhead of Man. It is this inward and inclusive, future-oriented spiritual attitude that renders Sri Aurobindo's practice of spiritual education unique. His non-conventional approach towards this type of education, as Nolini Kanta justly said, introduced a new wave in "decadent India." But it is not surprising that it attracted only the few who possessed the call within to strive spontaneously for a harmony yet unachieved.

Among these few who emerged most prominent was Dilip Kumar Roy and he was soon followed by others. In fact, Dilip Kumar was quite instrumental in bringing his poet-friend Harindranath Chattopadhyay (1898-1990) to Pondicherry Ashram right from Cambridge where both of them first met and became close friends. Harindranath and Dilip Kumar both went to Cambridge in the 1920s to do their higher studies and research and, both being bohemian in nature, leaving their studies incomplete finally returned to India to join the Sri Aurobindo Ashram.

Dilip Kumar and Harindranath, the celebrated singer and the poet, were attracted by Sri Aurobindo's "radicalism" as well as by his new approach to the Life Divine and they joined

2. *The Yoga of Sri Aurobindo*, Pondicherry Ashram, 1967, p. 23. It is interesting to note that Nolini Kanta, though a prolific writer writing remarkable essays on "poets and mystics" remained "silent" about Harindranath. It is this "silence" which has been maintained also in the autobiographical writings of other celebrated ashramites, Sahana Devi, for instance. To what extent Harindranath has justified this absolute "dismissal" from them is a question to be examined.

the Sri Aurobindo Ashram intending a "divinisation" of their life and art. Harindranath, while writing to his closest friend Dilip Kumar, disclosed his present mental state in the following words:

> Dilip, you do not know how I have been shrinking of late into a feeling of insignificance; nor can you imagine the deep veneration and awe with which I read every line that comes to me from the Ashram.

In order to depict the emptiness of his mind and failure to "contact the Nakedness behind all visibility" he wrote to Dilip:

> Rest assured, Dilip, I am hungry for something that will not pass away. Even beauty itself yields me little joy nowadays — the beauty whether of humanity or flower or mountain or water — I want to contact the Nakedness behind all visibility — I know you believe it because I am sincere about the quest, I am very swiftly outgrowing old yearnings — within the past month the speed has been unconscious but great. It has not left me shaken, but it has left me quiet — I know that *New Power which I have been wanting and begging for has consented to accept to unstain me of earthly shadow.*[3]

By "New Power" Harindranath seems to be referring to his spiritual mentor Sri Aurobindo who accepted Harindranath to "unstain" him of "earthly shadow" by his divine grace. The sincerity of his yearning and quest for "Life Divine" is quite evident here. His mental unrest for which he had been "shaken" earlier left him "quiet" now in the Ashram as a result of his living in a spiritual ambience with his new friends, Amal Kiran, Nolini Kanta, Nirodbaran, Arghav, Jyotirmoyi and others, all of whom were "charged" by Sri Aurobindo. These young followers find for the first time a spiritual ambience where they

3. For this correspondence between Dilip Kumar and Harindranath see the *Anami*, Kolkata, Bengali quarterly from 1933-34. This Bengali quarterly was edited by Dilip Kumar himself. All quotations from Harindranath's letters are from this volume, if not otherwise stated.

do not have to seek refuge in any fixed dogma or departure into other worlds. Rather it is a free association of the like-minded striving spontaneously for a harmony yet unachieved.

In Pondicherry Ashram Sri Aurobindo's objectives in regard to guidance of these young perceptive minds were quite clear. He called them *sādhaka* and he said in his book *On Himself*:[4]

> Each *sādhaka* has to be dealt with according to his nature, his capacities, his real needs (not his claims, or desires) and according to what is best for his spiritual welfare.

Sri Aurobindo eschews the path of a conventional spiritual guidance and instead of engaging the *sādhaka*s with his long religious discourses, inspires them to write poetry.

He does this with a purpose and this is quite evident in Sri Aurobindo and the Mother's *Treatise on Education*.[5] Here Sri Aurobindo observes that "sufficient knowledge of human psychology" is a *sine qua non* in any kind of education, be it academic, physical or spiritual. He believes that writing poetry is as good as making a voyage of self-discovery and a poet's soul helps him to see his "undiscovered self." It is this dimension of depth psychology or the Gestalt that justifies Sri Aurobindo's encouragement of his *sādhaka*s to write poetry. Poet's imagination, Sri Aurobindo affirms, may reach the level of "over-mind consciousness": "A fourth dimension of Aesthetic sense where all is in ourselves and ourselves in all."[6] In his *Upward Journey*, the poet crosses the boundaries of the unseen:

> And passes over the edge of mortal sight
> To a new vision of himself and things
> *He is a spirit in an unfulfilled world* — Emphasis mine

4. *Sri Aurobindo on Himself and the Mother*, Sri Aurobindo International University Centre, 1953.
5. Sri Aurobindo and the Mother, *Treatise on Education*, Sri Aurobindo Ashram, Pondicherry, 1956. see chapter "Human Mind".
6. H.R. Justa, *Aesthetic Vision of Sri Aurobindo*, Delhi, 1987, see Chapter "Poetic Aesthetic Vision".

Sri Aurobindo thus looks upon poetry as a step in evolution of consciousness, a process of "the outbreak of Godhood in man" and it is this ideal that he wants his *sādhaka*s to follow towards a divinisation of their life and art. As a helper and a guide of their spiritual education Sri Aurobindo assigns great emphasis on the significance of self-discovery without which spiritual education or any kind of education remains incomplete. He has made this fairly clear:

> The closer touch attempted with the psychical entity behind the vital and physical mentality and an increasing reliance on its possibilities must lead to the ultimate discovery that man is inwardly a soul and conscious Power of the Divine and that the evocation of this real man within is the right object of education and indeed of all human life. If it would find and live according to the hidden Truth and deepest law of its own being.[7]

His real objective in the Ashram is thus to make Harindranath and his young batchmates aware of the hidden Truth and deepest law of their own being. He believes that it is poetry which helps this opening the door of their "in world and the over world."

Sri Aurobindo as a practitioner of "overhead aesthetic" admits that there is no incompatibility between the "inner self-development and the growth of poetic power." He says:

> The expression in poetry and other forms must be, for the *yogī*, a flowing out from a growing self grows and the poetic power will grow with it.

As regards himself and his own practice Sri Aurobindo says in his *Letters on Poetry, Literature and Art*, "I myself never gave up poetry or other creative human activities out of *tapasyā*."[8] In

7. Sri Aurobindo, *SABCL*, vol. 15; also see, P.B. Saint Hilaric, *Education and the Aim of Human Life*, Delhi, 1996, 1997.
8. Sri Aurobindo, *Letters on Poetry, Literature and Art*, Pondicherry: Sri Aurobindo Ashram Trust, 1972, p. 506, "Poetic Activity and Yoga".

Sri Aurobindo's view, poetry like anything else can be made an instrumentation for the Divine Life but he knows that this practice cannot be imposed as necessary for everybody. He assigns this practice to Harindranath to help him opening his inner vision.

The kind of poetry that Sri Aurobindo practised and guided his *sādhakas* to do likewise is not the poetry of spiritual thought or ideas, but of spiritual experiences itself, as spiritual thought or ideas may be derivative or imitative. Sri Aurobindo appreciated Harindranath as he among his young batchmates has the flair for writing this kind of poetry that had appeal for Sri Aurobindo's "overhead aesthetics."

Sri Aurobindo had foreknowledge of Harindranath's poetic genius as he himself wrote a long perceptive review of his debutant work,[9] *The Feast of Youth* (1918); the review of the book was published in the November issue of Sri Aurobindo's own edited English journal, *Arya,* in 1918.[10] Sri Aurobindo had already foreseen the "promise" of a wonderful flowering of the young poet who was just nineteen years old. The spiritual joy of existence, of its primal colour and symbolic subtleties, a fusion of the Vedāntic and the Sūfī mentality in the lyrics of the *Feast of Youth* impressed Sri Aurobindo so much that he wrote in the review, "Here perhaps is the beginning of supreme utterance of the Indian soul in the rhythms of the English tongue."[11]

9. This debutant work was published by the Theosophical Society, Madras, in 1918 and "forewarded" by the well-known Irish poet James Henry Cousins, Sri Aurobindo's friend, who also settled in Madras since 1915. Cousins and Sri Aurobindo both could foresee the promise of the young poet Harindranath who was just nineteen then.

10. Sri Aurobindo, *Collected Works*, vol. 1, *Early Cultural Writings*. This is the longest review article that Sri Aurobindo had ever written to appreciate young Indian English poet, see pp. 614-23.

11. *Arya*, pp. 614-23.

Quite naturally, Sri Aurobindo was happy to see him after so many years as an inmate of the Ashram. He hoped to see possibilities of the fulfilment of the "promise" that he had foreseen in the young Harindranath:

> we may well hope to find him a supreme singer of the vision of God in nature and life and the meeting of the divine and the human which must be at first most vivifying and liberating part of India's message to humanity that is now touched everywhere by a growing will for the spiritualising of the earth existence.[12]

As a guide of the spiritual education Sri Aurobindo was delighted to see Harindranath's "growing will" to bring about a change in his life and art under his guidance in the Ashram. He appreciated Harindranath's poems that he wrote during his stay in the Ashram. These poems that shine with his authentic voice and marvel of a perfect verse form justified Sri Aurobindo's high hopes. Sri Aurobindo hoped that his "poet-*sādhaka*" would carry forward his spiritual quest and remain forever a wanderer in the realm of the spirit exploring new regions hewing fresh path.

Harindranath by way of gratitude (*gurudakṣiṇā*) dedicated his new poems to Sri Aurobindo. The book was published under the significant title *Crossroads* on a significant date 15 August 1934, Sri Aurobindo's birthday. Here Harindranath addressed Sri Aurobindo as the "God-man" whom he needed most in his moment of crisis and loss of inspiration. In the very title poem Harindranath expresses his yearning for his "Master of the Vision,"[13]

> O Master of the vision Come

---

12. On Harindranath, vol. 1, *Early Cultural Writings*.
13. His deep love and reverence for the "God-man" or Sri Aurobindo in this prefatory poem is quite clear. Here he seems to confide to his guru the innermost secret of his troubles and reveal his total surrender to Sri Aurobindo.

And free me from this martyrdom
Of untransmuted limbs which strive
To keep the smoky flame alive
Extinguishing in me thy white
Untroubled everlasting light.
Shatter me, Lord, on every side —
My little love, my human pride,
My empty dreams, poor plan on plan,
And all that makes me erring man.
O let thy strokes be swift and sure
Which would the glories that endure. — Emphasis mine

Harindranath's candid confession of being an "erring man," having his common human failings and his total surrender to his Master for a transformation bear the mark of his sincerity. The poems that Harindranath wrote in his successive volumes, *The Strange Journey* (1936), *The Edge Way and the Saint* (1947) and *The Divine Vagabond* (1950), all bear the direct influence of Sri Aurobindo.[14]

Pondicherry period under Sri Aurobindo's spiritual guidance and training thus bore fruits in Harindranath's life and career, and K.D. Sethna in his *Inspiration and Effort* (1955) rightly pointed out Harindranath's positive contribution to poetry : "Two glorious years in which he did poetic work of two lifetimes, so abundant and so uniformly excellent were the poems of various kinds."[15]

Harindranath, as K.D. Sethna says, did write "abundantly" poems, prose, plays, and other genres during and after the Pondicherry period. The "wonder" that K.D. Sethna noticed

14. Besides these poetical works, Harindranath during his stay in the Ashram wrote each day a paragraph in his diary to draw the attention of his master. These were later collected and published in a volume entitled *Reflections*: impressive flashes one comes across in them can be linked to Sri Aurobindo's vision of man's evolutionary journey. The volume was published by B.R. Publishing Corporation, Delhi, 1988.

15. K.D. Sethna, *Inspiration and Effort*, Delhi, 1955.

in Harindranath was not "short-lived." It continued till his death in June 1990. The poetry of Harindranath, like the poetry of Sri Aurobindo and Tagore, raises some fundamental questions pertaining to the relationship between poetry and philosophy. Take, for instance, the following lines he wrote long after he left Pondicherry.

> Do you seek liberation
> *Then come free of the unconscious,*
> The underlying sleeves of consciousness, which
> Because of its yearning off and on
> Gets blurred and fails in clarity.
>
> Once we come clear of this sad captivity,
> We become a *central glow*
> From which daybreak draws its colours
> *Irradiated by the centre.*[16] — Emphasis mine

Harindranath, being one of the aspirants under Sri Aurobindo's guidance, wanted to be "irradiated by the centre." Being an "erring man" he cannot raise his yearning to a higher plane; it "gets blurred" and "fails in clarity." He attempts sincerely to get rid of the "unconscious" and unfortunately fails to be free from it. A lifelong yearning and a gaze fixed on the beyond sound intensely in his poetry. His conflict between "light and darkness" is well expressed in a confessional poem where he explicitly states his spiritual problem. In this confessional poem he says:

> I have lived most strenuously
> Constant captive between light and darkness
> Dawnbreak and evenfall
> I am hardly able
> To be able to extract myself
> From the mystery of opposites
> Again the villain mind!

---

16. For these quotations from Harindranath's poems, see his latest publication, *Mirage and Mirror poem*, New World Literature Series, Delhi: B.R. Publishing Corporation, 1989, pp. 26-27.

Yes, *the mind is a villain*
Who loves to play against the other.[17] — Emphasis mine

Sri Aurobindo while assigning "spiritual education" delivered a warning to Harindranath and his young batchmates to get rid of this "villain mind" — he insisted that the aspirant must make a determined personal effort to rise above this "mind-body complex." Harindranath who considers himself an "erring man" having his "human pride" or ego failed to transcend mental barriers. "With the transforming pressure that Sri Aurobindo was putting on all his *sādhaka*s for a radical change of consciousness," said K.D. Sethna, "something in Harindranath proved too rigid and he rose in revolt and went away from the luminous fount of inspiration and was caught up in the currents of the common life of the external world."[18] No other explanation is being provided by K.D. Sethna than this vague statement just quoted here. Harindranath's persona seemed to have been split into non-cohesive selves. His untold story of direct personal interaction with Sri Aurobindo persuades researchers to not be unduly unkind to him though the so-called ashramites transformed him into a *bête noire*. Sri Aurobindo did not approve this unkind attitude of the ashramites to Harindranath.

Before his spiritual education in the Ashram was completed Harindranath left the Ashram in 1936. Some said that he went berserk. Some said that he was a creative mind and preferred to remain bohemian; the ashramites argued that he was impervious to the disciplined life in the Ashram. He

17. Ibid. These poems written few months before his death affirm that Harindranath's creativity did not come to a halt soon after his departure from Pondicherry Ashram — it is not worthwhile to conclude as most of the ashramites do, that Harindranath miserably failed to write anything during his post-Pondicherry period. The unforgettable impact of Sri Aurobindo's "spiritual education" left an indelible mark on Harindranath and this is reflected in some of his later poetry.

18. K.D. Sethna, *Inspiration and Effort*, Delhi, 1955, p. 55.

was, however, left to follow his bent. His sudden and silent departure from the Ashram caused a ripple of criticism in certain sections of the ashramites and this made Sri Aurobindo as well as Dilip Kumar quite unhappy.

Sri Aurobindo in one of his letters to Dilip Kumar written on 26 October 1934, volume II, said something significant about this unhappy incident. Here we are consistently reminded of the great seer's wisdom, his advocacy of moderation and acceptance while assigning spiritual education to his *sādhaka*s. Sri Aurobindo says:

> I have protected Harindranath for the most part by silence; it is only to you and one or two others that I have written about him and in your case my only attempt was to assuage in each the feelings that were rising against the other.
>
> As regards Harin, I am concerned not with defending or condemning him but only with ensuring so far as I can do it his spiritual welfare as with my other *sādhaka*. To lay stress on the good side, on the hopeful things, to abstain from public condemnation, *to stress with all my force the inner growth and development and to work silently, and patiently* and persistently for elimination of all that stands on the way is a course I have followed not only with many of the *sādhaka*s, but with most, though not with all.[19]
>
> — Emphasis mine

---

19. See, *Letters of Sri Aurobindo to Dilip Kumar*, vol. II, 1934-35, eds. Sujata Nahar & Shankar Bandyopadhyay, Pune: Harekrishna Mandir Trust, 2005.

    This volume of remarkable letters of Sri Aurobindo contains a brilliant photograph of young Harindranath sitting in contemplative mood with a *tānpūrā* in his lap. He had long hairs and black eyes of a *yogī*, see p. 200. The letters relating to Harindranath reveal Sri Aurobindo's love and concern for his "prodigal son" who was never deprived of his Master's grace. This is the only significant letter of Sri Aurobindo which highlights the dynamics of personal relationship between a guru and a *śiṣya*. This letter speaks manifold things about Sri Aurobindo's method of Spiritual education.

Thus, insistently Sri Aurobindo does with his integral approach, press home the thought that it is not enough either to condemn or admonish an erring or a truant mind like Harindranath's but to stress only on "the good side, the hopeful things" which are inherent in him.

It is this positive attitude of Sri Aurobindo as a spiritual and aesthetic guide which is also reflected in the following. While writing about the Ashram poets he observed:

> there were four here whose work seemed to me to contain already in a fairly ample way the ripe possibility of the thing I wanted . . . yourself (Dilip Kumar Roy), Arjava (Chadwick), Amal, Harin. . . . These four then I have encouraged and tried to push on towards a greater and richer expression.[20]

Sri Aurobindo also emphasises on the guide's drive *to encourage and to push on towards a greater and richer expression of his sādhakas*. But in this teaching-learning process he uses a categorical imperative that the guides must not be "insincere in their praise" of *sādhakas*. He says:

> I have praised but there was nothing insincere in my praise. What matters is the truth of inspiration and the power of what it utters.

Here Sri Aurobindo does speak all about the responsibility of the guide of the *sādhaka*. He wrote to Dilip Kumar Roy that the guide has to work "silently, patiently, persistently" for the *sādhaka*'s spiritual welfare.

Sri Aurobindo's letter to Dilip Kumar as well as his remarks on "the poets of the Ashram," just quoted above, help us to highlight the nature of his spiritual and aesthetic education. In his teaching and practice of spiritual and aesthetic education

---

20. See *SABCL*, vol. 27, p. 456, chapter, "The Poets of the Ashram" (emphasis mine).

he allows individual volition or will, and Harindranath quite naturally is left to follow his bent. He had his poetic mode differently channelled, and Sri Aurobindo had no objection to it. The goal of his spiritual and aesthetic education of Harindranath was based on tolerance, love, sympathy and understanding. His was a desire to help and guide and not to treat harshly the delinquent. Sri Aurobindo knew that these were more potent constructive forces than punishment, intimidation, domination and subjection. Sri Aurobindo's words as quoted from the letter to Dilip Kumar are still relevant and serve as a message to our understanding of the dynamics of relationship between a guru and his *sādhaka* — between a preceptor and his pupil.

Bibliography

Sri Aurobindo, *Basis of Yoga,* Pondicherry: Sri Aurobindo Ashram, 6th edn., 1952.

———, *On Himself,* Sri Aurobindo Birth Centenary Library, Pondicherry, vol. 26, 1972.

Sri Aurobindo and the Mother, *Treatise on Education,* Pondicherry, 1956.

Sri Aurobindo, *Letters on Poetry, Literature and Art,* Pondicherry, 1972

———, *Collected Works,* vol. 7, *Early Cultural Writings,* vol. 27.

———, *The Future Poetry,* Sri Aurobindo Birth Centenary, vol. 9, 1970-72.

Chaudhuri, Haridas and R.G. Spiegelberg, eds., *The Integral Philosophy of Sri Aurobindo,* London: George Allen and Unwin, 1958.

Chattopadhyay, Harindranath, *The Feast of Youth,* Madras: Theosophical Publishing House, 1918.

———, *Crossroads,* Madras: T.P. House, 1934.

———, *Life and Myself,* Bombay: Nalanda Publications, 1948.

———, *Mirage and Mirror Poems,* Delhi: B.R. Publishing Corporation, 1989.

Diwakar, R.R., *Mahayogi Sri Aurobindo,* Bombay: Bharati Vidya Bhavan, 1967.

Ghose, Sisir Kumar, *The Poetry of Sri Aurobindo,* Kolkata, 1969.

Gupta, Nolini Kanta, *Yoga of Sri Aurobindo,* Pondicherry, 1967.

Hilarie, P.B., *Education and the Aim of Human Life,* Delhi, 1996.

Justa, H.R, *Aesthetic Vision of Sri Aurobindo*, Delhi, 1987.

Nahar S. and Bandopadhyay, eds., *Letters of Sri Aurobindo to Dilip Kumar*, vols. I and II, Pune: Harekrishna Mandir 2005.

Roy, Dilip Kumar, *Sri Aurobindo Came to Me*, Pondicherry, 1952.

Sethna, K.D., *Inspiration and Effort*, Delhi, 1955.

———, *Sri Aurobindo the Poet*, Pondicherry, 1970.

The Contributors

Banerjee, Aparna, is Associate Professor in Philosophy at University of Calcutta. She is the author of *Explanation and Understanding in the Social Sciences* (2002) and co-editor of *Ethics: Classical and Contemporary Issues* (2010). She has also authored various articles in Anthologies and Journals, many of which are on Sri Aurobindo's philosophy. [*address*: 9/3C Rammohan Bera Lane, Kolkata – 700 046, W.B. *e-mail*: <aparna2316@yahoo.com>].

Banerji, Debashish, Ph.D., is the Dean of Academic Affairs at the University of Philosophical Research, Los Angeles, where he teaches topics in Indian Philosophy. He is an adjunct faculty member in Art History at the Pasadena City College, teaching courses on the history of South Asian, East Asian and Islamic Art. He is also an adjunct faculty in the Department of Asian and Comparative Studies at the California Institute of Integral Studies in San Francisco. Banerji has curated a number of exhibitions and is the author of a book, *The Alternate Nation of Abanindranath Tagore*. [*address*: 5900 Canterbury Drive, Apt. A303, CULVER CITY, CA 90230 (USA), *e-mail*:<debbanerji@yahoo.com>].

Bhowmik, Sushmita, completed her graduation and post-graduation in philosophy from Jadavpur University, Kolkata, and has been serving as an Assistant Professor in Philosophy for the last five years at Budge Budge College, Kolkata. She has also submitted her dissertation for a PhD to Jadavpur

University on the theme "Regeneration of Values: A Comparison between Mahatma Gandhi and Sri Aurobindo." Prof. Bhowmik has published several papers in different anthologies published by Jadavpur University focusing on the thoughts of Mahatma Gandhi and Sri Aurobindo [*address:* 23A/4, R.K. Sarani, Behala, Kolkata - 700 060, *e-mail:* <b_sushmita_79@yahoo.co.in>].

Chakrabarti, Mohit, D.Litt (b. 1941), former Professor of Education, Visva-Bharati and former Visiting Professor, Rabindra Bharati University. Presently, Visiting Professor, Ramakrishna Mission Sikshanamandira, Belurmath. A prolific author on education and philosophy of Gandhi, Tagore and Vivekananda, having over fifty scholarly books to his credit. Among them are *Gandhian Humanism; Gandhian Aesthetics; Gandhian Mysticism; Gandhian Philosophy of Man; Gandhian Religion; Gandhian Socio-Aesthetics; Gandhian Dimensions of Education; Mahatma Gandhi: A Revaluation; Gandhian Spiritualism; Fire sans Ire: A Critical Study of Gandhian Non-Violence; The Gandhian Philosophy of the Spinning Wheel; Mahatma Gandhi: A Miscellany*. Chairman of NAAC-NCTE Peer Team, he is a recipient of National award as Teacher Educator [*address*: *'Seemantika'* Seemanto Palli, Santiniketan – 731 235, West Bengal, *e-mail*: <mohit_chakrabarti@rediffmail.com>].

Chatterjee, Dilip Kumar (1952-), M.A., PhD, Associate Professor and Head of the Department of English, Bangabasi Morning College, Calcutta University, and Guest Faculty, Department of English, Rabindra Bharati University, Kolkata; completed a research project on "Harindranath Chattopadhyay: A Bio-Bibliographical Survey", approved by the U.G.C. which will be published shortly. His contribution to the Sri Aurobindo Number of the *Journal of South Asian Literature*, Asian Study Center, Michigan State University, USA, deserves special mention. His pioneering research on "James

H. Cousins" as published from Delhi under the title *James Henry Cousins and the Theosophical Movement in India and the West* (1994) is widely acclaimed. His edited volume of *James Cousins' "The Renaissance in India"* published by The Standard Book Agency, Kolkata, in 2005 was reviewed in the *Journal of Asiatic Society*, December 2010 and in the international journal, *The Irish Literary Supplement* (volume 27, number 2 Spring 2008), this is the only Indian publication reviewed in the American journal. Dr. Chatterjee's research on Indo-Irish cultural interaction was appreciated by Prof. Joseph Lennon in his book *Irish Orientalism: A Literary and Intellectual History* (Syracuse University Press, USA, in 2008). He also gave the 23rd Annual Sri Aurobindo Memorial Lecture in Jadavpur University, Kolkata, on Sri Aurobindo's Concept of Nationalism, in 2006. He is currently working on inter-cultural studies, East and West. [*address*: 129 Vivekananda Sarani, Indrani Apartment, A/2 Kolkata - 700 078, *e-mail*: <dilipchatter@gmail.com>].

Das, Manoj, who teaches English literature and Sri Aurobindo's works at the Sri Aurobindo International Centre of Education, Puducherry, is a bilingual writer writing in English and his mother tongue Oriya. He is the recipient of several honours including the Sahitya Akademi Award, the Saraswati Samman, the Padma Award as well as the Fellowship of the Sahitya Akademi. Five universities have conferred on him D.Litt. (Honoris Causa). [*address*: Sri Aurobindo Ashram, Pondicherry - 605 002, *e-mail*: <prof.manojdas@gmail.com>].

Ganguly, Anirban, interests lie in the areas of historical, civilisational, educational and cultural studies. He has written and spoken extensively on these issues and is presently occupied in trying to trace the evolution of Indian nationalism and also the impact of globalisation on local cultures. He is with Vivekananda International Foundation, a leading New Delhi based think-tank and is also a Research-Scholar with the Centre for Sri Aurobindo Studies, Dept. of Philosophy, Jadavpur University, Kolkata [*e-mail*: <anirbangan@gmail.com>].

Mohanty, Sachidananda, is Professor, Department of English, University of Hyderabad. He is the recipient of several national and international awards including those from the British Council, the Salzburg, the Katha and the Fulbright. He has to his credit 21 books in English and in Oriya, including *D.H. Lawrence Studies in India*, Writers' Workshop, 1990, Lawrence's *Leadership Politics and the Defeat of Fascism*, Academic Foundation,1992, *Understanding Cultural Exchange*, Vision Books 1997, *Literature and Culture*, Prestige, 2000 *Travel Writing and the Empire*, Katha, 2002; rpt. 2003, *Early Women's writing in Orissa, 1898-1950: A Lost Tradition*, Sage Publications, 2005, *Gender and Cultural Identity in Colonial Orissa*, Orient Longman 2008, and *Sri Aurobindo: A Contemporary Reader*, Routledge India, 2008; 2009. His essays and articles have appeared in some of the leading journals and forums in the country including *India Today, The Hindu, The Indian Express, The New Quest, The Book Review* and *Economic and Political Weekly* [*address:* Department of English, University of Hyderabad, Hyderabad – 500 046 (A.P), *e-mail*: <sachimohanty@yahoo.co.in>].

Moitra, Shefali, is retired Professor of Philosophy, Centre of Advanced Study, Jadavpur University, Kolkata. She is the author of *Naitikata O Naribad* (in Bangla), (New Age, 2003) *Feminist Thought* (Munshiram Manoharlal, 2002). She is the editor of *Kalyaniyashu* (letters written to Shefali Moitra by Kalidas Bhattacharyya, in Bangla), (Nandimukh Samsad, 2005). She is the editor of *Women Heritage and Violence* (Papyrus, 1996), and the co-editor of *Communication Identity and Self-Expression* (Oxford University Press, 1984). Her areas of specialisation are ethics, philosophy of language, feminist studies and Tagore [*address*: 193A/5 Picnic Garden Rd, Flat # 5, Kolkata – 700 039, *e-mail*: <smoitra22@rediffmail.com].

Sanyal, Indrani, is Professor in Philosophy at Jadavpur University. She is the author of *On Essentialist Claims* (2002), and co-editor of *Wittgenstein: Jagat Bhasa O Cintan* (1998), *Understanding Thoughts of Sri Aurobindo* (2006), *Sri Aurobindo and His Contemporary Thinkers* (2007), *Siksaksetre Parasparik Samparka* (2007), and *Dharmaniti O Shruti* (2009) [*address*: mail: Department of Philosophy, Jadavpur University, Kolkata - 700 032 (W.Bengal), *e-mail*: <indranisnyl@yahoo.co.in>].

Sinha, Atashee Chatterjee, did M.Phil. (1993) and PhD (2000) from Jadavpur University. She has published a book titled *The Many Faces of Reason and Violence* (Papyrus Publications, 2005). Presently engaged as Associate Professor of Philosophy at Jadavpur University, she has special interest in ethics (Indian and Western), feminist philosophy and cognitive science [*address*: 11/1 Selimpur Road, 1st Floor, Kolkata – 700 031, *e-mail*: <atashee2003@gmail.com>].

Index